THE

DEAD TOWNS

OF

GEORGIA

BY

CHARLES C. JONES, JR

Reprinted 1997
The Oglethorpe Press, Inc.

THE DEAD TOWNS OF GEORGIA

By Charles C. Jones, Jr.

First printed in 1878 as Volume Four of the
Collections of the Georgia Historical Society.

ISBN 1-891495-03-8

1. History - Georgia - 18th century

Reprinted 1997 by The Oglethorpe Press, Inc.
326 Bull Street
Savannah, Georgia 31401

TO

GEORGE WYMBERLEY-JONES DeRENNE, ESQ.,

OF SAVANNAH,

WHOSE INTELLIGENT RESEARCH, CULTIVATED TASTE, AND AMPLE FORTUNE HAVE BEEN

SO GENEROUSLY ENLISTED IN RESCUING FROM OBLIVION

THE EARLY MEMORIES OF GEORGIA,

THESE SKETCHES ARE RESPECTFULLY AND CORDIALLY INSCRIBED.

PREFATORY NOTE.

If it be praiseworthy in their descendants to erect monuments in honor of the illustrious dead, and to perpetuate in history the lives and acts of those who gave shape to the past and encouragement to the future, surely it will not be deemed inappropriate to gather up the fragmentary memories of towns once vital and influential within our borders, but now covered with the mantle of decay, without succession, and wholly silent amid the voices of the present.

Against the miasmatic influences of the swamps, Spanish perils, the hostility of the Aborigines, and the poverty and sometimes narrow mindedness of the Trust, did the Colonists grievously struggle in asserting their dominion over the untamed lands from the Savannah to the Alatamaha. Nothing indicates so surely the vicissitudes and the mistakes encountered during that primal period of development, as the DEAD TOWNS OF GEORGIA. From each comes in turn the whisper of hope, the sound of the battle with nature for life and comfort, the sad strain of disappointment, and then the silence of nothingness.

Of the chosen seats and characteristics of the primitive peoples who inhabited this territory prior to the advent of the European we have elsewhere spoken.*

Of the indications of a foreign occupancy antedating the colonization under Oglethorpe, such, for example, as those observed by DeBrahm† on Demetrius' island, and a few others which might be mentioned,—we refrain from writing, because the theories explanatory of their origin, possession, and abandonment, are so nebulous as to seem incapable of satisfactory solution.

In narrating the traditions and grouping the almost obsolete memories of these deserted villages we have endeavored to revive them, as far as practicable, in the language of those to whom we are indebted for their transmission.

CHARLES C. JONES, JR.

AUGUSTA, GEORGIA, February 1st, 1878.

* "Antiquities of the Southern Indians, particularly of the Georgia Tribes." New York, 1873.

† History of the Province of Georgia, pp. 29, 30. Wormsloe, 1849.

CONTENTS.

ILLUSTRATIONS.

Plan of the Town EBENEZER and its Fort

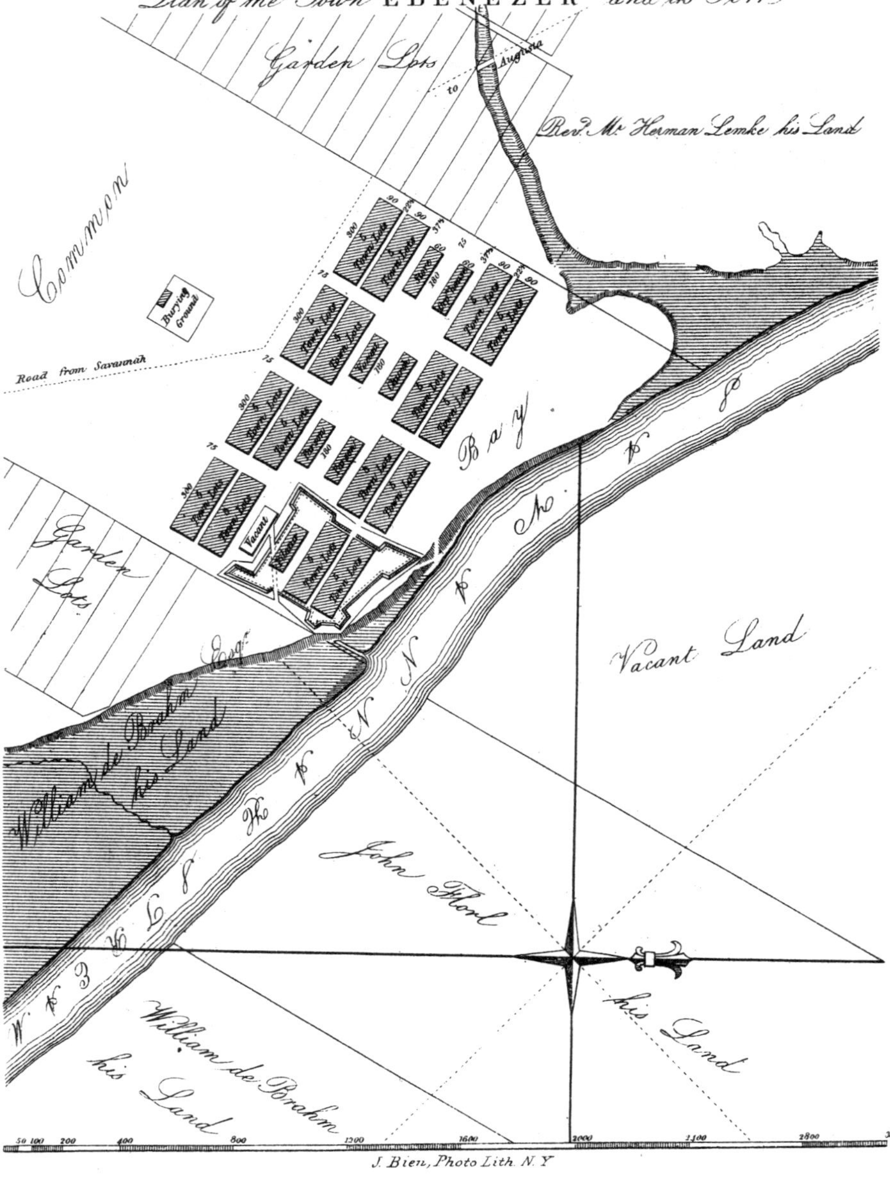

J. Bien, Photo Lith. N. Y

I.

OLD, AND NEW EBENEZER.

During the four years commencing in 1729 and ending in 1732, more than thirty thousand Saltzburgers, impelled by the fierce persecutions of Leopold, abandoned their homes in the broad valley of the Salza and sought refuge in Prussia, Holland, and England, where their past sufferings and present wants enlisted substantial sympathy and relief from Protestant communities. Persuaded by the "Society for the Propagation of Christian Knowledge," and acting upon the invitation of the Trustees of the Colony of Georgia,—who engaged not only to advance the funds necessary to defray the expenses of the journey and purchase the requisite sea-stores, but also to allot to each emigrant on his arrival in Georgia fifty acres of land in fee, and provisions sufficient to maintain himself and family until such land could be made available for support,—forty-two Saltzburgers, with their wives and children,—numbering in all seventy-eight souls,—set out from the town of Berchtolsgaden and its vicinity for Rotterdam, whence they were to be transported free of charge to Dover, England. At Rotterdam they were joined by their chosen religious teachers, the Reverend John Martin Bolzius and the Reverend Israel Christian Gronau. The oath of loyality having been administered to them at Dover by the Trustees, these pious, industrious, and honest emigrants, on the 28th of December, 1733, set sail in the ship Purisburg and, after a tedious and perilous passage, reached Charlestown, South Carolina, in safety. Mr. Oglethorpe, chancing to be there at the time, arranged that the Saltzburgers should proceed without delay to Savannah. The Savannah river was entered by them on the 10th of March, 1734. It was *Reminiscere* Sunday, according to the Lutheran calendar;—the gospel of the day being "Our Blessed Saviour came to the Borders of the Heathen after He had been persecuted in His own Country." "Lying in fine and calm weather, under the Shore of our beloved *Georgia*, where we heard the Birds sing melodiously, every Body in the ship was joyful." So wrote the Reverend Mr. Bolzius, the faithful attendant and spiritual guide of this Protestant band. He tells us also, that two days afterwards, when the ship arrived at the place of landing, "almost all the Inhabitants of the Town of *Savannah* were gather'd together; they fired off some Cannons, and cried Huzzah! which was answer'd by our Sailors, and other *English* People in our Ship in the same manner. Some of us were immediately fetch'd on Shore in a Boat, and carried about the City, into the woods, and the new Garden belonging to the Trustees. In the meantime a very good Dinner was prepared for us: And the *Saltzburgers*, who had yet fresh Meat in the Ship, when they came on shore, they got very good and wholesome *English* strong Beer. And besides the Inhabitants shewing them a great deal of Kindness, and the Country pleasing them, they were full of Joy and praised God for it."*

Leaving his people comfortably located in tents, and in the hospitable care of the Colonists at Savannah, Mr. Von

* Extract of the Journals of Mr. Commissary VonReck, &c., p. 32. London, 1734.

Reck set out on horseback with Mr. Oglethorpe to take a view of the country and select a spot where the Saltzburgers might form their settlement. At nine o'clock on the morning of the 17th of March they reached the place designated as the future home of the emigrants. It was about four miles below the present town of Springfield, in Effingham County, sterile and unattractive. To the eye of the Commissary, however, tired of the sea and weary of persecutions, it appeared a blessed spot, redolent of sweet hope, bright promise, and charming repose. Hear his description: "The Lands are inclosed between two Rivers, which fall into the *Savannah*. The *Saltzburg* Town is to be built near the largest, which is called *Ebenezer*,* in Remembrance that God has brought us hither; and is navigable, being twelve Foot deep. A little Rivulet, whose Water is as clear as Crystal, glides by the Town; another runs through it, and both fall into the *Ebenezer*. The Woods here are not so thick as in other Places. The sweet Zephyrs preserve a delicious coolness notwithstanding the scorching Beams of the Sun. There are very fine Meadows, in which a great Quantity of Hay might be made with very little Pains: there are also Hillocks, very fit for Vines. The Cedar, Walnut, Pine, Cypress and Oak make the greatest part of the Woods. There is found in them a great Quantity of Myrtle Trees out of which they extract, by boiling the Berries, a green Wax, very proper to make Candles with. There is much Sassafras, and a great Quantity of those Herbs of which Indigo is made, and Abundance of *China* Roots. The Earth is so fertile that it will bring forth anything that can be sown or planted in it; whether Fruits, Herbs, or Trees. There are wild Vines, which run up to

* The Stone of Help.

the Tops of the tallest Trees; and the Country is so good that one may ride full gallop 20 or 30 miles an end. As to Game, here are Eagles, Wild-Turkies, Roe-Bucks, Wild-Goats, Stags, Wild-Cows, Horses, Hares, Partridges, and Buffaloes."* Upon the return of Mr. Oglethorpe and the Commissary to Savannah, nine able bodied Saltzburgers were immediately dispatched, by the way of Abercorn, to Ebenezer, to cut down trees and erect shelters for the Colonists. On the 7th of April the rest of the emigrants arrived, and, with the blessing of the good Mr. Bolzius, entered at once upon the task of clearing land, constructing bridges, building shanties, and preparing a road-way to Abercorn. Wild honey found in a hollow tree greatly refreshed them, and parrots and patridges made them "a very good dish." Upon the sandy soil they fixed their hopes for a generous yield of peas and potatoes. To the "black, fat, and heavy" land they looked for all sorts of corn; and from the clayey soil they purposed manufacturing bricks and earthen ware. On the 1st of May lots were drawn upon which houses were to be erected in the town of Ebenezer. The day following, the hearts of the people were rejoiced by the coming of ten cows and calves,—sent as a present from the Magistrates of Savannah in obedience to Mr. Oglethorpe's order. Ten casks "full of all Sorts of Seeds" arriving from Savannah, set these pious peoples to praising God for all His loving kindnesses. Commiserating their poverty, the Indians gave them deer, and their English neighbors taught them how to brew a sort of beer made of molasses, sassafras, and pine tops. Poor Lackner dying, by common consent the little money he left was made the "Beginning of a Box for the Poor." The repeated thunder-

* An Extract of the Journals of Mr. Commissary VonReck, &c., pp. 16, 18. London, 1734.

storms and hard rains penetrated through the rude huts and greatly incommoded the settlers. The water disagreed with them, causing serious affections of the bowels, until they found a brook, springing from a little hill, which proved both palatable and wholesome. By appointment, Monday the 13th of May was observed by the congregation as a season of Thanksgiving.

Depending entirely upon the charity of the Trustees for supplies of all sorts, and having but few mechanics among them, these Saltzburgers labored under great disadvantages in building their little town in the depths of the woods, and surrounding themselves with fields and gardens. Patient of toil, however, and accustomed to work, they cut and delved away, day by day, rejoicing in their freedom, blessing the Giver of all good for His mercies, and observing the rules of honesty, morality, and piety, for which their sect had been so long distinguished. Communication with Savannah was maintained by way of Abercorn; to which place supplies were transported by water.

Early in 1735 the settlement was materially strengthened and encouraged by the arrival of fifty-seven more emigrants under the conduct of Mr. Vatt. Among the new-comers were several mechanics whose knowledge, industry, and skill were at once applied to hewing timber, splitting shingles, and sawing boards, to the manifest improvement of the dwellings in Ebenezer.

About a year afterwards occurred what is known as the *great embarcation.* Including some eighty Germans from the city of Ratisbon, under the control of Baron VonReck and Captain Hermsdorf, twenty-seven Moravians under the care of the Rev'd David Nitschman, the Rev'd John and Charles Wesley, and the Rev'd Mr. Ingham,—Missionaries to the Indians,—and a number of poor English families, this accession to the Colony of Georgia aggregated some two hundred and twenty-seven persons, of whom two hundred and two were conveyed upon the Trust's account. Francis Moore was appointed keeper of the stores. Oglethorpe in person accompanied the Colonists, and exercised a fatherly care over them during the voyage. They were transported in the Symond of 220 tons,—Capt. Joseph Cornish,—and the London Merchant, of like burthen, — Capt. John Thomas.* During the voyage the German Dissenters "sung psalms and served God in their own way." Turnips, carrots, potatoes, and onions, issued with the salt provisions, prevented scurvy. In order to promote comfort and good order, the ships had been divided into cabins, with gang-ways between them, in which the emigrants were disposed according to families. The single men were located by themselves. Weather permitting, the vessels were cleaned between decks and washed with vinegar to keep them sweet Constables were appointed "to prevent any disorders," and so admirably was discipline preserved, that there was no occasion for punishment except in the case of a boy, "who was whipped for stealing of turnips." The men were exercised with small arms, and instructed by Mr. Oglethorpe in the duties which would devolve upon them as free-holders in the new settlement. To the women were given thread, worsted, and knitting needles; and they were required to employ "their leisure time in making Stockings and Caps for their Family, or in mending their Cloaths and Linnen." In this sensible way were matters ordered on these emigrant ships, and the colonists, during a protracted voyage, prepared for lives of industry in their new homes.

* Moore's Voyage to Georgia, p. 11. London, 1744.

On the 5th of February, 1736, these ships, with the first of the flood, were carried over Tybee bar and found safe anchorage within. The emigrants were temporarily landed on Peeper island, where they dug a well and washed their clothes. It was Mr. Oglethorpe's purpose to send most of these Saltzburgers to Frederica that they might assist in the development of that town and the construction of its fortifications. Desiring the benefit of their ministers, not wishing to divide their congregation, and being reluctant to go to the Southward where "they apprehended blows,"—fighting being "against their religion,"—they persuaded Mr. Oglethorpe to permit them to join their countrymen at Ebenezer, whither they accordingly went some days afterwards and were heartily welcomed. It will be remembered, however, that Captain Hermsdorf, with his little company, assured Mr. Oglethorpe "that he would never forsake him, but serve with the English to the last." His offer was accepted, and on the 16th he set out with Mr. Oglethorpe for Frederica.

By this second accession the population of Ebenezer was increased so that it numbered in all some two hundred souls. Contentment and prosperity did not obtain in the town. In the fertility of the soil the inhabitants had encountered disappointment. Much sickness prevailed, and they were oppressed with the isolated character of their location. The creek upon which the town was situated was uncertain in volume, serpentine, and difficult of navigation. Although the distance from Old Ebenezer to the Savannah river by land did not exceed six miles, by following this, the only outlet by water, twenty-five miles must be passed before its confluence could be reached.*

Moved by these and other depressing considerations, the

* Strobels' Saltzburgers and their Descendants, p. 87. Baltimore, 1855.

Reverend Messrs. Bolzius and Gronau visited Savannah at the instance of their flock, and conferred with Mr. Oglethorpe as to the propriety of changing the location of the town. Moore says the Saltzburgers at Ebenezer were so discontented that they "demanded to leave their old Town, and to settle upon the Lands which the *Indians* had reserved for their own Use."*

Having patiently listened to the request, Mr. Oglethorpe, on the 9th of February, 1736, set out with the Saltzburger ministers and several gentlemen for Ebenezer, to make a personal inspection of the situation and satisfy himself with regard to the expediency of the removal. He was received with every mark of consideration, and proceeded at once to consider the causes which induced the inhabitants to desire a change. Admitting that the existing "dissatisfaction was not groundless, and that there were many embarrassments connected with their situation," he nevertheless endeavored to dissuade them from their purpose by reminding them that the labor already expended in clearing their lands, building houses, and constructing roads would, upon removal, be almost wholly lost. The hardships incident upon forming an entirely new settlement were urged upon their serious consideration. He also assured them that in clearing the forests, and in bringing the lands on the bank of the Savannah river under cultivation they would encounter the same diseases which afflicted them in their present location. He concluded, however, by assuring them that if they were resolved upon making the change he would not forbid it, but would assist them, as far as practicable, in compassing their design.

* Voyage to Georgia, &c., p. 23. London, 1741.

In reporting this change of location to the Trustees, Mr. Oglethorpe, on the 13th

After this conference, and upon Mr. Oglethorpe's return to Savannah, the question of a change of location was again considered by the Saltzburgers, who resolved among themselves that a removal was essential to the prosperity of their colony.* Acting upon this determination the community, without delay, set about migrating to the site selected for the new town. This was on a high ridge, near the Savannah river, called "Red Bluff" from the peculiar color of the soil. It received the name of New Ebenezer; and, to the simple-minded Germans, oppressed by poverty and saddened by the disappointments of the past, seemed to offer future happiness and much coveted prosperity. The labor of removal appears to have been compassed within less than two years. In June, 1738, Old Ebenezer ¶ had degenerated into a cow-pen, where Joseph Barker resided and "had the care of the Trust's Cattle." William Stephens gives us a pitiable view of the abandoned spot when he vis-

---

of February, wrote as follows: "The people at Ebenezer are very discontented and Mr. VonReck and they that come with him, refuse to settle to the Southward. I was forced to go to Ebenezer to quiet things there and have taken all the proceedings in writing. Finding the people were only ignorant and obstinate, but without any ill intention, I consented to the changing of their Town. They leave a sweet place where they had made great improvements, to go into a wood."*

*Collections of the Georgia Historical Society, vol. III, p. 13. Savannah, 1873. Compare Harris' Biographical Memorials of Oglethorpe, pp. 130, 132. Boston, 1841. Wright's Memoir of Oglethorpe, p. 113. London, 1867.

* Strobel's Saltzburgers and their Descendants, p. 89. Baltimore, 1855.

¶ Reverend Mr. John Wesley, writing in 1737, records in his Journal the following description of this abandoned settlement: "*Old Ebenezer*, where the *Saltzburghers* settled at first, lies twenty-five miles west of *Savannah*. A small Creek runs by the Town, down to the River, and many Brooks run between the little Hills: But the soil is a hungry, barren sand; and upon any sudden Shower, the Brooks rise several Feet perpendicular, and overflow whatever is near them. Since the *Saltzburghers* remov'd, two *English* Families have been placed there; but these too say, *That the Land is good for nothing; and that the Creek is of little Use; it being by Water twenty miles to the River; and the Water generally so low in Summer-time, that a Boat cannot come within six or sevem miles of the Town.*"*

*An Extract of the Rev. Mr. John Wesley's Journal, &c., &c., pp. 59, 60. Bristol, n. d.

ited it on the 26th of that month:—Indian traders, returning from Savannah, lodging for the night with Barker, who was unable to give due account of the cattle under his charge, and a servant, Sommers, moving about with "the Small-Pox out full upon him."* Thus early did "Old Ebenezer" take its silent place among the lost towns of Georgia. Its life of trials and sorrow, of ill-founded hope and sure disappointment, was measured by scarcely more than two years, and its frail memories were speedily lost amid the sighs and the shadows of the monotonous pines which environed the place.

The situation of the new Town, Mr. Strobel says, was quite romantic. "On the east lay the Savannah with its broad, smooth surface and its every varying and beautiful scenery. On the south was a stream, then called Little Creek, but now known as Lockner's Creek, and a large lake called 'Neidlinger's Sea;' while to the north, not very distant from the the town, was to be seen their old acquaintance, Ebenezer Creek, sluggishly winding its way to mingle with the waters of the Savannah. The surrounding country was gently undulating and covered with a fine growth of forest trees, while the jessamine, the woodbine and the beautiful azalia, with its variety of gaudy colors, added a peculiar richness to the picturesque scene. But unfortunately for the permanent prosperity of the town, it was surrounded on

*Journal of the Proceedings in Georgia, vol. I, pp. 226, 227. London, 1742.

In 1740 this Cow-Pen was still in existence at Old Ebenezer, the Trustees having a great number of cattle there. "But," continues the narrative, "they were much neglected, there not being Horses or Men sufficient to drive up the young and outlying cattle."*

*A State of the Province attested upon Oath in the Court of Savannah, November 10, 1740, p. 9. London, 1742.

Compare An Impartial Enquiry into the State and Utility of the Province of Georgia, p. 48. London, 1741.

Harris' Complete Collection of Voyages and Travels, &c., vol. II, p. 337. London, 1748.

three sides by low swamps which were subject to periodical inundation, and consequently generated a poisonous miasma prejudical to the health of the inhabitants."*

The plan adopted in laying out the town was prescribed by General Oglethorpe, and closely resembles that of Savannah ;—the size of the lots and the width of the streets and lanes being in each case quite similar. To John Gerar, William DeBrahm, his Majesty's Surveyor General for the Southern District of North America, who in 1757 erected a fort at Ebenezer, are we indebted for an accurate plan of that town.† As the village increased, this plan was extended ;—its distinctive characteristics being retained. From contemporaneous notices we learn that New Ebenezer, within a short time after its settlement, gave manifest token of substantial growth and prosperity. The houses there erected were larger and more comfortable than those which had been built in the old town. Gardens and farms were cleared, enclosed, and brought under creditable cultivation, and the sedate, religious inhabitants enjoyed the fruits of their industry and economy.

Funds received from Germany for that purpose were employed in the erection of an Orphan House, in which, for lack of a Church, the community worshipped for several years.

We presume the account of the condition of Ebenezer in 1738–9, furnished by Benjamin Martyn,‡ is as interesting and reliable as any that can be suggested. It is as follows: "Fifteen miles from *Purysburg* on the *Georgia* side, is *Ebenezer*, where the *Saltzburghers* are situated; their Houses are

* Strobel's Saltzburgers and their Descendants, p. 91. Baltimore, 1855.

† History of the Province of Georgia, &c., Plan facing p. 24. Wormsloe, 1849.

‡ An Impartial Enquiry into the State and Utility of the Province of Georgia, p. 47. London, 1741.

neat, and regularly set out in Streets, and the whole Œconomy of their town, under the Influence of their Ministers, Mess. *Bolzius* and *Gronau*, is very exemplary. For the Benefit of their Milch Cattle, a Herdsman is appointed to attend them in the Woods all the Day, and bring them Home in the Evening. Their Stock of out-lying Cattle is also under the Care of two other Herdsmen, who attend them in their Feeding in the Day, and drive them into Cow-Pens at night. This secures the Owners from any Loss, and the Herdsmen are paid by a small Contribution among the People. These are very industrious, and subsist comfortably by their Labour. Though there is no regular Court of Justice, as they live in Sobriety, they maintain great Order and Decency. In case of any Differences, the Minister calls three or four of the most prudent Elders together, who in a summary Way hear and determine as they think just, and the Parties always acquiesce with Content in their Judgment. They are very regular in their public Worship, which is on Week-Days in the Evening

---

Another contemporaneous account is almost identical; "On the *Georgia* side [of the Savannah river], twelve miles from *Purysburg*, is the Town of *Ebenezer*, which thrives very much; there are very good Houses built for each of the Ministers, and an Orphan House; and they have partly framed Houses and partly Huts, neatly built, and formed into regular streets; they have a great deal of Cattle and Corn-Ground, so that they sell Provisions at *Savannah;* for they raise much more than they can consume."*

---

* A State of the Province of Georgia attested upon Oath in the Court of Savannah, November 10, 1740, p. 5, London, 1742. See also idem, pp. 29, 31. "An Impartial Enquiry into the State and Utility of the Province of Georgia," p. 13. London, 1741.

Compare Harris' Complete Collection of Voyages and Travels, &c., vol. II, p. 337. London, 1748.

The Rev. Mr. John Wesley's description is as follows: "*New Ebenezer*, to which the *Saltzburghers* removed in *March*, 1736, lies six Miles Eastward from the *Old*, on a high bluff, near the *Savannah* River Here are some Tracts of Fruitful Land, tho' the greatest Part of that adjoining to the Town, is Pine-barren. The Huts, 60 in number, are neatly and regularly built; the little Piece of Ground allotted to each for a Garden, is everywhere put to the best Use, no spot being left unplanted. Nay, even one of the main Streets, being one more than was as yet wanted, bore them this year a crop of *Indian Corn.*"

An Extract of the Rev. Mr. John Wesley's Journal, &c., p. 60. Bristol, n. d.

after their Work; and in the Forenoon and Evening on Sundays. They have built a large and convenient House for the Reception of Orphans, and other poor Children, who are maintained by Benefactions among the People, are well taken Care of and taught to work according as their Age and Ability will permit. The Number computed by Mr. *Bolzius* in *June*, 1738, whereof his Congregation consisted, was one hundred forty-six, and some more have since been settled among them. They are all in general so well pleased with their condition, that not one of their People has abandoned the Settlement."

General Oglethorpe received a letter, dated Ebenezer, March 13, 1739, signed by forty-nine men of the Saltzburgers and verified by their Ministers, in which they assured him that they were well settled and pleased with the climate and condition of the country; that although the season was hotter than that of their native land, having become accustomed to it, they found it tolerable and convenient for working people; and that their custom was to commence their out-door labor early in the morning and continue it until ten o'clock; resuming it again from three in the afternoon until sun-set. During the heated term of mid-day, matters within their houses engaged their attention. The General was also informed that they had practically demonstrated the falsity of the tale told them on their arrival that rice could be cultivated only by negroes. "We laugh at such a Talking,"—so they wrote, "seeing that several People of us have had, in last Harvest, a greater Crop of Rice than they wanted for their own Consumption. Of Corn, Pease, Potatoes, Pumpkins, Cabbage, &c., we had such a good Quantity that many Bushels are sold, and much was spent in feeding Cows, Calves and Hogs." The letter concludes with an earnest petition that negroes should be excluded from their town and neighborhood, alleging as a reason that their houses and gardens would be robbed by them, and that, "besides other great inconveniences, white people were in danger of life from them."*

Of humble origin and moderate education, of primitive habits, accustomed to labor, free from covetousness and ambition, temperate, industrious, frugal and orderly, solicitous for the education of their children and the maintenance of the needy and the orphan, meddling not in the affairs of their neighbors, acknowledging allegiance to the Trustees and the King of England, maintaining direct connection with the Lutheran Church in Germany, and submitting without question to the decisions of their ministers and elders in all matters, whether of a civil or ecclesiastical nature, engaging in no pursuits save of an agricultural or a mechanical character, and little given either to excitement or wandering, these Saltzburgers for years preserved the integrity of their community and their religion, and secured for themselves a comfortable existence. As early as 1738 the Saltzburgers at Ebenezer made some limited experiment in growing cotton and were much encouraged;—the yield being abundant, and of an excellent quality. The Trustees, however, having fixed their hopes upon silk and wine, the cultivation of this plant was not countenanced.†

It was estimated by Mr. Benjamin Martyn, Secretary of the Trustees, that up to the year 1741, not less than twelve

---

* An Impartial Enquiry into the State and Utility of the Province of Georgia, pp. 69, 72. London, 1741.

Compare A State of the Province of Georgia attested upon Oath, &c., pp. 5, 29, 30, 32. London, 1742.

An Account showing the Progress of the Colony of Georgia in America, &c., pp. 66, 69. London, 1741.

† See McCall's History of Georgia, vol. I, p. 199. Savannah, 1811.

hundred German Protestants had arrived in the Colony. Their principal settlements were at Ebenezer, Bethany, Savannah, Frederica, Goshen, and along the road leading from Savannah to Ebenezer. They were all characterized by industry, sobriety, and thrift.

About the year 1744 the Saltzburgers at Ebenezer and along the line of the public road running from that town to Savannah, through the assistance of friends in Germany, were enabled to build two comfortable and substantial houses for public worship,—one at New Ebenezer, called *Jerusalem Church*, and the other about four miles below, named *Zion Church*. The joy experienced upon the dedication of these sacred buildings was soon turned to grief by the death of one of their faithful pastors,—the Reverend Israel C. Gronau,—who, in the supreme moments of a lingering fever, desiring a friend to support his hands uplifted in praise of the Great Master whom he had so long and so truthfully served, exclaimed "Come, Lord Jesus! Amen!! Amen!!!" and with these words,—the last upon his lips,—entered into peace.*

Reverend Mr. Bolzius continued to be the principal pastor and, as an assistant, the Reverend Mr. Lembke was associated with him.

As early as January 31, 1732, Sir Thomas Lombe† certified to the Trustees of the Colony that silk produced in Carolina possessed "as much natural Strength and Beauty as the Silk of Italy." In his "New and Accurate Account of the Provinces of South Carolina and Georgia,"‡ Mr. Oglethorpe enumerated among the chief revenues which

* See Strobel's Saltzburgers and their Descendants, p. 123. Baltimore, 1855.

† An Account showing the Progress of the Colony of Georgia, &c., pp. 39, 40. London, 1741.

‡ Chapter V, pp. 55, 59. London, 1733.

might be anticipated from the settlement of Georgia, profits to arise from the manufacture of silk. His opinion was that between forty and fifty thousand people might be advantageously employed in this business. In view of the encouragement which might reasonably be expected from Parliament, and the cheapness of the labor and land, he estimated that the cost of production would be at least twenty-five per cent. lower than that then current in Piedmont. Sharing in this belief, the Trustees sent to Italy for silk-worm eggs, and engaged the services of several Piedmontese to go to Georgia and instruct the Colonists in the production of silk.* In the grants of land to parties emigrating to Georgia either at their own expense or at the charge of the Charity, may be found covenants on the part of the grantees to "keep a sufficient number of white mulberry trees standing on every acre," or else to "plant them where they were wanted." A special plea is entered by Benjamin Martyn in behalf of silk-culture in Georgia and the manifest benefits to be expected.†

The early accounts all agree in representing the production of silk as one of the most important matters to be considered and fostered in connection with the establishment and development of the Colony of Georgia.

In 1735, Queen Caroline, upon the King's birth-day, appeared in a full robe of Georgia silk; and in 1739 a parcel of raw silk, brought from Georgia by Samuel Augspourguer, was exhibited at the Trustees' office in London to "Mr. John Zachary,—an eminent raw-silk merchant,—and to Mr. Booth,—one of the greatest silk-weavers in England,"—both

* An Account showing the Progress of the Colony of Georgia in America, p. 13. London, 1741.

† Martyn's Reasons for establishing the Colony of Georgia with regard to the Trade of Great Britain, p. 9. London, 1733.

of whom "declared it to be as fine as any Italian silk, and worth at least twenty shillings a pound."*

With that industry and patience so characteristic of them as a people, the inhabitants of New Ebenezer were among the earliest and the most persevering in their efforts to carry into practical operation Mr. Oglethorpe's wishes in regard to the production of silk. In 1736 each Saltzburger there was presented with a mulberry tree, and two of the congregation were instructed by Mrs. Camuse in the art of reeling.

Under date of May 11th, 1741, Mr. Bolzius, in his journal, records the fact that within the preceding two months twenty girls succeeded in making seventeen pounds of cocoons which were sold at Savannah for £3, 8s. The same year £5 were advanced by General Oglethorpe to this Clergyman for the purchase of trees. With this sum he procured twelve hundred, and distributed them among the families of his parish.

On the 4th of December, 1742, five hundred trees were sent by General Oglethorpe to Ebenezer, with a promise of more should they be needed. Near Mr. Bolzius' house a machine for the manufacture of raw-silk was erected, and the construction of a public Filature was contemplated. Of the eight hundred and forty-seven pounds of cocoons raised in the Colony of Georgia in 1747, about one-half was produced by the Saltzburgers at Ebenezer. Two years afterwards this yield was increased to seven hundred and sixty-two pounds of cocoons, and fifty pounds thirteen ounces of spun silk. Two machines were in operation in Mr. Bolzius' yard, capable of reeling twenty-four ounces per day. It was

* An Account showing the Progress of the Colony of Georgia in America, &c., p. 32. London, 1741.

apparent, however, that while, by ordinary labor, about two shillings could be earned, scarcely a shilling per diem could be expected by one engaged in the manufacture of silk. This fact proved so discouraging to the Colonists that, except at Ebenezer, silk culture was generally relinquished. The Germans persevered, and as the result of their energy, over a thousand pounds of cocoons and seventy-four pounds, two ounces of raw-silk were raised at Ebenezer in 1750, and sold for £110 sterling. The community was now pretty well supplied with copper basins and reeling machines. Considerable effort was made in England to attract the notice of the Home Government to this production of silk in Georgia, and to enlist in its behalf fostering influences at the hands of those in authority. In 1755 a paper was laid before the Lords of Trade and Plantations, signed by about forty eminent silk throwsters and weavers, declaring that "having examined about 300 wt. of Georgia raw-silk they found it as good as the Piedmontese, and better than the common Italian silks." Assurance was given that there was the utmost reason to afford "all possible encouragement for the raising of so valuable a commodity."*

In 1764 fifteen thousand two hundred and twelve pounds of cocoons were delivered at the Filature in Savannah, then under the charge of Mr. Ottolenghe, of which eight thousand six hundred and ninety-five pounds were contributed by the Saltzburgers. In 1766 the production of silk in Georgia reached its acme, and from that time, despite the encouragement extended by Parliament, continued to decline until it was practically abandoned a few years before the inception of the Revolution. Operations at the Filature

* Gentleman's Magazine for 1755, p. 185.
London " " " p. 186.

in Savannah were discontinued in 1771; and Sir James Wright, in his message to the Commons House of Assembly, under date 19th of January, 1774, alludes to the fact that the Filature buildings were falling into decay, and suggests that they be put to some other use.

Despite the disinclination existing in other portions of the Colony to devote much time and labor to the growing of trees and the manufacture of silk, the Saltzburgers,—incited by their worthy magistrate, Mr. Wertsch,—redoubled their efforts, and in 1770, as the result of their industry, shipped two hundred and ninety-one pounds of raw-silk. At the suggestion of the Earl of Hillsborough, who warmly commended the zeal of these Germans and interested himself in procuring from Parliament a small sum to be expended in aid of the more indigent of the community, Mr. Habersham distributed among them the basins and reels then being in the unused public Filature in Savannah.

"So popular had the silk business become at Ebenezer that Mr. Habersham, in a letter dated the 30th of March, 1772, says: 'Some persons in almost every family there understand its process from the beginning to the end.' In 1771 the Germans sent four hundred and thirty-eight pounds of raw silk to England, and in 1772 four hundred and eighty-five pounds:—all of their own raising. They made their own reels, which were so much esteemed that one was sent to England as a model, and another taken to the East Indies by Pickering Robinson."*

In the face of the distractions encountered upon the commencement of hostilities between the Colonies and the Mother Country, silk culture languished even among these

*Silk Culture in Georgia, by Dr. Stevens. Harris' Memorials of Oglethorpe, pp. 410, 411. Boston, 1841.

Germans, and was never afterwards revived to any considerable degree. The unfriendliness of climate, the high price of labor, the withdrawal of all bounty—which had been the chief stimulus to exertion,—and the larger profits to be derived from the cultivation of rice and cotton combined to interrupt silk-raising, and, in the end, caused its total abandonment.

The construction of a bridge over Ebenezer creek materially promoted the interests and the convenience of those residing at Ebenezer; and the erection of Churches at Bethany and Goshen,—the former about five miles northwest of Ebenezer, and the latter some ten miles below and near the road leading to Savannah,—indicated the growth of the German plantations along the line of the Savannah river.

The settlement at Bethany was effected in 1751 by John Gerar William DeBrahm, who there located one hundred and sixty Germans. Eleven months afterwards these Colonists were joined by an equal number,—"the Relations and Acquaintance of the former." The Saltzburgers then numbered about fifteen hundred souls.* Alluding to the location and growth of these plantations, and the agricultural pursuits of their cultivators, Surveyor-General DeBrahm says: "The German Settlements have since Streatched S: Eastwardly about 32 miles N: W-ward from the Sea upon Savannah Stream, from whence they extend up the same Stream through the whole Salt Air Zona. They cultivate European and American Grains to Perfection; as Wheat, Rye, Barley, Oats; also Flax, Hemp, Tobacco and Rice, Indigo, Maize, Peas, Pompions, Melons—they plant Mulberry, Apple, Peach, Nectorins, Plumbs and Quince Trees,

* History of the Province of Georgia, &c. p. 20. Wormsloe, 1749.

besides all manner of European Garden Herbs, but, in particular, they Chose the Culture of silk their principal Object, in which Culture they made such a Progress, that the Filature, which is erected in the City of Savannah could afford to send in 1768 to London 1,084 Pounds of raw Silk, equal in Goodness to that manufactured in Piemont; but the Bounties to encourage that Manufactory being taken off, they discouraged, dropt their hands from that Culture from year to year in a manner, that in 1771 its Product was only 290 Pounds in lieu of 1,464, which must have been that year's Produce, had this Manufactory been encouraged to increase at a 16 years rate. In lieu of Silk they have taken under more Consideration the Culture of Maize, Rice, Indigo, Hemp & Tobacco: But the Vines have not as yet become an Object of their Attention, altho' in the Country especially over the German Settlements, Nature makes all the Promises, yea gives yearly full Assurances of her Assistance by her own Endeavours producing Clusture Grapes in Abundance on its uncultivated Vines; yet there is no Person, who will listen to her Addresses, and give her the least Assistance, notwithstanding many of the Inhabitants are refreshed from the Sweetness of her wild Productions. The Culture of Indigo is brought to the same Perfection here, as in South Carolina, and is manufactured through all the Settlements from the Sea Coast, to the Extent of the interior Country."*

On the 19th of November, 1765, the Ebenezer congregation was called upon to mourn the loss of its venerable Spiritual Guide, the Reverend Mr. Bolzius, who had been at once teacher and magistrate, counsellor and friend during the thirty years of poverty and privation, labor and sorrow, hope and joy, passed in the wilds of Georgia. He was

* History of the Province of Georgia, &c., pp. 21, 22. Wormsloe, 1849.

interred, amid the lamentations of his people, in the cemetery near Jerusalem Church, and no stone marks his grave.

After his demise the conduct of the Society devolved upon Messrs. Lembke and Rabenhorst. This involved not only the spiritual care of this people, but also the preservation and proper management of the mill-establishments and public property belonging to the Ebenezer Congregation. "These two faithful men," writes the Reverend P. A. Strobel,* "labored harmoniously and successfully in the discharge of their heavy civil and religious obligations, and gave entire satisfaction to those with whose interests they were intrusted." During their administration the large brick house of worship, known as Jerusalem Church, was built at Ebenezer. The materials used in its construction were, for the most part, supplied by the Saltzburgers, while the funds necessary to defray the cost of erection were contributed by friends in Germany.

Upon the death of Mr. Lembke, the Reverend Christopher F. Triebner "was sent over by the reverend fathers in Germany as an adjunct to Mr. Rabenhorst. Being a young man of talents, but of an impetuous and ambitious disposition, he soon raised such a tumult in the quiet community that all the efforts of the famous Mr. Muhlenburg, who was ordered on a special mission to Ebenezer in 1774 to heal the disturbances which had arisen, scarce saved the congregation from disintegration. The schism was, however, finally cured, and peace was restored." For the better government of the Society, articles of discipline were prepared by Dr. Muhlenburg, which were formally subscribed by one hundred and twenty-four male members. This occurred at Jerusalem Church on the 16th of January, 1775,

* The Saltzburgers and their Descendants, &c., p. 149. Baltimore, 1855.

and affords substantial evidence of the strength of the congregation.

The property belonging to the Church, according to an inventory made by Dr. Muhlenburg in 1775, consisted of the following:

"1. In the hands of Pastor Rabenhorst a capital of £300. 16s. 5d.

2. In the hands of John Casper Wertsch, for the store, £300.

3. In the mill treasury, notes and money, £229. 16s. 2d.

4. Pastor Triebner has some money in hands, (£400) the application of which has not been determined by our Reverend Fathers.

5. Belonging to the Church is a Negro Boy at Mr. John Flöerls', and a Negro Girl at Mr. David Steiner's.

6. A town-lot and an out-lot, of which Mr. John Triebner has the grant in his hands.

7. An inventory of personal goods in the mills belonging to the estate.

8. And, finally, real estate, with the mills, 925 acres of land."

Including certain legacies from private individuals, and donations from patrons of the Colony in Germany, which were received within a short time, it is conjectured that this church property was then worth not much less than twenty thousand dollars.

So long as the congregation at Ebenezer preserved its integrity, direct allegiance to the parent Church in Germany was acknowledged, its precepts, orders and deliverances were obeyed, its teachers welcomed and respected, and accounts of all receipts, disbursements, and important transactions regularly rendered. Its pastors continued to be charged with the administration of affairs, both spiritual and temporal, and were the duly constituted custodians of all church funds and property. Upon their arrival in Georgia these Saltzburgers, wearied with persecutions and stripped of the small possessions which were once theirs, were at first quite dependent upon public and private charity for bare subsistence. They were then unable, by voluntary contributions, to sustain their pastors and teachers, and build churches. Foreign aid arrived, however, from time to time, and this was supplemented in a small, yet generous way, by the labor of the parishioners and such sums and articles as could be spared from their slow accumulations. With a view to providing for the future, all means thus derived were carefully invested for the benefit of church and pastor. This system was maintained for more than fifty years, so that in the course of time not only were churches built, but reasonable provision was made for clergyman, teacher, and orphan, aside from the yearly voluntary contributions of the members of the Society. The education of youths was not neglected; and DeBrahm assures us that in his day a library had been accumulated at Ebenezer in which "could be had Books wrote in the Caldaic, Hebrew, Arabec, Siriac, Coptic, Malabar, Greek, Latin, French, German, Dutch and Spanish, beside the English, viz: in thirteen Languages."*

In the division of the Province of Georgia into eight Parishes, which occurred on the 15th of March, 1758, "the district of Abercorn and Goshen, and the district of Ebenezer—extending from the northwest boundaries of the parish of Christ Church up the river Savannah as far as the Beaver Dam, and southwest as far as the mouth of Horse-Creek on the river Great Ogechee"—were declared a Parish under

* History of the Province of Georgia, &c., p. 24. Wormsloe, 1849.

the name of "The Parish of St. Matthew."* The parish just below, on the line of the Savannah river, and embracing the town of Savannah, was known as "Christ Church Parish."

The Parish of St. Matthew, and the upper part of St. Philip lying above the Canouchee river, were, by the Constitution of Georgia adopted at Savannah on the 5th of February, 1777, consolidated into a county called Effingham.†

In the opinion of the Reverend Mr. Strobel, to whose valuable sketch of the Saltzburgers and their descendants we are indebted for much of the information contained in these pages, Ebenezer attained the height of its importance about 1774. The population of the town proper was not less than five hundred, embracing agriculturists, mechanics, and shop-keepers, who pursued their respective avocations with energy and thrift. Trade with Savannah and Charleston was carried on by means of sloops and schooners. In a contemporaneous picture, representing the general appearance of the town, may be seen two schooners riding at anchor near the Ebenezer landing.‡

Although there arose a sharp division of sentiment when the question of direct opposition to the acts of Parliament was discussed at Ebenezer in 1774, and although quite a number of the inhabitants favored "passive obedience and non-resistance," the response of the majority was: "We have experienced the evils of tyranny in our own land;

---

* Marbury and Crawford's Digest, pp. 150, 151.

Under the Writs of Election issued by Sir James Wright in 1761, the following gentlemen were returned as members from St. Matthew's Parish:

Abercorn and Goshen—William Francis.

Ebenezer—William Ewen, N. W. Jones, and James de Veaux.¶

¶ McCall's History of Georgia, vol I, p. 285.

† Watkins' Digest, p. 8.

‡ See Strobel's Saltzburgers and their Descendants, p. 194. Baltimore, 1855.

for the sake of liberty we have left home, lands, houses, estates, and have taken refuge in the wilds of Georgia; shall we now submit again to bondage? No, never." Among the delegates from the Parish of St. Matthew to the Provincial Congress which assembled in Savannah on the 4th of July, 1775, were the following Saltzburgers: John Stirk, John Adam Treutlen, Jacob Waldhauer, John Flöerl, and Christopher Craemer. Despite the fact that as a community the Saltzburgers espoused the cause of the Revolutionists, a considerable faction, headed by Mr. Triebner, maintained an open and a strenuous adherence to the Crown. Between these parties sprang up an angry controversy, replete with the bitterest feelings, and very prejudicial to the peace and prosperity of the congregation. In the midst of the discussion the Reverend Mr. Rabenhorst, who exerted his utmost influence to curb the dominant passions and inculcate mutual forbearance, crowned his long and useful life with a saintly death.

Three days after the capture of Savannah by Colonel Campbell, a strong force was advanced, under the command of Lieut. Col. Maitland, to Cherokee Hill. The following day [January 2, 1779,] Ebenezer was occupied by the British troops. Upon their arrival they threw up a redoubt within a few hundred yards of Jerusalem Church and fortified the position.‡ The remains of this work are said to be still visible. The moment he learned that Savannah had fallen before Colonel Campbell's column, Mr. Triebner hastened to that place, proclaimed his loyalty, and took the oath of allegiance. The intimation is that he counselled the immediate occupation of Ebenezer, and in person accom-

‡ In 1776, Ebenezer had been partially fortified by the Revolutionists.*

* See letter of Sir James Wright to Lord George Germain under date March 20, 1776. Collections of the Georgia Historical Society, vol. III, p. 239, Savannah, 1873.

panied the detachment which compassed the capture of his own town and people. He was a violent, uncompromising man,—at all times intent upon the success of his peculiar views and wishes. Influenced by his advice and example, not a few of the Saltzburgers subscribed oaths of allegiance to the British Crown, and received certificates guaranteeing Royal protection to person and property. Prominent among those who maintained their adherence to the Rebel cause were Governor John Adam Trentlen, William Holsendorf, Colonel John Stirk, Secretary Samuel Stirk, John Schnider, Rudolph Strohaker, Jonathan Schnider, J. Gotlieb Schnider, Jonathan Rahn, Ernest Zittrauer, and Joshua and Jacob Helfenstein.

"The citizens at Ebenezer and the surrounding country," says Mr. Strobel, "were made to feel very severely the effects of the war. The property of those who did not take the oath of allegiance was confiscated, and they were constantly exposed to every species of insult and wrong from a hired and profligate soldiery. Besides this, some of the Saltzburgers who espoused the cause of the Crown became very inveterate in their hostility to the Whigs in the settlement, and pillaged and then burnt their dwellings. The residence on the farm of the pious Rabenhorst was among the first given to the flames. Among those who distinguished themselves for their cruelty was one Eichel,—who has been properly termed an 'inhuman miscreant,'—whose residence was at Goshen, and Martin Dasher, who kept a public house five miles below Ebenezer. These men placed themselves at the head of marauding parties, composed of British and Tories, and laid waste every plantation or farm whose occupant was even suspected of favoring the Republican cause. In these predatory excursions the most revolting cruelty and unbridled licentiousness were indulged, and the whole country was overrun and devastated. * * * The Salzburgers, nevertheless, were to experience great annoyances from other sources. * * * A line of British posts had been established all along the western bank of the Savannah river to check the demonstrations of the Rebel forces in Carolina. Under these circumstances, Ebenezer, from its somewhat central position, became a kind of thoroughfare for the British troops in passing through the country from Augusta to Savannah. To the inhabitants of Ebenezer, particularly, this was a source of perpetual annoyance. British troops were constantly quartered among them, and to avoid the rudeness of the soldiers and the heavy tax upon their resources, many of the best citizens were forced to abandon their homes and settle in the country, thus leaving their houses to the mercy of their cruel invaders.

"Besides all this, they were forced to witness almost daily acts of cruelty practised by the British and Tories toward those Americans who happened to fall into their hands as prisoners of war; for it will be remembered that Ebenezer, while in the hands of the British, was the point to which all prisoners taken in the surrounding country were brought and from thence sent to Savannah. It was from this post that the prisoners were carried who were rescued by Sergeant Jasper and his comrade, Newton, at the Jasper Spring, a few miles above Savannah.

"There was one act performed by the British commander which was peculiarly trying and revolting to the Salzburgers. Their fine brick church was converted into a hospital for the accommodation of the sick and wounded, and subsequently it was desecrated by being used as a stable for their horses. To this latter use it was devoted until the close of the war and the removal of the British troops from Georgia. To show their contempt for the church and their disregard for the religious sentiments of the people, the church records were nearly all destroyed, and the soldiers would discharge their guns at different objects on the church; and even to this day the metal "*Swan*" (Luther's coat of arms) which surmounts the spire on the steeple, bears the mark of a musket ball which was fired through it by a reckless soldier. Often, too, cannon were discharged at the houses; and there is a log-house now standing not far from Ebenezer, which was perforated by several cannon shot. * * * The Salzburgers endured all these hardships and indignities with becoming fortitude; and though a few were overcome by these severe measures, yet the great mass of them remained firm in their attachment to the principles of liberty."*

It is suggested that the establishment of tippling houses in Ebenezer, during its occupancy by the British, and constant intercourse with a licentious soldiery, corrupted the lives of not a few of the once sober and orderly Germans. That the protracted presence of the enemy, the confiscation of estates, the interruption of regular pursuits, the expulsion of such as clave to the Confederate cause, and the general demoralization cosnequent upon a state of war, tended to the manifest injury and depopulation of the town, cannot, for a moment, be questioned. Indications of decay and ruin were patent in Ebenezer before the cessation of hostilities. From the time of its occupation by Maitland, shortly after the capture of Savannah by Colonel Campbell in December, 1778,—with the exception of the limited period when its garrison was called in to assist in the

* Strobel's Saltzburgers and their Descendants, pp. 203, 207. Baltimore, 1855.

defense of Savannah against the operations of the allied army under the command of Count DeEstaing and General Lincoln in the fall of 1779,—Ebenezer continued in the possession of the British until a short time prior to the evacuation of Savannah in July, 1783. In his advance toward Savannah, General Anthony Wayne established his head quarters at this town. The Tory pastor, Triebner, who, during the struggle had sided with the Royalists and remained unmoved amid the sufferings and oppressions of his people, betook himself to flight so soon as the English forces were withdrawn, and found a refuge in England, where he ended his days in seclusion.

Upon the evacuation of Savannah, many of the Saltzburgers returned to Ebenezer. Its aspect was sadly changed. Not a few of the abandoned dwellings had been burned. Others had fallen into decay. Smiling gardens had been trampled into desert places, and the impress of stagnation, neglect, and desolation was upon everything. Jerusalem Church was a mass of filth, and very dilapidated. Notwithstanding this sad condition of affairs, much energy was displayed in the purification and renovation of this temple of worship, and in the rehabilitation of the town.

The arrival of the Reverend John Ernest Bergman,—a clergyman of decided talents and of considerable literary attainments,—and the revival of the parochial school greatly encouraged the depressed inhabitants and promoted the general improvement of the place. The population began to increase. It assumed an apparently permanent character, and countenanced the hope that the ante-bellum quiet, good order, thrift, and prosperity would be regained. This expectation, however, was not fully realized. The former trade never revived. The mills were never again put in motion. Silk-culture was renewed only to a limited degree. Having for twenty-five years more remained about stationary, New Ebenezer commenced visibly to decline; and, when scarcely more than a century old, took its place, in silence and nothingness, among the dead towns of Georgia.*

The act of February 26th, 1784,† provided for the erection of the "Court House and Gaol" and for holding public elections in Effingham County at Tuckasee-King, near the present line of Scriven County. The situation proving inconvenient, three years afterwards the county-seat was removed to Elberton, near Indian Bluff, on the north side of the Great Ogeechee river.

On the 18th of February, 1796, the Legislature of Georgia‡ appointed Jeremiah Cuyler, John G. Neidlinger, Jonathan Rawhn, Elias Hodges, and John Martin Dasher "commissioners for the town and common of Ebenezer," with instructions to have the town "surveyed and laid out as nearly as possible in conformity to the original plan thereof, to sell all vacant lots, and such as had become vested in the State, [reserving such only as were necessary for public uses,] and appropriate the proceeds to the erection of a County Court House and Jail." Any over-plus was to be applied to building a public Academy. For three years only did Ebenezer remain the County Town of Effingham County. In 1799, its public buildings were sold, and the village of Springfield was designated by the Legislature as "the permanent seat for the public buildings of the County of Effing-

---

* Ebenezer is not mentioned among the principal towns of Georgia enumerated by George Sibbald in 1801.

See "Notes and Observations on the Pine Lands of Georgia," &c., pp. 58 to 66. Augusta, 1801.

† Watkins' Digest, p. 298.

‡ Marbury and Crawford's Digest, pp. 154, 155.

ham."* David Hall, Joshua Loper, Samuel Ryals, Godhelf Smith, and Drurias Garrison were appointed commissioners to carry this change into effect.

In 1808 the Ebenezer Congregation received legislative permission to sell the glebe lands which it owned. By degrees all the real estate held by the society was disposed of. The proceeds arising from these sales were invested in lands, mortgages, and securities;—the interest accruing being applied to the payment of the pastor's salary and the current expenses of the church.†

Until about the year 1803 all the religious services observed by the Saltzburgers were conducted in the German language; and, in the church at Ebenezer, for a long time subsequent to that date, the religious exercises continued in that tongue. Methodist and Baptist Churches springing up in the neighborhood drew away many of the younger members of the congregation. The introduction of the English language into all the Saltzburger Churches was effected in 1824 through the instrumentality of the Reverend Christopher F. Bergman.

Year by year Ebenezer became more sparsely populated. Many of its citizens removed into the interior and upper parts of the county. Quite a number formed settlements in Scriven County, while others went to Savannah, and to Lowndes, Liberty, and Thomas counties. Others still,—more enterprizing than their fellows,—sought new homes in South Carolina, Alabama, Florida, Pennsylvania, and Ohio.

We close this sketch with a picture of Ebenezer painted by one of the late Pastors‡ of Jerusalem Church,—a gen-

* Marbury and Crawford's Digest, p. 158.

† See Strobel's Saltzburgers and their Descendants, p. 234. Baltimore, 1855.

‡ Rev'd P. A. Strobel.

tleman of cultivation and of piety, who saw the last waves of oblivion as they closed over the town and obliterated its decayed traces from the grass covered bluff of the Savannah.

"To one visiting the ancient town of Ebenezer, in the present day [1855] the prospect which presents itself is anything but attractive; and the stranger who is unacquainted with its history would perhaps discover very little to excite his curiosity or awaken his sympathies. The town has gone almost entirely to ruins. Only two residences are now remaining, and one of these is untenanted. The old church, however, stands in bold relief upon an open lawn, and by its somewhat antique appearance seems silently, yet forcibly, to call up the reminiscences of former years. Not far distant from the church is the cemetery, in which are sleeping the remains of the venerable men who founded the colony and the church, and many of their descendants who, one by one, have gone down to the grave to mingle their ashes with those of their illustrious ancestors.

"Except upon the Sabbath, when the descendants of the Saltzburgers go up to their temple to worship the God of their fathers, the stillness which reigns around Ebenezer is seldom broken, save by the warbling of birds, the occasional transit of a steamer, or the murmurs of the Savannah as it flows on to lose itself in the ocean. The sighing winds chant melancholy dirges as they sweep through the lofty pines and cedars which cast their sombre shades over this 'deserted village.' Desolation seems to have spread over this once-favored spot its withering wing, and here, where generation after generation grew up and flourished, where the persecuted and exiled Saltzburgers reared their offspring in the hope that they would leave a numerous progeny of pious, useful, and prosperous citizens, and where everything seemed to betoken the establishment of a thrifty and permanent colony, scarcely anything is to be seen, except the sad evidences of decay and death."

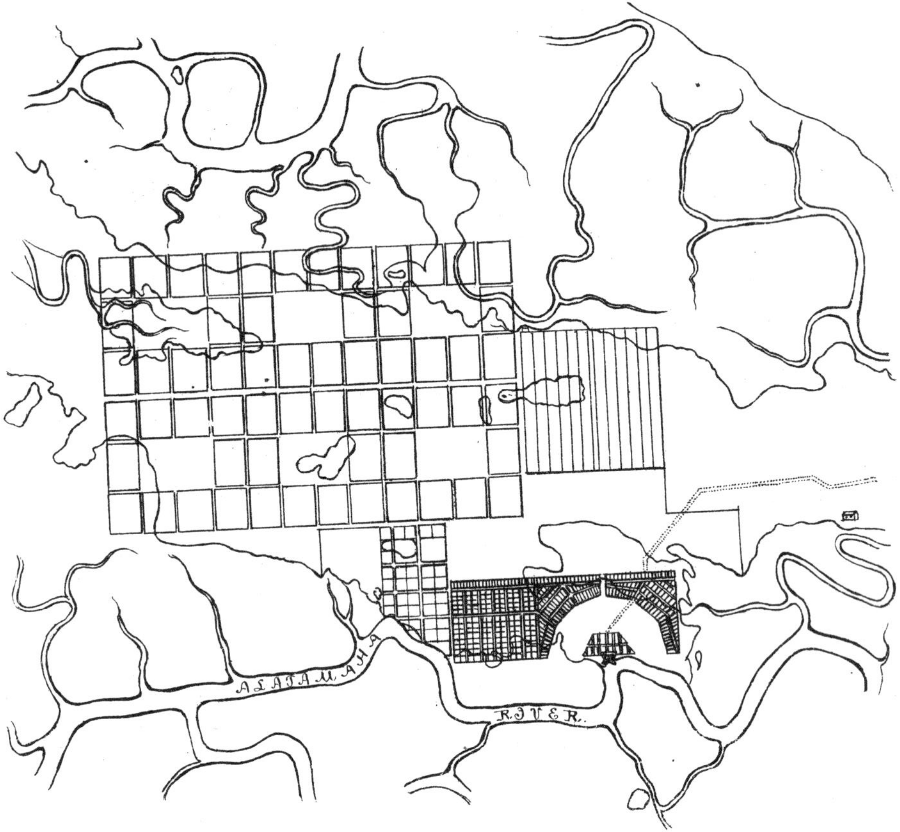

Plan of the Town of Frederica, on St Simon's Island, Georgia.

J. Bien Photo. Lith. N.Y.

II.

FREDERICA.

"As the Mind of Man cannot form a more exalted Pleasure than what arises from the Reflexion of having relieved the Distressed; let the Man of Benevolence, whose Substance enables him to contribute towards this Undertaking, give a Loose for a little to his Imagination, pass over a few Years of his Life, and think himself in a Visit to *Georgia*. Let him see those, who are now a Prey to all the Calamities of Want, who are starving with Hunger, and seeing their Wives and Children in the same Distress; expecting likewise every Moment to be thrown into a Dungeon, with the cutting Anguish that they leave their Families expos'd to the utmost Necessity and Despair: Let him, I say, see these living under a sober and orderly Government, settled in Towns, which are rising at Distances along navigable Rivers: Flocks and Herds in the neighbouring Pastures, and adjoining to them Plantations of regular Rows of Mulberry-Trees, entwin'd with Vines, the Branches of which are loaded with Grapes; let him see Orchards of Oranges, Pomegranates, and Olives; in other Places extended Fields of Corn, or Flax and Hemp. In short, the whole Face of the Country chang'd by Agriculture, and Plenty in every Part of it. Let him see the People all in Employment of various Kinds, Women and Children feeding and nursing the Silkworms, winding off the Silk, or gathering the Olives; the Men ploughing and planting their Lands, tending their Cattle, or felling the Forest, which they burn for Potashes, or square for the Builder; let him see these in Content and Affluence, and Masters of little Possessions which they can leave to their Children; and then let him think if they are not happier than those supported by Charity in Idleness. Let him reflect that the Produce of their Labour will be so much new Wealth for his Country, and then let him ask himself, Whether he would exchange the Satisfaction of having contributed to this, for all the trifling Pleasures the Money, which he has given, would have purchas'd.

"Of all publick-spirited Actions, perhaps none can claim a Preference to the Settling of Colonies, as none are in the End more useful. * * * Whoever then is a Lover of Liberty will be pleas'd with an Attempt to recover his fellow Subjects from a State of Misery and Oppression, and fix them in Happiness and Freedom.

"Whoever is a Lover of his Country will approve of a Method for the Employment of her Poor, and the Increase of her People and her Trade. Whoever is a Lover of Mankind will join his wishes to the Success of a Design so plainly calculated for their Good: Undertaken, and conducted with so much Disinterestedness."

By such suggestions did Benjamin Martyn* seek to enlist the public sympathy in behalf of the then projected but not established Colony of Georgia.

Mr. Oglethorpe, in a contemporaneous publication,† had

---

* Reasons for Establishing the Colony of Georgia with regard to the Trade of Great Britain, &c., pp. 38–41. London, 1733.

† A New and Accurate Account of the Provinces of South Carolina and Georgia, &c London, 1733.

assigned, among the weightiest reasons for founding the Colony, the ample opportunity which would be afforded in Georgia for persons reduced to poverty at home and constituting a positive charge upon the Nation, to be made happy and prosperous abroad and profitable to England. The conversion of the Indians, the confirmation of the development and security of Carolina, and a lucrative trade in silk, rice, cotton, wine, indigo, grain, and lumber, were enumerated as additional inducements to the enterprize.

On the 9th of June, 1732, his Majesty, George the Second, by Charter, granted to the Trustees for establishing the Colony of Georgia in America and their successors, all the Lands and Territories from the most northern stream of the Savannah river along the sea-coast to the southward unto the most southern stream of the Alatamaha river, and westward from the heads of the said rivers respectively in direct lines to the south seas. Not only the lands lying within these boundaries, but also all islands within twenty leagues of the coast were, by this Royal feoffment, conveyed "for the better support of the Colony."*

During the first year of the foundation of the Colony, Mr. Oglethorpe's attention was directed to providing for the emigrants suitable homes at Savannah, Joseph's Town, Abercorn, and Old Ebenezer, to concluding necessary treaties of cession and amity with the Natives, and the erection of a fort on the Great Ogeechee river to command the main passes by which the Indians had invaded Carolina during the late wars, and afford the settlers some security against anticipated incursions from the Spaniards. This fortified post,—as a compliment to his honored patron John, Duke of

* See Copy of Charter, McCall's History of Georgia, Vol. I, p. 329 et seq: Savannah, 1811. Reasons for establishing the Colony of Georgia, &c., p. 29. London, 1733.
A State of the Province of Georgia attested upon oath, &c., p. 1. London, 1742.

Argyle,—was called *Fort Argyle,* and was garrisoned by Captain McPherson and his detachment of Rangers. At this time no English plantations had been established south of the Great Ogeechee river. Having confirmed the Colonists in their occupation of the right bank of the Savannah, and engaged the friendship of the venerable Indian Chief, Tomo-chi-chi, and the neighboring Lower Creeks and Uchees, in January, 1734, Mr. Oglethorpe set out to explore the coast, and determine upon such settlement as appeared most advantageous for the protection of the southern confines of the Colony. During a heavy rain on the 26th of that month, he and his party landed "on the first Albany bluff of St. Simon's island" and "lay all night under the shelter of a large live-oak-tree and kept themselves dry." This reconnoissance, which was continued as far as the sea-point of St. Simon's island, and Jekyll island, convinced Mr. Oglethorpe it was expedient and necessary for the proper defence of the Colony that a military station and settlement should be formed, at the earliest practicable moment, near the mouth of the Alatamaha river; and that, as an outpost, a strong fort should be built on St. Simon's island.

This plan was in part compassed in January, 1735, when one hundred and thirty Highlanders, and fifty women and children, who had been enrolled for emigration at Inverness and its vicinity, arrived at Savannah, and, a few days afterwards, were conveyed in periaguas to the southward. Ascending the Alatamaha river to a point about sixteen miles above St. Simon's island, they there landed and entered upon a permanent settlement, which they called New Inverness. Here they erected a fort,—mounting four pieces of cannon,—built a guard-house, a store, and a chapel, and constructed huts for temporary accommodation preparatory to putting up more substantial structures. These Scots were a brave, hardy people,—just the men to occupy this advanced position. In their plaids, and with their broad-swords, targets, and firearms, Oglethorpe says they presented "a most manly appearance."

Upon their arrival in Savannah some of the Carolinians endeavored to dissuade them from going to the southward by telling them that the Spaniards, from the houses in their fort, would shoot them upon the spot selected by the Trustees for their future home. Nothing daunted, these doughty countrymen of Bruce and Wallace responded* "we will beat them out of their fort and shall have houses ready built to live in." This valiant spirit found subsequent expression in the effective military service rendered by these Highlanders during the wars between the Colonists and the Spaniards, and by their decendants in the primal struggle for independance. To John Moore McIntosh, Captain Hugh MacKay, Ensign Charles MacKay, Colonel John McIntosh, General Lachlan McIntosh, and their gallant followers, Georgia, both as a Colony and a State, owes a special debt of gratitude.

On the 5th of February, 1735,† two hundred and two persons, upon the Trust's account, conveyed in the *Symond* and the *London Merchant*, and conducted by Oglethorpe in person, arrived at the mouth of the Savannah river. It was his intention to locate all these emigrants at St. Simon's island, but, in compliance with their earnest entreaty, such of them as were German Lutherans were permitted to join

---

* See Letter of Gen'l Oglethorpe to the Trustees under date February 27th, 1735-6. Collections of the Georgia Historical Society, Vol. III, p. 15. Savannah, 1873.

† A Voyage to Georgia, begun in the year 1735 by Francis Moore, p. 17. London 1744.

Compare Harris' Complete Collection of Voyages and Travels, Vol. II, p. 330. London, 1748.

An Account Showing the Progress of the Colony of Georgia, &c., p. 20. London, 1741.

their friends at Ebenezer. Upon leaving London it was contemplated that the Symond and the London Merchant should sail directly for Jekyll sound, and land their passengers at the point where it was proposed that the new town should be located. The timidity of the captains, however, who, in the absence of experienced pilots, feared the dangers of an unknown entrance, caused this deviation in the voyage.

Having engaged the services of fifty Rangers and one hundred workmen, and having dispatched Captain McPherson with a part of his command to march by land to the suppport of the Highlanders on the Alatamaha, Mr. Oglethorpe who, since his arrival, had been busily occupied in arranging matters at Savannah and Old Ebenezer, returned to the ships which were still lying in Tybee roads. Finding their captains unwilling to risk their ships without having previously acquired a knowledge of the entrance into Jekyll sound, he bought the cargo of the sloop *Midnight*, which had just arrived, on condition that it should be at once delivered at Fredrica, and with the understanding that captains Cornish and Thomas should go on board of her, acquaint themselves with the coast and entrance, and then return and conduct their vessels to Frederica. During their absence these ships,—the Symond and the London Merchant,—their cargoes still on board,—were to remain at anchor at Tybee roads in charge of Francis Moore, who was appointed keeper of the stores. Mr. Horton and Mr. Tanner, with thirty single men of the Colony, and cannon, arms, ammunition and entrenching tools, were ordered to proceed to the southward with the sloop Midnight. The workmen who had been engaged at Savannah, and Tomo-chi-chi's Indians were directed to rendezvous at convenient points whence they might be transported as occasion required. The sloop sailed for St. Simon's island on the morning of the 16th, and at evening of the same day Mr. Oglethorpe set out in the scout boat to meet the sloop at Jekyll sound. Captain Hermsdorf, two of the Colony, and some Indians went with him, and Captain Dunbar accompanied him with his boat. They passed through the inland channels lying between the outer islands and the main. "Mr. Oglethorpe being in haste," says one of the party, "the Men rowed Night and Day, and had no other Rest than what they got when a Snatch of Wind favoured us. They were all very willing, though we met with very boisterous Weather. * * * The Men vied with each other who should be forwardest to please Mr. Oglethorpe. Indeed he lightened their Fatigue by giving them Refreshments, which he rather spared from himself than let them want. The Indians seeing the Men hard laboured, desired to take the Oars, and rowed as well as any I ever saw, only differing from the others by taking a short and long Stroke alternately, which they called the Yamasee Stroke." On the morning of the 18th they reached St. Simon's island and found that the sloop had come in ahead of, and was waiting for them. Mr. Oglethorpe at once set all hands to work. The tall grass growing upon the bluff at Frederica was burnt off, a booth was marked out "to hold the stores,—digging the ground three Foot deep, and throwing up the Earth on each Side by way of Bank,—and a roof raised upon Crutches with Ridge-pole and Rafters, nailing small Poles across, and thatching the whole with Palmetto-leaves. Mr. Oglethorpe afterwards laid out several Booths without digging under Ground, which were also covered with Palmetto Leaves, to lodge the Families of the Colony in when they should come up; each of these Booths was between thirty and forty Foot long, and upwards of twenty Foot wide. * * We all made merry that Evening, having a plentiful Meal of Game brought in by the Indians.

"On the 19th, in the Morning, Mr. Oglethorpe began to mark out a Fort with four Bastions, and taught the Men how to dig the Ditch, and raise and turf the Rampart. This Day and the following Day were spent in finishing the Houses, and tracing out the Fort." *

Such was the simple beginning of Frederica.† Near the town Mr. Oglethorpe fixed the only home he ever owned in the Province. In its defence were enlisted his best energies, military skill, and valor. Brave are the memories of St. Simon's island. None prouder belong to the colonial history of Georgia.

Three days afterwards arrived from Savannah a periagua with workmen, provisions, and cannon, for the new settlement. Captains Cornish and Thomas returned from the southward to Tybee roads on the 26th and, although assured of the fact that there was ample water for the conveyance of their vessels to Frederica, still refused to conduct the Symond and the London Merchant to the southward. Mr. Oglethorpe was consequently compelled to consent that their cargoes should be unloaded into the "*Peter and James*," which could not carry above one hundred tons, and the rest transferred in sloops to Savannah for safe storage until such time as opportunity offered for conveying it to its destination. He was also put to the great inconvenience of collecting periaguas‡ sufficient for the transportation of the Colonists.

---

* Moore's Voyage to Georgia, &c., p. 44. London, 1744.

† Named by Oglethorpe after *Frederick*, Prince of Wales.

‡ These are "long flat-bottomed boats carrying from 20 to 35 Tons. They have a kind of a Forecastle and a Cabbin; but the rest open, and no Deck. They have two Masts, which they can strike, and Sails like Schooners. They row generally with two Oars only."

Much incensed at the conduct of the Captains of the transports, and inconvenienced by the demurrage consequent upon their timidity, he was also indignant at the delay thus caused in the consummation of his plans, annoyed at the additional charges for transfer of passengers and cargo, and solicitous for the health of the colonists who would be exposed in open boats, at an inclement season, during the passage from Tybee roads to Jekyll sound.

It was not until the 2nd of March that the fleet of periaguas and boats, with the families of the Colonists on board, set out from the mouth of the Savannah river. Spare oars had been rigged for each boat. With their assistance,—the men of the Colony rowing with a will,—the voyage to Frederica was accomplished in five days. Mr. Oglethorpe accompanied them in his scout-boat, keeping the fleet together, and taking the hindermost craft in tow. As an incentive to unity of movement, he placed all the strong beer on board one boat. The rest labored diligently to keep up; for, if they were not all at the place of rendezvous each night, the tardy crew lost their ration. Frederica was reached on the 8th, and there was general joy among the colonists.

So diligently did they labor in building their town and its fortifications, that by the 23rd of March a battery of cannon, commanding the river, had been mounted, and the fort was almost finished. Its ditches had been dug, although not to the required depth or width, and a rampart raised and covered with sod. A store-house, having a front of sixty feet, and intended to be three stories in height, was completed as to its cellar and first story. The necessary streets were all laid out. "The Main Street that went from the Front into the Country was 25 yards wide. Each Free-holder had 60 Foot in Front by 90 Foot in Depth, upon the high Street, for their House and Garden; but those which fronted the River had but 30 Foot in Front, by 60 Foot in Depth. Each Family had a Bower of Palmetto Leaves, finished upon the back Street in their own Lands: The Side towards the front Street was set out for their Houses: These Palmetto Bowers were very convenient Shelters, being tight in the hardest Rains; they were about 20 Foot long and 14 Foot wide, and, in regular Rows, looked very pretty, the Palmetto Leaves lying smooth and handsome, and of a good Colour. The whole appeared something like a Camp; for the Bowers looked liked Tents, only being larger and covered with Palmetto Leaves instead of Canvas. There were 3 large Tents, two belonging to Mr. *Oglethorpe*, and one to Mr. *Horton*, pitched upon the Parade near the River."

Such is the description of the town in its infancy as furnished by Mr. Moore, whose "Voyage to Georgia" is one of the most interesting and valuable tracts we have descriptive of the colonization.

That there might be no confusion in their constructive labors, Mr. Oglethorpe divided the Colonists into working parties. To some was assigned the duty of cutting forks, poles, and laths for building the bowers. Others set them up. Others still gathered palmetto leaves, while a fourth gang,—under the superintendence of a Jew workman, bred in Brazil and skilled in the matter,—thatched the roofs "nimbly and in a neat manner."

Men accustomed to the agriculture of the region, instructed the Colonists in hoeing and planting. Potatoes, Indian corn, flax, hempseed, barley, turnips, lucern-grass, pumpkins, and water-melons were planted. The labor was common and enured to the benefit of the entire community. As it was rather too late in the season to prepare the ground fully and get in such a crop as would promise a yield sufficient to subsist the settlement for the coming year, many of the men were put upon pay and set to work upon the fortifications and the public buildings.

Mr. Hugh MacKay, about this time, arrived in Frederica and reported, that with the assistance of Messrs. Augustine and Tolme, and the guides furnished by Tomo-chi-chi, he had surveyed and located a road, practicable for horses, between Savannah and Darien. This information was very gratifying to the Colonists on St. Simons, assuring them, as it did, that their situation was not so isolated as they at first supposed.

Frederica was located in the midst of an Indian field* containing between thirty and forty acres of cleared land. The grass in this field yielded an excellent turf which was freely used in sodding the parapet of the fort. The bluff upon which it stood rose about ten feet above high-water mark, was dry and sandy, and exhibited a level expanse of about a mile into the interior of the island. The position of the fort was such that it fully commanded the reaches in the river both above and below. With their situation the Colonists were delighted. The harbor was land-locked,† having

*The Aborigines cleared considerable spaces on the Sea Islands along the Georgia Coast, planting them with maize, pumpkins, gourds, beans, melons, &c. These indications of early agriculture were not infrequent in various portions of the State. The richest localities were selected by the Aborigines for cultivation: their principal towns and maize-fields being generally found in rich valleys where a generous soil yielded, with least labor, the most remunerative harvest. The trees were killed by girdling them by means of stone axes. They then decayed and fell piecemeal. So old were these Indian fields that in them no traces appeared of the roots and stumps even of the most durable trees. The occupancy of these islands by the Red race was general and of long duration. Prominent bluffs are to this day marked by their refuse heaps, composed chiefly of the shells of oysters, conchs, and clams, and the bones of the animals, reptiles, birds, and fishes upon which they subsisted, intermingled with sherds of pottery, and broken articles, and relics of various sorts. Many localities are hoary with ancient shell-mounds, while sepulchral tumuli of earth are not infrequent. Besides the primitive population permanently domiciled on these islands, at certain seasons of the year, large numbers of Indians from the main here congregated and spent much time in hunting and fishing.

† An Impartial Enquiry into the State and Utility of the Province of Georgia, pp. 40 and 41. London, 1741.

a depth of twenty-two feet of water at the bar, and capable of affording safe anchorage to a large number of ships of considerable burden. Surrounded by beautiful forests of live-oak, water oaks, laurel, bay, cedar, sweet-gum, sassafras, and pines, festooned with luxuriant vines, [among which those bearing the Fox-grape and the Muscadine were peculiarly pleasing to the Colonists,] and abounding in deer, rabbits, raccoons, squirrels, wild-turkeys, turtle-doves, red-birds, mocking birds, and rice birds,* with wide extended marshes frequented by wild geese, ducks, herons, curlews, cranes, plovers, and marsh-hens,—the adjacent waters teeming with fishes, crabs, shrimps, and oysters, and the island fanned by South-East breezes prevailing with the regularity of the trade winds—the strangers were charmed with their new home. Within their fort were enclosed and preserved several of those grand old live-oaks which for centuries had crowned the bluff, and whose shade was refreshing beyond any shelter the hand of man could devise. The town sprang into being as a military post. It was ordered and grew day by day under the immediate supervision of Oglethorpe. The soil of the island was fertile, and its health unquestioned. Lieutenant George Dunbar, on the 20th of January, 1739, made oath before Francis Moore, Recorder of the Town of Frederica, that since his arrival with the first detachment of Colonel Oglethorpe's regiment the preceding June, all the carpenters and many of the soldiers had been continuously occupied in building clap-board huts, carrying lumber and bricks, unloading vessels, [often working up to their necks in water,] in clearing the parade, burning wood and rubbish, making lime, and in other out-door exercises,—the hours of labor being from daylight until

* Buffalo and quail were found on the Main.

eleven or twelve M. and from two or three o'clock in the afternoon until dark. Despite these exposures, continues the Affiant, "All the time the men kept so healthy that often no man in the camp ailed in the least, and none died except one man who came sick on board and never worked at all; nor did I hear that any of the men ever made the heat a pretence for not working."*

Beyond question Frederica was the healthiest of all the early settlements in Georgia, and St. Simon's island has always enjoyed an enviable reputation for salubrity. Until marred by the desolations of the late war, this island was a favorite summer resort, and the homes of the planters were the abodes of beauty, comfort, and refinement. A mean temperature of about fifty degrees in winter, and not above eighty-two degrees in summer, gardens adorned with choice flowers, and orchards enriched with plums, peaches, nectarines, figs, melons, pomegranates, dates, oranges and limes,—forests rendered majestic by the live-oak, the pine, and the magnolia grandiflora, and redolent with the perfumes of the bay, the cedar and the myrtle,—the air fresh and buoyant with the South-East breezes, and vocal with the notes of song-birds,—the adjacent sea, sound, and inlets, replete with fishes,—the shell roads and broad beach affording every facility for driving and riding,—the woods and fields abounding with game in their season, and the culture and generous hospitality of the inhabitants, impressed all visitors with the delights of this favored spot. Sir Charles Lyell, among others, alludes with marked satisfaction to the pleasures he there experienced.

---

* State of the Province of Georgia attested upon Oath, &c., p. 25. London, 1742.

Compare Affidavits of Lieut. Raymond Demare, Hugh MacKay, and John Cuthbert, to same effect.

An Impartial Enquiry into the State and Utility of the Province of Georgia, pp. 61, 63, 64. London, 1741.

Among the reptiles which not only attracted the notice of, but, to a considerable degree, upon first acquaintance, disquieted the early Colonists, the alligators were the most noted. Listen to this description furnished by an eye-witness* in 1736: "They are terrible to look at, stretching open an horrible large Mouth, big enough to swallow a Man, with Rows of dreadful large sharp Teeth, and Feet like Draggons, armed with great Claws, and a long Tail which they throw about with great Strength, and which seems their best Weapon, for their Claws are feebly set on, and the Stiffness of their Necks hinders them from turning nimbly to bite." In order that the public mind might be disabused of the terror which pervaded it with respect to these reptiles, Mr. Oglethorpe, having wounded and caught one, had it brought to Savannah and made the boys bait it with sticks and finally pelt and beat it to death.

The rattle snakes, too, were objects of special dread.

Leaving his people busily occupied with the labors assigned to them at Frederica, Mr. Oglethorpe set out on the 18th of March† for the frontiers, "to see where his Majesty's Dominions and the Spaniards joyn."‡ He was accompanied by "Toma-Chi-Chi, Mico, and a Body of Indians, who, tho' but few, being not forty, were all chosen Warriors and good Hunters." They were conveyed in two Scout Boats, and the next day were joined by the periagua, commanded by Captain Hugh MacKay, with thirty Highlanders, ten men of the Independent Company, and entrenching tools and provisions on board. Upon the north-western point of Cumber-

---

* Francis Moore, Voyage to Georgia, &c., p. 57. London, 1744.

† Moore says April. See A Voyage to Georgia, p. 63. London, 1744.

‡ Oglethorpe's letter to the Lieutenant Governor of South Carolina.

Collections of the Georgia Historical Society, vol. III, p. 28. Savannah, 1873.

land island* washed by the bay on the one side, and on the other by the channel running to the southward, Oglethorpe marked out a fort, called it St. Andrews, and left Captain MacKay with his command to build it, and some Indians to hunt and shoot for them while thus employed.

Proceeding on his voyage, Mr. Oglethorpe named the next large Island to the South, Amelia,†—"it being a beautiful Island, and the Sea-shore cover'd with Myrtle, Peach-Trees, Orange-Trees, and Vines in the wild Woods." Tomo-chi-chi conducted him to the mouth of the St. Johns, pointed out the advanced post occupied by the Spanish Guard, and indicated the dividing line. It was with difficulty that the old chief and his followers could be restrained from making a night attack upon the Spaniards, upon whom they thirsted to take revenge for the killing of some Indians during the Mico's absence in England. Stopping at fort St. Andrews on his way back, Oglethorpe was surprised to find the work in such a state of "forwardness,—the Ditch being dug, and the Parapet raised with Wood and Earth on the Land-side, and the small Wood clear'd fifty yards round the Fort." This seemed the more extraordinary, adds Francis Moore, because Mr. MacKay had no engineer, or any assistance other than the directions which Mr. Oglethorpe gave. The ground consisting of loose sand, it was a difficult matter to construct the parapets: "therefore they used the same Method to support it as Cæsar mentions in the Wars of *Gaul*, laying Trees and Earth alternately, the Trees prevent-

* This island was named *Wissoo* by the Indians, signifying *Sassafras*. It was called Cumberland in memory of his Royal Highness, the Duke of Cumberland, at the suggestion of Toonahowi,—nephew of Tomo-chi-chi,—to whom, during his visit to England, the Duke had given a gold repeating watch, that he "might know how the time went." "We will remember him at all times," said Toonahowi, "and therefore will give this Island this name."

† Called by the Spaniards *Santa Maria*.

ing the Sand from falling, and the Sand the Wood from Fire."

Upon their return to Frederica the Indians encamped near the town, and, on the 26th, favored Mr. Oglethorpe and all the people with a War Dance. "They made a Ring, in the middle of which four sat down, having little Drums made of Kettles, cover'd with Deer-skins, upon which they beat and sung: Round them the others danced, being naked to their Waists, and round their Middles many Trinkets tied with Skins, and some with the Tails of Beasts hanging down behind them. They painted their Faces and Bodies, and their Hair was stuck with Feathers: In one Hand they had a Rattle, in the other Hand the Feathers of an Eagle, made up like the Caduceus of *Mercury*: They shook these Wings and the Rattle, and danced round the Ring with high Bounds and antick Postures, looking much like the Figures of the Satyrs.

"They shew'd great Activity, and kept just Time in their Motions; and at certain times answer'd by way of Chorus, to those that sat in the Middle of the Ring. They stopt, and then stood out one of the chief Warriors, who sung what Wars he had been in, and described (by Actions as well as by Words) which way he had vanquish'd the Enemies of his Country. When he had done, all the rest gave a Shout of Approbation, as knowing what he said to be true. The next Day Mr. Oglethorpe gave Presents to Toma-chi-chi and his *Indians*, and dismiss'd them with Thanks for their Fidelity to the King."*

For the further protection of the approaches to Frederica by the inland passages, a strong battery,—called Fort St. Simons,—was erected at the south end of St. Simons' island.

---

* Moore's Voyage to Georgia, p. 71. London, 1744.

It was designed to command the entrance to Jekyll sound. Adjacent to it was laid out a camp containing barracks and huts for the soldiers. At the southern extremity of Cumberland island Fort William was afterwards built with a view to controlling Amelia sound and the inland passage to St. Augustine. Upon San Juan island to the south, and near the entrance of the St. Johns river, Oglethorpe had observed the traces of an old fort. Thither he sent Captain Hermsdorf, and a detachment of Highlanders, with instructions to repair and occupy it. Having ascertained that this island was included in the cession of lands made by the Indians to his Majesty, he named the island George, and called the fortification fort St. George. With the exception of one or two posts of observation, this constituted the most southern defense of the Colony, and was regarded as an important position for holding the Spaniards in check, and for giving the earliest intelligence of any hostile demonstration on their part.* The energy and boldness displayed by the Commander in Chief in developing his line of occupation so far to the south, and in the very teeth of the Spaniards in Florida, are quite remarkable, and indicate on his part not only a daring bordering upon rashness, but also no little confidence in the courage and firmness of the small garrisons detailed to fortify and hold these advanced and isolated positions.

Returning to Frederica from this tour of observation, Mr. Oglethorpe found the workmen busily occupied in constructing the fort, whose outer works were being "palisaded with Cedar Posts to prevent our Enemies turning up the green Sod." Upon the bastions, platforms of two inch plank were

*On the South-west side of Cumberland island, and upon a high neck of land commanding the water approaches each way, Fort St. Andrews was subsequently built. "Its walls were of wood, filled in with earth. Round about were a ditch and a palisade."†

† Wesley's Journal, p. 61. Bristol, n. d.

laid for the cannon. A piece of marsh lying below the fort was converted into a water battery, called "the Spur," the guns of which,—being on a level with the water,—were admirably located for direct and effective operation against all vessels either ascending or descending the river.

A well was dug within the fort which yielded an abundant supply of "tolerable good water." The people having no bread, and the store of biscuits being needed for the crews of the boats which were kept constantly moving from point to point, an oven was built, and an indented servant,—a baker by trade,—was detailed to bake bread for the Colony. For the flour furnished by each individual an equal weight was returned in bread, "the difference made by the water and salt" being the baker's gain. This fresh bread, in the language of one who partook of it, was a great comfort to the people. Venison brought in by the Indians was frequently issued in lieu of salt provisions; and poultry, hogs, and sheep were occasionally killed for the sick. Such domestic animals, however, were, at that early period, so scarce in the settlement, that they were carefully guarded for the purpose of breeding. A little later, live stock came forward in abundance, by boats from Port Royal and Savannah.

Grave apprehensions were entertained of an attack from the Spaniards, and Mr. Oglethorpe was untiring in his efforts to place the southern frontier in the best possible state of defense. It is remarkable how much was accomplished under the circumstances. His energy was boundless, his watchfulness unceasing. Scout boats were constantly on duty observing the water approaches from the south as far as the mouth of the St. Johns. Indian runners narrowly watched the walls of St. Augustine, and conveyed intelligence of every movement by the enemy. Look-outs were maintained at all necessary points to give warning of threatened danger. Mr. Bryan and Mr. Barnwell promised, in case Frederica or its out-posts were attacked, to come to their support with a strong body of volunteers from Carolina. Chiefs of the Cheehaws and the Creeks volunteered their assistance.

Acting upon the belief that it was better to confront the Spaniards upon the confines of the Colony than abide the event of their invasion, volunteers came in such numbers from Carolina and Georgia that General Oglethorpe was compelled to issue orders that all who had plantations should remain at home and cultivate them until actually summoned to arms.

Hearing a report that the Spaniards were intent upon dislodging the settlers from Frederica, Ensign Delegal, taking thirty men of the Independent Company under his command, and rowing night and day, reached Frederica on the 10th of May and tendered his services. Without permitting them to land, Oglethorpe ordered English strong beer and provisions on board, sent a present of wine to Ensign Delegal, and, upon the same tide, in his scout boat conducted the party to the east point of St. Simons island where it is washed by Jekyll sound, and there posted the company, locating a spot for constructing a fort, and commanding a well to be dug. By the 16th, Ensign Delegal had succeeded in casting up a considerable entrenchment and in mounting several cannon.

This post,—strengthened on the 8th of June by the arrival of Lieutenant Delegal, with the rest of the Independent Company and thirteen pieces of cannon belonging to them,—was subsequently known as Delegal's Fort at the Sea-point.

The workmen at Frederica were diligently employed in

building a powder magazine under one of the bastions of the fort. It was made of heavy timber covered with several feet of earth. The construction of a large store-house, a smith's forge, a wheelwright's shop, and a corn-house also engaged their attention. The men capable of bearing arms were trained in military exercises each day by Mr. McIntosh. The Colonists were in a state of constant alarm, and everything was made subservient to the general defense. Even the feeble avowed their willingness to sacrifice their lives in protecting their new homes. Inspired by the intrepidity and vigilance, the fearlessness and the activity of the General,—who was constantly on the move, visiting the advanced works, pressing his reconnoissances even within the enemy's lines, and making every available disposition of men and munitions which could conduce to the common safety,—soldiers and citizens kept brave hearts, labored incessantly and cheerfully, observed a sleepless watch upon the sea and its inlets, and stood prepared to offer stout resistance to the Spaniard. It was a manly sight, that little colony fearlessly planting itself upon island and headland, separated from all substantial support, and yet extending itself on land and water to the very verge of hostile lines held by an enemy greatly superior in men and the appliances of warfare.

This state of uncertainty and alarm continued along the southern frontier of Georgia until, by conference between Mr. Oglethorpe and the Spanish Commissioners in Jekyll sound on the 19th of June, there occurred an amicable adjustment of pending disputes. The healths of the King and Royal Family of Great Britain, and of the King and Queen of Spain, were drank amid salvos of artillery from the sloop Hawk and the Sea-Point Battery; and when the Spaniards set out on the 22d to return to St. Augustine, they expressed themselves pleased with their reception and amicably inclined towards the Colony and its knightly General. This period of tranquility was of but short duration. In the fall of the year a peremptory demand was made by the Spanish Government for the evacuation by the English of all territory lying south of St. Helena's sound.

Perceiving that vigorous measures and a stronger force were requisite for the preservation of the Colony, and yielding to the solicitations of the Trustees that he should be present at the approaching meeting of Parliament to influence larger supplies for Georgia, Mr. Oglethorpe, having made the best possible arrangements for the government and protection of the province during his absence, embarked for England on the 29th of November, 1736.*

During his absence in England, nothing of special moment transpired on the southern frontiers. Mr. Horton appears to have been left in general charge of the defenses in that quarter. He established himself at Frederica, whence he made frequent tours of inspection to its out-posts and dependent works. Of a visit which he paid to the town early in February, 1737, Mr. Stephens, Secretary of the Colony, gives us rather a stupid account,† from which we gather that the inhabitants were living "in perfect Peace and Quiet, without Fear of any Disturbance from Abroad, and without any Strife or Contention at Law at Home, where they sometimes opened a Court, but very rarely had any Thing to do in it." Only slight improvements had been made during the preceding year in clearing and cultivating land, because of the constant apprehension of incursion by the Spaniards,

---

* See Wright's Memoir of Gen'l James Oglethorpe, p. 167. London, 1867.

†See A Journal of the Proceedings in Georgia, &c., vol. I, p. 98. London, 1742.

and the amount of military service the able-bodied men were obliged to perform.

Moved by the indications of hostility on the part of the Spaniards, and yielding to the entreaties of the Trustees* that additional troops be provided for the protection of the Colony, his Majesty, in June, 1737, appointed Oglethorpe General of all forces in Carolina as well as in Georgia, and authorized him to raise a regiment. In October of that year, and before his regiment had been fully recruited, he was commissioned as Colonel. The relief of Georgia being regarded as important, a body of troops was sent thither from Gibraltar, which reached Savannah early in May, 1738, and was transferred from that point to the South for the defense of the frontiers. The famous clergyman George Whitefield, detailed to take Mr. Wesley's place in the Colony, was a passenger on board the ship in which these soldiers were transported. About the same time two or three companies of the General's own regiment, under the command of Lieutenant-Colonel James Cochrane, arrived in Charleston, and were marched southward by the road which ran from Port Royal to Darien.† Oglethorpe's regiment was limited to six companies of one hundred men each, exclusive of non-commissioned officers and drummers. To it a grenadier company was subsequently attached. Disdaining to "make a market of the service of his country" by selling commissions, the General secured the appointment, as officers, only of such persons as were gentlemen of family and character in their respective counties. He also engaged about twenty young gentlemen of no fortune to serve as cadets. These he subsequently promoted as vacancies occurred. So far

* See one of the Memorials of the Trustees in "An Account Shewing the Progress of the Colony of Georgia," &c., p. 58. London, 1741.

† See Wright's Memoir of Oglethorpe, p. 191. London, 1867.

from deriving any pecuniary benefit from these appointments, the General, in some cases, from his private fortune advanced the fees requisite to procure commissions, and provided moneys for the purchase of uniforms and clothing. At his own expense he engaged the services of forty supernumeraries,—"a circumstance," says a contemporaneous writer, "very extraordinary in our armies, especially in our plantations."

In order to engender in the hearts of the enlisted men an interest in and an attachment for the Colony they were designed to defend, and with a view to induce them eventually to become settlers, permission was granted to each to take a wife with him. For the support of the wife, additional pay and rations were provided.* So carefully was this regiment recruited and officered, that it constituted one of the best military organizations in the service of the King.

Sailing from Portsmouth on the 5th of July, 1738, with the rest of his regiment,—numbering, with the women, children, and supernumeraries who accompanied, between six and seven hundred souls,—in five transports convoyed by the men of war Blandford and Hector, General Oglethorpe arrived safely in Jekyll sound on the 18th of the following September.† The next day the troops were landed at the Soldiers Fort, on the south end of St. Simon's island. This arrival was welcomed by an artillery salute from the battery, and by shouts from the garrison. Upon coming within soundings off the Georgia coast on the 13th, Sir Yelverton Peyton, in the Hector, parted company and sailed for Virginia. Until the 21st, the General encamped near the

* See Harris' Memorials of Oglethorpe, pp. 188, 189. Boston, 1841.
Wright's Memoir of Oglethorpe, p. 191. London, 1867.
Gentleman's Magazine, vol. VIII, p. 164.

† Stephens' Journal of Proceedings, vol. I, pp. 294, 295. London, 1742.

Fort, superintending the disembarcation and issuing necessary orders. His regiment was now concentrated, and every officer is represented to have been at his post.

Frederica was visited on the 21st, and there Oglethorpe was saluted with fifteen guns from the fort. The Magistrates and towns-people waited upon him in a body, tendering their congratulations upon his return. Several Indians were present who assured him that the Upper and Lower Creeks were in readiness to come and see him so soon as they should be notified of his presence.* In a letter† to Sir Joseph Jekyll, under date 19th September, 1738, General Oglethorpe, alluding to the fact that the Spaniards, although having fifteen hundred men at St. Augustine,—there being nothing but the militia in Georgia,—had delayed their contemplated attack until the arrival of the Regular Troops, acknowledges that God had thus given "the greatest marks of his visible Protection to the Colony." He advises Sir Joseph that the passage had been fine,—but one soldier having died,—and that the inhabitants who had hitherto been so harrassed by Spanish threats were now cheerful, believing that the worst was over, and that,—relieved from the constant guard duty which they had been compelled to perform, some times two days out of five, to the neglect of their crops and improvements,—they might now prosecute their labors and make comfortable provision for the future. Realizing the necessity of opening direct communication between Frederica and the Soldiers Fort at the south end of the island, on the 25th General Oglethorpe set every male to work cutting a road to connect those points. So energetically was the labor prosecuted, that although the woods

* Gentleman's Magazine for January, 1739, p. 22.

† Collections of the Georgia Historical Society, vol. III, p. 48. Savannah, 1873.

were thick and the distance nearly six miles, the task was compassed in three days.

To the Honorable Thomas Spalding* are we indebted for the following description of this important avenue of communication: "This road after passing out of the town of Frederica in a south-east direction, entered a beautiful prairie of a mile over, when it penetrated a dense, close oak wood; keeping the same course for two miles, it passed to the eastern marsh that bounded St. Simon's seaward. Along this marsh, being dry and hard, no road was necessary, and none was made. This natural highway was bounded on the east by rivers and creeks and impracticable marshes; it was bounded on the west, (the island side) by a thick wood covered with palmetto and vines of every character so as to be impracticable for any body of men, and could only be traveled singly and alone. This winding way along the marsh was continued for two miles, when it again passed up to the high land which had become open and clear, and from thence it proceeded in a direct line to the fort, at the sea entrance, around which, for two hundred acres, five acre allotments of land for the soldiers had been laid out, cleared, and improved. I have again been thus particular in my description, because it was to the manner in which this road was laid out and executed, that General Oglethorpe owed the preservation of the fort and town of Frederica. * * * His fort and batteries at Frederica were so situated as to water approaches, and so covered by a wood, that no number of ships could injure them. And he now planned his land route in such a manner, that again the dense wood of our eastern islands became a rampart mighty to save. And

* Sketch of the Life of General James Oglethorpe. Collections of the Georgia Historical Society, vol. I, p 261. Savannah, 1840.

fifty Highlanders and four Indians occupying these woods did save."

We learn from that admirable "History of the Rise, Progress, and Present State of the Colony of Georgia," contained in Dr. Harris' Complete Collections of Voyages and Travels,* that "on the arrival of the Regiment of which Mr. *Oglethorpe* was appointed Colonel, he distributed them in the properest manner for the Service of the Colony; but notwithstanding this was of great Ease to the Trustees, and a vast Security to the Inhabitants, yet Colonel Oglethorpe still kept up the same Discipline, and took as much Care to form and regulate the Inhabitants with respect to military Affairs as ever. He provided likewise different Corps for different Services; some for ranging the Woods; others, light armed, for sudden Expeditions; and he likewise provided Vessels for scouring the Sea Coasts, and for gaining Intelligence. In all which Services he gave at the same time his Orders and his Example; there being nothing he did not which he directed others to do; so that if he was the first Man in the Colony, his Pre-eminence was founded upon old *Homer's* Maxims: He was the most fatigued, and the first in Danger, distinguished by his Cares and his Labours, not by any exterior Marks of Grandeur, more easily dispensed with, since they were certainly needless."

The finances of the Trust being in a depressed condition, the General drew largely upon his private fortune and pledged his individual credit in conducting the operations necessary for the security of the southern frontiers and in provisioning the settlers. To Alderman Heathcote he writes: "I am here" [at Frederica] "in one of the most delightful situations as any man could wish to be. A

* Vol. II, p. 332. London, 1748.

great number of Debts, empty magazines, no money to supply them, numbers of people to be fed, mutinous soldiers to command, a Spanish Claim and a large body of their Troops not far from us. But as we are of the same kind of spirit, these Difficulties have the same effect upon me, as those you met with in the City, had upon you. They rather animate than daunt me."*

Again, on the 16th of November, 1739, he advises the Trustees :† "I am fortifying the Town of Frederica & hope I shall be repaid the Expences; from whom I do not know, yet I could not think of leaving a number of good houses and Merch'ts Goods and, which was more valuable, the Lives of Men, Women and Children in an open Town at the mercy of every Party, and the Inhabitants obliged either to fly to a Fort and leave their Effects, or suffer with them."

That the Trustees might be fully informed of the condition and needs of the Province, Mr. Horton,—who commanded the Southern Division during Oglethorpe's absence,—was sent to London about the close of the year 1739. The letter‡ of advice which he bore, contains an interesting account of the affairs of the Colony. In it General Oglethorpe states that his Regiment of Foot being unable to perform garrison duty and undertake the requisite marches on the main to overtake Indians and horsemen, he had been compelled to associate Indian allies whom he had armed, supplied with ammunition, fed, and clothed, in consideration of their services. Sixty Rangers, to act as scouts, had been recruited and mounted. By means of his boats, and the Colony Periagua,—which had been fitted out with four guns and a crew of forty men,—he had succeeded in

* Collections of the Georgia Historical Society, vol. III, p. 62. Savannah, 1873.

† Idem, p. 94.

‡ See Collections of the Georgia Historical Society, vol. III, pp. 97, 101. Savannah, 1873.

driving the Spaniards out of the mouth of the St. Johns river. The forts having been originally built of earth and hastily constructed, had fallen sadly out of repair. To place them in proper condition was then his earnest endeavor. "Upon the Hostilities being committed," so runs the letter, "I thought I should be answerable for the blood of these people before God and man if I had left them open to be surprised by Spanish Indians, and murdered in the night and their houses burnt, and if I did not take all proper means for their defence, they being under my charge." With this end in view, he resolved to enclose the town of Frederica with fortifications. This defensive work is thus described: "It is half an Hexagon with two Bastions, and two half Bastions and Towers, after Monsieur Vauban's method, upon the point of each Bastion. The Walls are of earth faced with Timber, 10 foot High in the lowest place, and in the highest 13, and the Timbers from eight inches to twelve inches thick. There is a wet Ditch 10 foot wide, and so laid out that if we had an allowance for it, I can by widening the Ditch double the thickness of the Wall and make a covered way. I hope in three months it will be entirely finished, and in that time not only to fortify here but to repair the Forts on Amelia and Saint Andrews. The Expence of these small above mentioned Works, which is all that I can now make, will not be great. Frederica will come within £500, St. Andrews £400, and Amelia £100."*

In the midst of his multifarious engagements and perplexities, in which General Oglethorpe exhibited the highest executive ability, and an activity and self abnegation worthy of all admiration, he was embarrassed by treachery within

---

* Compare Harris' Complete Collection of Voyages and Travels, vol. II, p. 337. London, 1748.

his camp which well nigh eventuated in the most serious consequences. A plan,—set on foot by one of the soldiers who had been in the Spanish service,—to murder the officers and escape to the enemy with such plunder as could be secured, was discovered in time to prevent its execution. The ring-leaders were tried, convicted, whipped, and drummed out of the regiment.

Early in November, 1738, General Oglethorpe took up his temporary quarters at Fort St. Andrew, on Cumberland island, that he might personally superintend and encourage the construction of the military defenses which were being there erected. This island was then garrisoned by the companies which had been detailed from Gibraltar. In addition to their pay these troops, for a limited period after their arrival in Georgia, had been allowed extra provisions from the King's store. When, in November, these rations were discontinued, conceiving themselves wronged and defrauded of their rights, the men became dissatisfied. As the General was conversing at the door of his hut with Captain MacKay, a turbulent fellow had the temerity to come up unannounced and demand a renewal of the allowance. Oglethorpe replied that the terms of enlistment had been fully complied with: and that if he desired any favor at his hand such rude and disrespectful behavior was not calculated to secure a favorable consideration of his application. The fellow thereupon became outrageously insolent. Captain MacKay drew his sword, which the desperado wrested from him, broke in half, and, having thrown the hilt at that officer's head, rushed away to the barracks. There snatching up a loaded gun and crying aloud "One and All," he ran back, followed by five or more of the conspirators, and fired at the General. Being only a few paces distant, the ball whizzed close by

Oglethorpe's ear, while the powder scorched his face and singed his clothes. Another soldier presented his piece and attempted to discharge it. Fortunately it missed fire. A third drew his hanger and endeavored to stab the General, who, however, having by this time unsheathed his sword, parried the thrust. An officer coming up ran the ruffian through the body. Frustrated in their attempt at assassination, the mutineers sought safety in flight, but were apprehended and put in irons. After trial by court martial the ring-leaders were found guilty and shot.*

Thus wonderfully was the General preserved for the important trusts committed to his care, and so narrowly was a calamity averted which would have plunged the Colony into the depths of uncertainty and peril. Had she been deprived, at this trying moment, of Oglethorpe's guidance, Georgia, feeble and uncertain, would have been left well-nigh naked to her enemies.

Spanish emissaries from St. Augustine endeavored to inaugurate an insurrection among the negroes of South Carolina. To them freedom and protection were promised. Every inducement was offered which could encourage not only desertion from, but also massacre of their owners. Of the run-away slaves the Governor of Florida had formed a regiment, appointing officers from among them, and placing both officers and enlisted men upon the pay and rations allowed to the regular Spanish soldiers. Of this fact the Carolina negroes were ad-

---

* Compare Gentleman's Magazine, vol. IX, pp. 214, 215.
Stephens' Journal of Proceedings, vol. I, p. 326. London, 1742.
McCall's History of Georgia, vol. I, pp. 124, 125. Savannah, 1811.
Hewitt's Historical Account of the Rise and Progress of the Colonies of South Carolina and Georgia, vol. II, pp. 70, 71. London, 1779.
Stevens' History of Georgia, vol. I, pp. 154, 155. New York, 1847.
Wright's Memoir of Oglethorpe, pp. 204, 205. London, 1867.
Harris' Biographical Memorials of Oglethorpe, pp. 194, 195, 369. Boston, 1841.

vised.* The pernicious influence of such tampering with this servile population may be more readily conjectured than described. Thus did Spain grow daily more and more offensive in the development of her plans for the destruction of the English Colonies adjacent to her possessions in Florida. To the vigilance of Oglethorpe is Carolina largely indebted for her escape from the horrors of a servile insurrection.†

By his personal interview with the Indians at Coweta town, Oglethorpe had secured the good will of the Creeks, the Cousees, the Tallapousees, the Cowetas, the Choctaws and the Chickesas, thus thwarting the machinations of the Spanish and French, and relieving the Colony from apprehensions of a most serious character. His energies were all directed to a careful preparation to meet the Spanish storm which was gathering and almost ready to burst upon the southern frontier of the Province. Referring to this perilous and protracted journey performed by General Oglethorpe to propitiate these Indian tribes and secure from them pledges whose observance was essential to the continuance of the Colony, Mr. Spalding‡ justly remarks, "When we call into remembrance the then force of these tribes,—for they could have brought into the field twenty thousand fighting men,—when we call to remembrance the influence the French had everywhere else obtained over the Indians,—when we call to remembrance the distance he had to travel through solitary pathways from Frederica,

* See McCall's History of Georgia, vol. I., pp. 125, 126. Savannah, 1811.

† Hewitt's Account of the Rise and Progress of the Colonies of South Carolina and Georgia, vol. II., pp. 72–74. London, 1779.

‡ Sketch of the Life of General James Oglethorpe. Collections of the Georgia Historical Society, vol. I, p. 263. Savannah, 1840.

exposed to summer suns, night dews, and to the treachery of any single Indian who knew, and every Indian knew, the rich reward that would have awaited him for the act from the Spaniards in St. Augustine or the French in Mobile; surely we may proudly ask what soldier ever gave higher proof of courage? What gentleman ever gave greater evidence of magnanimity? What English governor of an American province ever gave such assurance of deep devotion to public duty?"

But for this manly conference with the Red men in the heart of their own country, and the admiration with which his presence, courage, and bearing inspired the assembled Chiefs, Oglethorpe could not have compassed the pacification and secured that treaty of amity so essential to the welfare of the Colony now on the eve of most serious difficulties with the Spaniards in Florida.

On the 5th of October, 1739, at his little town four miles from Savannah, the venerable Tomo-chi-chi,—Oglethorpe's earliest and best friend among the Indians,—yielding to the effects of a lingering illness, died at the advanced age of ninety-seven years. The General acted as one of the pall-bearers, and the body of the old Chief, in accordance with his wish, was interred, with becoming honors, in one of the public squares in Savannah. In his last moments he expressed no little concern that he was about to be taken away at a time when his services might prove of special value to his friends, the English, against the Spaniards, and counseled his people never to forget the favors he had received, when in England, from the King, and to persevere in their amicable relations with the colonists.* These injunctions were not unheeded. Toonahowi—the favorite nephew of the aged Mico—accompanied General Oglethorpe in his expedition against St. Augustine; and again, leading a party of Creek Indians, brought off from the very walls of that city Don Romualdo Ruiz del Moral, lieutenant of Spanish horse and nephew to the late governor of Florida, and delivered him a prisoner to Oglethorpe. During the memorable and successful resistance maintained when St. Simon's island was attacked by the Spaniards in 1742, this brave Indian, illustrating the valor, personal courage, and friendship which characterized his distinguished uncle, remained firm in his attachment to the colonists and rendered valuable military service. On the 7th of July, although wounded in the right arm by Captain Mageleto, he drew his pistol with the left, and shot the Captain dead on the spot. This brave warrior and faithful ally was finally killed in 1743, at Lake di Papa, while valiantly fighting for the English against the Yemasee Indians.†

The disputes existing between England and Spain culminated in a declaration of war in October, 1739. On the 15th of November intelligence was brought to Frederica that a party of Spaniards had recently landed on Amelia island in the night, and, concealing themselves in the woods, had, on the ensuing morning, shot two

* See Stephens' Journal of Proceedings, etc., vol. II., p. 153. London, 1742.
Gentleman's Magazine, vol. x., p. 129.
Historical Sketch of Tomo-chi-chi, C. C. Jones, Jr., p. 120, *et seq.* Albany, 1868.
For the precise location of Tomo-chi-chi's grave, see Plan of the City of Savannah and its Fortifications by John Gerar William DeBrahm, History of the Province of Georgia, etc., p. 36. Wormsloe, 1849.

† See Jones' Historical Sketch of Tomo-chi-chi, pp. 107, 108. Albany, 1868.
Gentleman's Magazine, vol. XII, p. 497.
Harris' Memorials of Oglethorpe, pp. 256, 257. Boston, 1841.

unarmed Highlanders who were in quest of fuel, and then, in the most inhuman manner, hacked their bodies with their swords. Francis Brooks,—commanding the scout-boat,—heard the firing and gave the alarm to the fort, which was garrisoned by a detachment from Oglethorpe's regiment. Although pursued, the enemy escaped, leaving behind them the proofs of their inhuman butchery.* Informed of the outrage, Oglethorpe manned a gunboat and followed in the hope of overtaking the party. The effort proved futile, and the General, by way of retaliation, passing up the St. Johns drove in the guards of Spanish horse posted on that river, and detached Captain Dunbar to ascertain the location and force of the enemy's fort at Picolata. This incursion was followed by another in January, which resulted in the capture of Forts Picolata and St. Francis, the garrisons being made prisoners of war. In the assault upon the latter work General Oglethorpe narrowly escaped death from a cannon shot.†

Chafing under these repeated annoyances experienced at the hands of the Spaniards, advised that the garrison at St. Augustine was suffering for lack of provisions, and ascertaining that the galleys having been sent to Havana for reinforcements and supplies, the St. Johns river and the Florida coast were in a comparatively defenseless condition, the General deemed it a fitting

---

* In the account of this transaction contained in the Gentleman's Magazine for 1740, (volume x, page 129,) it is stated that after they were shot, the heads of these two Highlanders were cut off and their bodies cruelly mangled by the enemy. The perpetrators of this outrage consisted of Spaniards, negroes, and Indians. See Letter of General Oglethorpe to the Lieutenant Governor of South Carolina, dated November 16th, 1739.

"The Spanish Hireling detected," etc., pp. 50, 51. London, 1743.

† For full details of these incursions see letter of Gen. Oglethorpe to Col. Stephens, dated Frederica, 1st February, 1740.

Collections of the Georgia Historical Society, vol. III., pp. 105-108. Savannah, 1873.

opportunity to attempt the reduction of St. Augustine and the expulsion of the Spaniards from Florida. Admiral Vernon was instructed to assume the offensive against the Spanish possessions in the West Indies, while General Oglethorpe should conduct all available forces against the seat of their dominion in Florida. The assistance of Carolina was urgently invoked, but the authorities at first would not acquiesce in the feasibility of the enterprise.* A rapid movement being regarded essential to success, General Oglethorpe repaired to Charleston to urge early and potent co-operation. As a result of the conference which there ensued, the Legislature, by an act passed April 5th, 1740, agreed to contribute a regiment of five hundred men to be commanded by Colonel Vanderdussen, a troop of Rangers, presents for the Indians, and three months' provisions. A large schooner,—conveying ten carriages and sixteen swivel guns, and fifty men under the command of Captain Tyrrell,—was also furnished for the expedition. Com-

---

*In a letter dated Frederica, December 29th, 1739, General Oglethorpe explained to the Carolina authorities his designs against St. Augustine, and the assistance he desired to receive from that Province. A requisition was therein made for twelve 18-pounder guns with two hundred rounds of ammunition for each piece, one mortar with proper complement of powder and bombs, eight hundred pioneers, either negroes or white men, and the requisite tools "such as spades, hoes, axes, and hatchets to dig trenches, make gabelines, and fascines." Vessels and boats sufficient to transport the artillery, men, and provisions, and six thousand bushels of corn or rice to feed the thousand Indians who were to unite in the expedition, were also demanded. He also desired that as many horsemen as could be collected, should, under the guidance of Mr. McPherson or Mr. Jones, cross the Savannah and rendezvous at the ferry on the "Alata" river, from which point they would be conducted into "Spanish Florida." It was suggested that fifty good horsemen might be raised at "Purrisburg," and that four months' provisions for four hundred men of his regiment should be contributed, and also boats sufficient to transport them. Of artillery on hand the General reported thirty-six coehorns and about eighteen hundred shells. In addition to the four hundred men drawn from his regiment, and the Indians whom he had engaged, he expected to be able to arm and utilize for the expedition about two hundred men of the Georgia Colony, if arrangements could be made for paying and feeding them.

For this letter in full, see Harris' Complete Collection of Voyages and Travels, vol. II, pp. 338, 339. London, 1748.

See also "The Spanish Hireling detected," etc., pp. 52-57. London, 1743.

modore Vincent Price, with a small fleet, pledged his assistance.

On the first of April General Oglethorpe published a manifesto, in which, recognizing Alexander Vanderdussen, Esq., as Colonel of the Carolina regiment, he empowered him for the space of four months to hold regimental court martials for the trial of all offenders. At the expiration of that period all connected with that regiment were to be suffered to return to their homes. To the naval forces uniting in the expedition a full share of all plunder was guaranteed. To the maimed and wounded, and to the widows and orphans of such as might perish in the service, was promised whatever share of the spoils should fall to the lot of the General in Chief. Indian enemies, if taken captive, were to be treated as prisoners of war, and not as slaves.*

The mouth of the St. Johns was designated as the point of rendezvous.

Runners were sent from the Uchee town to the Indian allies to inform them of the contemplated demonstration against St. Augustine, and to request a junction of their forces at Frederica at the earliest moment. This done, the General returned at once to St. Simons island where he devoted himself to equipping his forces and collecting the requisite munitions of war.

Anticipating the concentration of his forces, and wishing to reduce the posts through which the enemy derived supplies from the country, General Oglethorpe, with four hundred men of his own regiment and a considerable force of Indians led by Molochi,—son of Prim, the late Chief of the Creeks,—Raven, war chief of the Cherokees, and

* See Harris' Memorials of Oglethorpe, pp. 378, 380. Boston, 1841.

Toonahowi, nephew of Tomo-chi-chi, on the 9th of May passed over into Florida, and within a week succeeded in capturing Fort Francis de Papa* seventeen miles north of St. Augustine, and Fort Diego† situated on the plains twenty-five miles from St Augustine. The latter work was defended by eleven guns and fifty regulars, besides Indians and negroes. Leaving Lieutenant Dunbar and sixty men to hold this post, the General returned with the rest of his command to the place of rendezvous where, on the 19th of May, he was joined by Captain McIntosh with a company of Highlanders, and by the Carolina troops under Colonel Vanderdussen. The anticipated horsemen, pioneers, and negroes, however, did not arrive.

From the best information he could obtain,—gathered from prisoners and otherwise,—General Oglethorpe ascertained that the Castle of St. Augustine at that time consisted of a fort, built of soft stone. Its curtain was sixty yards in length, its parapet nine feet thick, and its rampart twenty feet high, "casemated underneath for lodgings, and arched over and newly made bomb-proof." Its armament consisted of fifty cannon,—sixteen of brass,—and among them some twenty-four pounders. The garrison had been for some time working upon a covered-way, but this was still in an unfinished condition. The town of St. Augustine was protected by a line of intrenchments with ten salient angles, in each of which some field pieces were mounted.

* The object of this fort was to guard the passage of the St. Johns river and maintain communication with St. Marks and Pensacola. It was a place of some strength, and the traces of the earth-works there thrown up may still be seen about a fourth of a mile north of the termination of the Bellamy road.

Fairbanks' History and Antiquities of St Augustine. pp. 144, 145. New York, 1858.

† This work had been erected by Don Diego de Spinosa upon his own estate. Its remains, with one or two cannon, are still visible.

Idem, p. 144.

In January, 1740, the Spanish forces in Florida, by establishment, consisted of the following organizations :*

1 Troop of Horse,	numbering	100	officers	and	men.
1 Company of Artillery,	"	100	"	"	"
3 Independent Companies of old Troops, each	"	100	"	"	"
2 Companies of the Regiment of Austurias, "	"	53	"	"	"
1 Company " " " Valencia,	"	53	"	"	"
1 " " " " Catalonia,	"	53	"	"	"
2 Companies " " " Cantabria, "	"	53	"	"	"
2 " " " " Mercia, "	"	53	"	"	"
Armed Negroes,		200	"	"	"
White Transports for labor,		200			
1 Company of Militia, (strength unknown.)					
Indians, (number not ascertained.)					

It was General Oglethorpe's original purpose, as foreshadowed in his dispatch of the 27th of March, 1740,† with four hundred regular troops of his regiment, one hundred Georgians, and such additional forces as South Carolina could contribute, to advance directly upon St. Augustine, and attack, by sea and land, the town and the island in its front. Both of these, he believed, could be taken "sword in hand." He would then summon the castle to surrender, or surprise it. Conceiving that the castle would be too small to afford convenient shelter for the two thousand one hundred men, women, and children of the town, he regarded the capitulation of the fortress as not improbable. Should it refuse to surrender, however, he proposed to shower upon it "Granado-shells from the Cohorns and Mortars, and send for the Artillery and Pioneers and the rest of the Aid promised by the Assembly;‡ also for Mortars and Bombs from *Providence;*" and, if the castle should not have yielded prior to the

* See Letter of General Oglethorpe to the Lieutenant Governor of South Carolina, under date December 29, 1739. "The Spanish Hireling detected," etc., pp. 57, 58. London, 1743. Collections of the Georgia Historical Society, vol. III, pp. 108, 109. Savannah, 1873.

† "Spanish Hireling detected," etc., pp. 59–61. London, 1743.

‡ Of South Carolina.

arrival of "these Aids," he was resolved to open trenches and conduct a siege which he reckoned would be all the easier, the garrison having been weakened by the summer's blockade.

About the time of the concentration of the Georgia and Carolina forces for combined operations against St. Augustine, that town was materially reinforced by the arrival of six Spanish half-galleys,—manned by two hundred regular troops and armed with long brass nine-pounder guns,—and two sloops loaded with provisions.

Warned by the preliminary demonstration which eventuated, as we have seen, in the capture of forts Francis de Papa and Diego, the enemy massed all detachments within the lines of St. Augustine, collected cattle from the adjacent region, and prepared for a vigorous defense.

Apprehending that he might not be able to carry the town by assault from the land side,—where its entrenchments were strong and well armed,—unless supported by a demonstration in force from the men of war approaching the town where it looks toward the sea and where it was not covered by earth-works, and being without the requisite pioneer corps and artillery train for the conduct of a regular siege, before putting his army in motion General Oglethorpe instructed the naval commanders to rendezvous off the bar of the north channel, and blockade that and the Matanzas pass to St. Augustine. Captain Warren, with two hundred sailors, was to land on Anastasia island and erect batteries for bombarding the town in front. When his land forces should come into position and be prepared for the assault, he was to notify Sir Yelverton Peyton, commanding the naval forces, and St. Augustine would thus be attacked on all sides. Shortly after the middle of May, 1740, General Oglethorpe, with a land army numbering over two thousand regulars, militia, and Indians, moved upon St. Augustine. Fort Moosa,* situated within two miles of that place, lay in his route. Upon his approach the garrison evacuated it and retired within the lines of the town. Having burnt the gates of this fort and caused three breaches in its walls, General Oglethorpe, on the 5th of June, made his reconnoissances of the land defenses of St. Augustine and prepared for the contemplated assault. Everything being in readiness, the signal previously agreed upon to insure the cooperation of the naval forces was given; but, to the General's surprise and mortification, no response was returned. His forces being disposed and eager for the attack, the signal was repeated, but failed to evoke the anticipated answer. Satisfied that the town could not be carried without the assistance of the naval forces, and being ignorant of the cause of their non-action, the General reluctantly withdrew his army and placed it in camp at a convenient distance, there to remain until he could ascertain the reason of the failure on the part of the navy to coöperate in the plan which had been preconcerted. This failure was explained in this wise. Inside the bar, and at such a remove that they could not be affected by the fire of the British vessels of war,—the Flamborough, the Phœnix, the Squirrel, the Tartar, the Spence, and the Wolf,—Spanish gallies and half gallies were moored so as to effectually prevent the ascent of the barges intended for the attack, and preclude a landing of troops upon Anastasia island. The shallowness of the

* This was an out-post on the North river, about two miles north of St. Augustine. A fortified line,—a considerable portion of which may now be traced,—extended across from the stoccades on the St. Sebastian to Fort Moosa. A communication by a tide creek existed through the marshes, between the Castle at St. Augustine and Fort Moosa.

Fairbanks' History and Antiquities of St. Augustine, p. 144. New York, 1858.

water was such that the men of war could not advance near enough to dislodge them. Under the circumstances therefore, Sir Yelverton Peyton found himself unable to respond to the important part assigned him in the attack.

Advised of this fact, and chagrined at the non-realization of his original plan of operations, Oglethorpe determined at once to convert his purposed assault into a siege. The ships of war lying off the bar of St. Augustine were directed to narrowly observe every avenue of approach by water, and maintain a most rigid blockade. Colonel Palmer, with ninety-five Highlanders and forty-two Indians, was left at Fort Moosa with instructions to scout the woods incessantly on the land side and intercept any cattle or supplies coming from the interior. To prevent surprise and capture, he was cautioned to change his camp each night, and keep always on the alert. He was to avoid anything like a general engagement with the enemy. Colonel Vanderdussen, with his South Carolina regiment, was ordered to take possession of a neck of land known as Point Quartel, about a mile distant from the castle, and there erect a battery. General Oglethorpe, with the men of his regiment and most of the Indians, embarked in boats and effected a landing on Anastasia island, where, having driven off a party of Spaniards there stationed as an advanced guard, he, with the assistance of the sailors from the fleet, began mounting cannon with which to bombard the town and castle.* Having by these dispositions completed his investment, Oglethorpe summoned the Spanish Governor to

* The main battery on Anastasia island, called the Poza, was armed with four eighteen pounders and one nine pounder. Two eighteen pounders were mounted on the point of the wood of the island. The remains of the Poza battery are still to be seen, almost as distinctly marked as on the day of its erection. Four mortars and forty cohorns were employed in the siege.

See Fairbanks' History and Antiquities of St. Augustine, p. 146. New York, 1868.

a surrender. Secure in his strong-hold, the haughty Don "sent him for answer that he would be glad to shake hands with him in his castle." Indignant at such a response, the General opened his batteries upon the castle and also shelled the town. The fire was returned both by the fort and the half gallies in the harbor. So great was the distance, however, that although the cannonade was maintained with spirit on both sides for nearly three weeks, little damage was caused or impression produced.* It being evident that the reduction of the castle could not be expected from the Anastasia island batteries, Captain Warren offered to lead a night attack upon the half gallies in the harbor which were effectually preventing all ingress by boats. A council of war decided that in as much as those galleys were covered by the guns of the castle, and could not be approached by the larger vessels of the fleet, any attempt to capture them in open boats would be accompanied by too much risk. The suggestion was therefore abandoned.

Observing the besiegers uncertain in their movements, and their operations growing lax, and being sore pressed for provisions, the Spanish Governor sent out a detachment of three hundred men against Colonel Palmer. Unfortunately that officer, negligent of his instructions and apprehending no danger from the enemy, remained two or three consecutive nights at Fort Moosa. This detachment, under the command of Don Antonio Salgrado, passed quietly out of the gates of St. Augustine during the night of June 14th, and after encountering a most desperate resistance, succeeded in capturing Fort Moosa at day light, the

---

* The light guns, from their long range, caused trifling effect upon the strong walls of the castle. When struck, they received the balls in their spongy, infrangible embrace, and sustained comparatively little injury. The marks of their impact may be noted to this day.

next morning. Colonel Palmer fell early in the action. The Highlanders "fought like lions," and "made such havoc with their broadswords as the Spaniards cannot easily forget." This hand-to-hand conflict was won at the cost to the enemy of more than one hundred lives. Colonel Palmer, a Captain, and twenty Highlanders were killed. Twenty-seven were captured. Those who escaped made their way to Colonel Vanderdussen at Point Quartel. Thus was St. Augustine relieved from the prohibition which had hitherto estopped all intercourse with the surrounding country.

Shortly after the occurrence of this unfortunate event, the vessel which had been blockading the Matanzas river was withdrawn. Taking advantage of the opportunity thus afforded, some small vessels from Havana, with provisions and reinforcements, reached St. Augustine by that narrow channel, bringing great encouragement and relief to the garrison. This reinforcement was estimated at seven hundred men, and the supply of provisions is said to have been large. "Then," writes Hewitt,* whose narrative we have followed in the main, "all prospects of starving the enemy being lost, the army began to despair of forcing the place to surrender. The Carolinean troops, enfeebled by the heat, dispirited by sickness, and fatigued by fruitless efforts, marched away in large bodies. The navy being short of provisions, and the usual season of hurricanes approaching, the commander judged it imprudent to hazard his Majesty's ships by remaining longer on that coast. Last of all, the General himself, sick of a fever, and his regiment worn out with fatigue and rendered unfit for

---

* Historical Account of the Rise and Progress of the Colonies of South Carolina and Georgia, vol. II, p. 81. London, 1779.

action by a flux, with sorrow and regret followed, and reached Frederica about the 10th of July, 1740."

The Carolineans, under Colonel Vanderdussen, proved themselves inefficient, "turbulent, and disobedient." They lost not a single man in action, and only fourteen deaths occurred from sickness and accident. Desertions were frequent.*

Upon Oglethorpe's regiment, and the Georgia companies, devolved the brunt of the siege. On the 5th of July the artillery and stores on Anastasia island were brought off, and the men crossed over to the mainland.† Vanderdussen and his regiment at once commenced a disorderly retreat in the direction of the St. Johns, leaving Oglethorpe and his men within half-cannon shot of the castle. In his dispatch to the Secretary of State, dated Camp on St. Johns in Florida, July 19th, 1740, the General thus describes his last movements: "The Spaniards made a sally, with about 500 men, on me who lay on the land side. I ordered Ensign Cathcart with twenty men, supported by Major Heron and Captain Desbrisay with upwards of 100 men, to attack them; I followed with the body. We drove them into the works and pursued them to the very barriers of the covered way. After the train and provisions were embarked and safe out of the harbour, I marched with drums beating and colours flying, in the day, from my camp near

*Stephens says, * * Most of the gay Volunteers run away by small Parties, basely and cowardly, as they could get Boats to carry them off during the Time of greatest Action; and Capt. *Bull*, (a son of the Lieutenant-Governor) who had the Command of a Company in that Regiment, most scandalously deserted his Post when upon Duty, and not staying to be relieved regularly, made his Flight privately, carrying off four Men of his Guard with him, and escaped to *Charles Town;* for which he ought in Justice to have been tried as a Deserter; but he was well received at home.

Journal of Proceedings, &c., vol. II, p. 462. London, 1742.

Compare Ramsay's History of South Carolina, vol. I, p. 143. Charleston, 1809.

†Wright's Memoir of General James Oglethorpe, p. 254. London, 1867.

the town to a camp three miles distant, where I lay that night. The next day I marched nine miles, where I encamped that night. We discovered a party of Spanish horse and Indians whom we charged, took one horseman and killed two Indians; the rest ran to the garrison. I am now encamped on St. Johns river, waiting to know what the people of Carolina would desire me farther to do for the safety of these provinces, which I think are very much exposed to the half-galleys, with a wide extended frontier hardly to be defended by a few men."

In one of the Indian chiefs Oglethorpe found a man after his own heart. When asked by some of the retreating troops to march with them, his reply was, "No! I will not stir a foot till I see every man belonging to me marched off before me; for I have always been the first in advancing towards an enemy, and the last in retreating."*

This failure to reduce St. Augustine may be fairly attributed

I; to the delay in inaugurating the movement, caused mainly, if not entirely, by the tardiness on the part of the South Carolina authorities in contributing the troops and provisions for which requisition had been made;

II; to the reinforcement of men and supplies from Havanna introduced into St. Augustine just before the English expedition set out; thereby materially repairing the inequality previously existing between the opposing forces;

---

* See Harris' Memorials of Oglethorpe, pp. 239, 240. Boston, 1841, quoting from the Gentleman's Magazine.

III; to the injudicious movement against forts Francis de Papa and Diego, which put the Spaniards on the alert, encouraged concentration on their part, and foreshadowed an immediate demonstration in force against their stronghold; and

IV; to the inability on the part of the fleet to participate in the assault previously planned, and which was to have been vigorously undertaken so soon as General Oglethorpe with his land forces came into position before the walls of St. Augustine.

V. The subsequent destruction of Colonel Palmer's command,—thereby enabling the enemy to communicate with and draw supplies from the interior,—the lack of heavy ordnance with which to reduce the castle from the batteries on Anastasia island,—the impossibility of bringing up the larger war vessels that they might participate in the bombardment,—the inefficiency of Colonel Vanderdussen's command,—the impatience and disappointment of the Indian allies who anticipated early capture and liberal spoils,—hot suns, heavy dews, a debilitating climate, sickness among the troops, and the arrival of men, munitions of war, and provisions through the Matanzas river, in the end rendered quite futile every hope which at the outset had been entertained for a successful prosecution of the siege.

Great was the disappointment upon the failure of the expedition, and unjust and harsh the criticisms levelled by not a few against its brave and distinguished leader.* We

*See "An Impartial Account of the late Expedition against St. Augustine under General Oglethorpe," &c., London, 1742, which called forth "The Spanish Hireling detected," &c., London, 1743.

agree with the Duke of Argyle who, in the British House of Peers, declared "One man there is, my Lords, whose natural generosity, contempt of danger, and regard for the public prompted him to obviate the designs of the Spaniards, and to attack them in their own territories; a man whom by long acquaintance I can confidently affirm to have been equal to his undertaking, and to have learned the art of war by a regular education, who yet miscarried in the design only for want of supplies necessary to a possibility of success."

Although this attempt,—so formidable in its character when we consider the limited resources at command, and so full of daring when we contemplate the circumstances under which it was undertaken,—eventuated in disappointment, its effects were not without decided advantages to the Colonies. For two years the Spaniards remained on the defensive, and General Oglethorpe enjoyed an opportunity for strengthening his fortifications on St. Simons island, so that when the counter blow was delivered by his adversary he was in condition not only to parry it, but also to severely punish the uplifted arm."*

For two months after the termination of this expedition, Oglethorpe lay ill of a continued fever contracted during

---

* For fuller account of this demonstration against St. Augustine see Harris' "Complete Collection of Voyages and Travels," &c., pp. 339, 340. London, 1748. "An Impartial Account of the late Expedition against St. Augustine," &c. London, 1742. "The Spanish Hireling detected," &c. London, 1743. Stephens' "Journal of Proceedings," &c., vol. II, pp. 438, 444–448, 461 et aliter. London, 1742. Hewitt's "Historical Account of the Rise and Progress of the Colonies of South Carolina and Georgia," vol. II, chap. viii, pp. 65–82. London, 1779. McCall's "History of Georgia," vol. I, pp. 143–151. Savannah, 1811. Stevens' "History of Georgia," vol. I., pp. 167–179. New York, 1847. Spalding's "Sketch of the Life of General James Oglethorpe," Collections of the Georgia Historical Society, vol. I, pp. 265–272. Savannah, 1840. Harris' "Biographical Memorials of James Oglethorpe," pp. 222–242. Boston, 1841. Wright's "Memoir of General James Oglethorpe," &c., pp. 235–255. London, 1867. Ramsay's "History of South Carolina," vol. I., pp. 140–144. Charleston, 1809, &c., &c., &c.

Fairbanks' History and Antiquities of St. Augustine, pp. 141–152. New York, 1858.

the exposures and fatigues incident upon his exertions and anxieties during the siege. When, on the second of September, Mr. Stephens called to see him at Frederica, he found him still troubled with a lurking fever and confined to his bed. His protracted sickness had so "worn away his strength" that he "seldom came down stairs, but retained still the same vivacity of spirit in appearance to all whom he talked with, though he chose to converse with very few."*

Four companies of the regiment were now encamped at the south-east end of St. Simons island, and the other two at Frederica. So soon as the men recovered from the malady contracted at St. Augustine, they were busily occupied in erecting new fortifications and strengthening the old. From these two camps detachments garrisoned the advanced works, St. Andrew, Fort William, St. George, and the outposts on Amelia island;—the details being relieved at regular intervals.†

During the preceding seven years, which constituted the entire life of the Colony, General Oglethorpe had enjoyed no respite from his labors. Personally directing all movements,—supervising the location, and providing for the comfort, safety, and good order of the settlers,—accommodating their differences,—encouraging and directing their labors,—propitiating the Aborigines,—influencing necessary supplies, and inaugurating suitable defences, he had been constantly passing from point to point finding no rest for the soles of his feet. Now in tent at Savannah,—now in open boat reconnoitering the coast,—now upon the southern islands,—his only shelter the wide-spreading live-oak,—

* Stephens' "Journal of Proceedings," &c., vol. II, pp. 467–468, 494–495. London, 1742.

† Idem, p. 496.

designating sites for forts and look-outs, and with his own hands planning military works and laying out villages,—again in journeys oft along the Savannah, the Great Ogeechee, the Alatamaha, the St. Johns, and far off into the heart of the Indian country,—frequently inspecting his advanced posts,—undertaking voyages to Charlestown and to England in behalf of the Trust, and engaged in severe contests with the Spaniards, his life had been one of incessant activity and solicitude. But for his energy, intelligence, watchfulness, and self-sacrifice, the enterprise must have languished. As we look back upon this period of trial, uncertainty, and poverty, our admiration for his achievements increases the more narrowly we scan his limited resources and opportunities, the more intelligently we appreciate the difficulties he was called upon to surmount. Always present wherever duty called or danger threatened, he never expected others to press on where he himself did not lead. The only home he ever owned or claimed in Georgia was on St. Simons island. The only hours of leisure he ever enjoyed were spent in sight and sound of his military works along the southern frontier, upon whose safe tenure depended the salvation of the Colony. Just where the military road connecting Fort St. Simon with Frederica, after having traversed the beautiful prairie,—constituting the common pasture land of the village,—entered the woods, General Oglethorpe established his cottage. Adjacent to it were a garden, and an orchard of oranges, figs and grapes. Magnificent oaks threw their protecting shadows above and around this quiet, pleasant abode, fanned by delicious sea-breezes, fragrant with the perfume of flowers, and vocal with the melody of song-birds. To the westward, and in full view, were the fortifications and the white houses of Frederica. Behind rose a dense forest of oaks. "This cottage and fifty acres of land attached to it," says the honorable Thomas Spalding in his "Sketch of the life of General James Oglethorpe,"* "was all the landed domain General Oglethorpe reserved to himself, and after the General went to England it became the property of my father. * * * After the Revolutionary war, the buildings being destroyed, my father sold this little property. But the oaks were only cut down within four or five years past, and the elder people of St. Simons yet feel as if it were sacrilege, and mourn their fall." Here the defences of St. Simons island were under his immediate supervision. His troops were around him, and he was prepared, upon the first note of warning, to concentrate the forces of the Colony for active operations. In the neighborhood several of his officers established their homes. Among them, "Harrington Hall,"—the country seat of the wealthy Huguenot, Captain Raymond Demeré, enclosed with hedges of cassina,—was conspicuous for its beauty and comfort.

Including the soldiers and their families, Frederica in 1740 is said to have claimed a population of one thousand.† This estimate is perhaps somewhat exaggerated, although much nearer the mark than that of the discontents Tailfer, Anderson, and Douglas, who, in their splenetic and jacobinical tract entitled "A True and Historical Narrative of the Colony of Georgia in America," assert that of the one hundred and forty-four lots into which the town was divided,

---

* Collections of the Georgia Historical Society, vol. I, p. 273. Savannah, 1840.

† Collections of the Georgia Historical Society, vol. I, p. 274. Savannah, 1840.

Bancroft's History of the United States, vol. III, p. 434. Boston, 1852.

In this estimate may properly be included such officers and men of Oglethorpe's regiment as were there stationed.

only "about fifty were built upon," and that "the number of the Inhabitants, notwithstanding of the Circulation of the Regiment's money, are not over *one hundred and twenty* Men, Women, and Children, and these are daily stealing away by all possible Ways."*

As we have already seen, the town was regularly laid out in streets called after the principal officers of Oglethorpe's regiment; and, including the military camp on the north, the parade on the east, and "a small wood on the south which served as a blind to the enemy in case of attack from ships coming up the river," was about a mile and a half in circumference. The fort was strongly built of tabby and well armed. Several eighteen pounders, mounted on a ravelin in front, commanded the river, and the town was defended on the land side by substantial intrenchments. The ditch at the foot of these intrenchments was intended to admit the influx of the tide, thus rendering the isolation of Frederica complete, and materially enhancing the strength of its line of circumvallation. We reproduce from "An Impartial Enquiry into the State and Utility of the Province of Georgia"† the following contemporaneous notice: "There are many good Buildings in the Town, several of which are Brick. There is likewise a Fort and Store-house belonging to the Trust. The People have a Minister who has a Salary from the Society for propagating the Gospel. In the Neighbourhood of the Town, there is a fine Meadow of 320 Acres ditch'd in, on which a number

---

* Page 106. Charles-Town, South Carolina, 1741.

† Pages 51 and 52. London, 1741.

Compare "A State of the Province of Georgia attested upon Oath," &c., p. 11. London, 1742.

"An Account Shewing the Progress of the Colony of Georgia," &c., p. 36. London, 1741.

Wright's Memoir of Gen'l James Oglethorpe, pp. 263, 264. London, 1867.

of Cattle are fed, and good Hay is likewise made from it. At some Distance from the Town is the Camp for General *Oglethorpe's* Regiment. The Country about it is well cultivated, several Parcels of Land not far distant from the Camp having been granted in small Lots to the Soldiers, many of whom are married, and fifty-five Children were born there in the last year. These Soldiers are the most industrious, and willing to plant; the rest are generally desirous of Wives, but there are not Women enough in the Country to supply them. There are some handsome Houses built by the Officers of the Regiment, and besides the Town of *Frederica* there are other little Villages upon this Island. A sufficient Quantity of Pot-herbs, Pulse, and Fruit is produced there to supply both the Town and Garrison; and the People of *Frederica* have begun to malt and to brew; and the Soldiers Wives Spin Cotton of the Country, which they Knit into Stockings. At the Town of *Frederica* is a Town-Court for administring Justice in the Southern Part of the Province, with the same Number of Magistrates as at *Savannah*."

At the village of St. Simon, on the south point of the island, was erected a watch-tower from which the movements of vessels at sea might be conveniently observed. Upon their appearance, their number was at once announced by signal guns, and a horseman dispatched to head quarters with the particulars. A look-out was kept by a party of Rangers at Bachelor's Redoubt on the main, and a Corporal's guard was stationed at Pike's Bluff. To facilitate communication with Darien a canal was cut through General's island. Defensive works were erected on Jekyll island, where Captain Horton had a well improved plantation, and there a brewery was established for supplying the troops with beer. On Cumberland island were three batteries,—Fort St. Andrew,—built in 1736, on high commanding ground, at the north-east point of the island,—a battery on the west to control the inland navigation,—and Fort William,—a work of considerable strength and regularity,—commanding the entrance to St. Mary's river. Two companies of Oglethorpe's regiment were stationed near Fort St. Andrew. As many of the soldiers were married, lots were assigned to them which they cultivated and improved. Near this work was the little village of Barrimacké of twenty-four families.

Upon Amelia island, where the orange trees were growing wild in the woods, were stationed the Highlanders with their scout boats. They had a good plantation,—upon which they raised corn enough for their subsistence,—a little fort, and "a stud of horses and mares."*

"Nowhere," remarks Mr. Spalding,† "had mind, with the limited means under its control, more strongly evinced its power. And it will be seen hereafter, that it was to the great ability shown in the disposition of these works, that not Georgia only, but Carolina owed their preservation; for St. Simon's was destined soon to become the Thermopylæ of the southern Anglo American provinces." Besides compassing the improvement of, and garrisoning his defensive works along the southern frontier with the men of his regiment, Oglethorpe kept in active service considerable bodies of Indians whose mission was to harrass the Spaniards in Florida, annoy their posts, and closely invest St. Augustine. So energetically did these faithful

*See an Impartial Enquiry into the State and Utility of the Province of Georgia, &c., p. 53. London, 1743.

Wright's Memoir of Oglethorpe, p. 264. London, 1867.

†Collections of the Georgia Historical Society, vol. I, p. 258. Savannah, 1840.

13

allies discharge the duty assigned them, and so narrowly did they watch and thoroughly plague the garrison and inhabitants of St. Augustine, that they dared not venture any distance without the walls. Adjacent plantations remained uncultivated; and, within the town, food, fuel, and the necessaries of life became so scarce that the Spanish government was compelled to support the population by stores sent from Havana. To the efficient aid of his Indian allies was Oglethorpe on more than one occasion indebted for the consummation of important plans. It would not be an exaggeration to affirm that to their friendship, fidelity, and valor, was the Colony largely beholden not only for its security, but even for its preservation. "If we had no other evidence," writes Mr. Spalding, "of the great abilities of Oglethorpe but what is offered by the devotion of the Indian Tribes to him, and to his memory afterwards for fifty years, it is all-sufficient; for it is only master minds that acquire this deep and lasting influence over other men."

In his letter to the Duke of Newcastle, dated Frederica, May 12th, 1741, Oglethorpe advises the Home Government of a reinforcement of eight hundred men newly arrived at St. Augustine, and of a declared intention on the part of the Spanish authorities to invade the provinces of Georgia and Carolina so soon as the result of Admiral Vernon's expedition in the West Indies should have been ascertained. He makes urgent demand for men-of-war to guard the water approaches, for a train of artillery, arms, and ammunition, and for authority to recruit the two troops of Rangers to sixty men each, and the Highland company to one hundred, to enlist one hundred boatmen, and to purchase or build, and man two half-galleys. Alluding to the expected advance of the Spaniards, the writer continues: "If our men of war will not keep them from coming in by sea, and we have no succour, but decrease daily by different accidents, all we can do will be to die bravely in his Majesty's service. * * I have often desired assistance of the men-of-war, and continue to do so. I go on in fortifying this town, making magazines, and doing everything I can to defend the Province vigorously, and I hope my endeavors will be approved of by his Majesty, since the whole end of my life is to do the duty of a faithful subject and grateful servant. I have thirty Spanish prisoners in this place, and we continue so masters of Florida that the Spaniards have not been able to rebuild any one of the seven forts which we destroyed in the last expedition."

It does not appear that the men-of-war and ordnance requested were ever furnished.

With a little squadron composed of the Guard sloop, the sloop "Falcon," and Captain Davis' schooner "Norfolk" carrying a detachment of his regiment under command of Major Heron, General Oglethorpe on the 16th of August, 1741, bore down upon a large Spanish ship lying at anchor, with hostile intent, off the bar of Jekyll sound. A heavy storm intervening, the Spanish vessel put to sea and was lost to sight. Unwilling to dismiss his miniature fleet until he had performed more substantial service, the General boldly continued down the coast, attacked and put to flight a Spanish man-of-war, and the notorious privateer "Black-Sloop" commanded by Destrade, a French officer, challenged the vessels lying in the inner harbor of St. Augustine to come out and engage his small squadron, remained at anchor all night within sight of the castle, cruised for some days off the Matanzas, and, after having alarmed the whole coast, returned in safety to Frederica.

In the midst of these labors and anxieties incident upon his preparations to resist the threatened Spanish invasion, and at a time when harmony and content were most essential to the well-being of the Colony, Oglethorpe was annoyed by sundry complaints from evil-minded persons. Most of them were frivolous, and a few quite insulting in their character. The publication of two tracts, one entitled "An Impartial Enquiry into the State and Utility of the Province of Georgia,"* and the other "A State of the Province of Georgia attested upon Oath in the Court of Savannah, November 10, 1740,"†—both presenting favorable views of the Colony and disseminated in the interest of the Trust,—irritated these malcontents and gave rise to several rejoinders, among which, as particularly reflecting upon the conduct of the commander-in-chief and his administration of affairs, may be mentioned "A Brief Account of the Causes that have Retarded the Progress of the Colony of Georgia in America, attested upon Oath, being a Proper Contrast to 'A State of the Province of Georgia attested upon Oath,' and some other misrepresentations on the same subject."‡ The charge was openly made that some of the magistrates at Savannah and Frederica (the principal towns in Georgia) had wilfully injured the people by declaring "from the Bench that the Laws of England were no laws in Georgia," by causing "false imprisonments," by "discharging Grand Juries while matters of Felony lay before them," by "intimidating Petit Juries," and, in short, "by sticking at nothing to oppress the

* London, 1741.
† London, 1742.
‡ London, 1743.

people." It was further alleged that there was no way of applying for redress to his Majesty. General Oglethorpe was accused of partiality and tyranny in his administration. In support of these charges various affidavits were obtained from parties claiming to be residents of Frederica, Darien, Savannah, Ebenezer, and Augusta,—most of them, however, being sworn to and verified outside the limits of Georgia. Those who are curious with regard to the contents of these affidavits, so far as they reflect upon the conduct of the Frederica magistrates, are referred to the depositions of Samuel Perkins, John Roberson, and Samuel Davison.*

A desire to sell forbidden articles, and to ply trades for which special permission had been granted to others, opposition to the regulation which prohibited the owners of hogs and cattle from allowing them to run at large on the common and in the streets of Frederica, alleged misfeasance in the conduct of bailiffs and under-magistrates in the discharge of their duties, the unprofitableness of labor, overbearing acts committed by those in authority, and similar matters formed the burthen of these sworn complaints. While they tended to distract the public mind and to annoy those upon whose shoulders rested the administration of affairs, they fortunately failed in producing any serious impression either within the Colony or in the mother country. We allude to the subject in its proper connection simply as a matter of history, and to show how ill-judged and ill-timed were these efforts of the malcontents, among whom Pat Tailfer, M. D., Hugh Anderson, M. A., and Da: Douglas should not be forgotten.

---

*A Brief Account of the Causes that have retarded the Progress of the Colony of Georgia, &c., Appendix, pp. 1–19. London, 1743.

The utter destruction of the provinces of Georgia and South Carolina was the avowed object of the Spaniards, who promised to extend no quarter to English or Indians taken with arms in their hands. The struggle was to be desperate in the extreme. To the urgent applications for assistance forwarded by General Oglethorpe, Lieutenant-Governor Bull turned a deaf ear; and the Carolinians, instead of furnishing supplies and munitions of war, and marching to the south to meet the invader where the battle for the salvation of both Colonies was to be fought, remained at home, leaving the Georgians single-handed to breast the storm.*

The Gentleman's Magazine† contains the following estimate of the Spanish forces under the command of Don Manuel de Monteano, Governor of Augustine and Commander-in-Chief of the expedition, and Major General Antonio de Rodondo, Engineer General, participating in the attack upon St. Simons island:

"2 Colonels with Brevits of Brigadiers.

"One Regiment of Dragoons, dismounted, with their Saddles and Bridles.

"The Regiment call'd The Battalion of the *Havannah*.

"10 Companies of 50 each, draughted off from several Regiments of *Havannah*.

"One Regiment of the *Havannah* Militia, consisting of 10 Companies of 100 Men each.

"One Regiment of Negroes, regularly officer'd by Negroes.

"One ditto of Mulattas, and one Company of 100 Miguelets.

---

* See Letter of General Oglethorpe, dated Frederica, June 8th, 1742. Wright's Memoir of Oglethorpe, p. 298. London, 1867.

† For 1742. Vol. XII, p. 694.

"One Company of the Train with proper Artillery.

"*Augustine* Forces consisting of about 300 Men.

"Ninety Indians.

"And 15 Negroes who ran away from *South Carolina.*"

From the various accounts of this memorable struggl we select that prepared by Oglethorpe himself, written on the spot, with the scars of battle fresh around him, and the smoke of the conflict scarce lifted from the low-lying shores and dense woods of St. Simons island. The commanding eye that saw, the stern lips which answered back the proud defiance, and the strong arm which, under Providence, pointed the way to victory, are surely best able to unfold the heroic tale. We present the report as it came from his pen:*

"FREDERICA IN GEORGIA,
30th July, 1742.

"The Spanish Invasion which has a long time threatened the Colony, Carolina, and all North America has at last fallen upon us and God hath been our deliverance. General Horcasilas, Governour of the Havannah, ordered those Troops who had been employed against General Wentworth to embark with Artillery and everything necessary upon a secret expedition. They sailed with a great fleet:† amongst them were two half Galleys carrying 120 men each & an 18 pound Gun. They drew but five feet water which satisfied me they were for this place. By good great Fortune one of the half Galleys was wrecked coming out.‡ The Fleet sailed for St. Augustine in Florida. Capt.

---

* See Collections of the Georgia Historical Society, vol. III, p. 133 et seq. Savannah, 1873.

† Consisting of fifty-six sail, and between seven and eight thousand men.

‡ This was a large Settee having one hundred and fifty men on board. A few days afterwards the fleet was dispersed by a storm so that all the shipping did not arrive at St. Augustine.

Homer the latter end of May called here for Intelligence. I acquainted him that the Succours were expected and sent him a Spanish Pilot to shew him where to meet with them. He met with ten sail* which had been divided from the Fleet by storm, but having lost 18 men in action against them, instead of coming here for the defence of this Place he stood again for Charles Town to repair, and I having certain advices of the arrival of the Spanish Fleet at Augustine wrote to the Commander of His Majesty's Ships at Charles Town to come to our assistance.†

"I sent Lieut. Maxwell who arrived there and delivered the letters the 12th of June, and afterwards Lieut. MacKay, who arrived and delivered letters on the 20th of June.

"Lieut. Colonel Cook who was then at Charles Town, and was Engineer, hastened to England, and his son-in-law Ensign Eyre, Sub-Engineer, was also in Charles Town, and did not arrive here till the action was over; so, for want of help, I myself was obliged to do the duty of Engineer.

"The Havannah Fleet, being joined by that of Florida, composed 51 sail, with land men on board, a List of whom is annexed: they were separated, and I received advice from Capt. Dunbar (who lay at Fort William with the Guard Schooner of 14 Guns and ninety men) that a Spanish Fleet of 14 sail had attempted to come in there,‡ but being

---

* These he attacked, driving some of them ashore.

† "Never did the Carolineans," says Mr. Hewitt, "make so bad a figure in the defence of their country. When union, activity and dispatch were so requisite, they ingloriously stood at a distance, and suffering private pique to prevail over public spirit, seemed determined to risk the safety of their country, rather than General Oglethorpe by their help should gain the smallest degree of honour and reputation. * * * The Georgians with justice blamed their more powerful neighbors, who, by keeping at a distance in the day of danger, had almost hazarded the loss of both provinces."

Historical Account of the Rise and Progress of the Colonies of South Carolina and Georgia, vol. II, pp. 119, 120. London, 1779.

‡ This was on the 21st of June. Most of the accounts place the number of Spanish vessels, then attempting to enter Amelia Sound, at *nine*, instead of *fourteen*.

drove out by the Cannon of the Fort and Schooner they came in at Cumberland Sound. I sent over Capt. Horton to land the Indians and Troops on Cumberland. I followed myself and was attacked in the Sound, but with two Boats fought my way through. Lieut. Tolson, who was to have supported me with the third and strongest boat, quitted me in the fight and run into a River where he hid himself till next day when he returned to St. Simons with an account that I was lost but soon after found. I was arrived there before him, for which misbehaviour I put him in arrest and ordered him to be tryed. The Enemy in this action suffered so much* that the day after they ran out to sea and returned for St. Augustine and did not join their great Fleet till after their Grenadiers were beat by Land.

"I drew the Garrison from St. Andrews, reinforced Fort William, and returned to St. Simons with the Schooner.

"Another Spanish Fleet appeared the 28th off the Barr: by God's blessing upon several measures taken I delayed their coming in till the 5th of July. I raised another Troop of Rangers, which with the other were of great service.

"I took Captain Thomson's ship† into the service for defence of the Harbour. I imbargoe'd all the Vessells, taking their men for the service, and gave large Gifts and promises to the Indians so that every day we increased in numbers. I gave large rewards to men who distinguished themselves upon any service, freed the servants,‡ brought down the Highland Company, and Com-

*In endeavoring to reach St. Augustine for repairs, four of their vessels foundered at sea.

†This was the merchant ship "*Success*," mounting twenty guns. The General sent one hundred soldiers on board of her and filled her with necessary military stores. Thus she became, in the language of one of her crew, "ready for twice the number of Spaniards."

‡For their passage and outfit, they had agreed to labor for the Trust for a given period.

pany of Boatmen, filled up as far as we had guns. All the vessels being thus prepared* on the 5th of July with a leading Gale and Spring Tide 36 sail of Spanish vessels run into the Harbour in line of Battle.

"We cannonaded them very hotly from the Shipping and Batterys. They twice attempted to board Capt. Thomson† but were repulsed. They also attempted to board the Schooner, but were repulsed by Capt. Dunbar with a Detachment of the Regiment on board.

"I was with the Indians, Rangers, and Batterys, and sometimes on board the ships, and left Major Heron with the Regiment. It being impossible for me to do my duty as General and be constantly with the Regiment, therefore it was absolutely necessary for His Majesty's service to have a Lieut. Colonel present, which I was fully convinced of by this day's expérience. I therefore appointed Major Heron to be Lieut. Colonel, and hope that your Grace will move His Majesty to be pleased to approve the same.

"The Spaniards after an obstinate Engagement of four hours, in which they lost abundance of men, passed all our Batterys and Shipping and got out of shot of them towards Frederica. Our Guard Sloop was disabled and sunk: one of our Batterys blown up, and also some of our Men on

* This little fleet consisted of the "Success," Captain Thompson, of twenty guns and one hundred and ten men, with springs upon her cables,—General Oglethorpe's schooner of fourteen guns and eighty men,—and the sloop "St. Philip," of fourteen guns and eighty men. Eight York sloops were close in shore, with one man on board each of them, whose instructions were, in case the enemy were about to capture, to sink or run them on shore.

Gentleman's Magazine, vol. XII, p. 495.

† This attempt was made by the Spanish Commodore with a ship of twenty-two guns, and a settee with an eighteen pounder and two nine pounders in her bow. So stout was the resistance offered by Captain Thompson with the great guns of his ship, by Captain Carr and his company of Marines, and by Lieutenant Wall and Ensign Otterbridge in charge of a detachment from Oglethorpe's Regiment, that the Spaniards were obliged to retire with loss. A snow of sixteen guns at the same time attempted to board the Guard Schooner, but was repulsed by Captain Dunbar.

See Harris' Complete Collection of Voyages and Travels, vol. II, p. 341. London, 1748.

board Capt. Thomson, upon which I called a Council of War at the head of the Regiment where it was unanimously resolved to march to Frederica to get there before the Enemy and defend that Place. To destroy all the Provisions, Vessels, Artillery, &c., at St. Simon's, that they might not fall into the Enemy's hands.

"This was accordingly executed, having first drawn all the Men on shoar which before had defended the shipping. I myself staid till the last, and the wind coming fortunately about I got Capt. Thompson's Ship, our Guard Schooner, and our Prize Sloop to sea and sent them to Charles Town. This I did in the face and spite of thirty-six sail of the Enemy: as for the rest of the Vessells, I could not save them, therefore was obliged to destroy them.

"I must recomend to His Majesty the Merchants who are sufferers thereby, since their loss was in great measure the preserving the Province.

"We arrived at Frederica, and the Enemy landed at St. Simon's.*

"On the 7th a party of their's marched toward the Town: our Rangers discovered them and brought an account of their march, on which I advanced with a party of Indians, Rangers, and the Highland Company, ordering the Regiment to follow, being resolved to engage them in the Defiles of the Woods before they could get out and form in the open Grounds. I charged them at the head of our Indians,

* From the statement made by five Spanish prisoners captured and brought in by the Creek Indians, it appeared that Don Manuel de Monteano, Governor of St. Augustine, was the Commander in Chief of the Expedition, and that Major General Antonio de Redondo was Chief Engineer. He and two Brigadier Generals accompanied the forces which came from Cuba. The aggregate strength of the expedition was about five thousand men, of whom four thousand three hundred were landed on St. Simons.

Heavy scouting parties were sent out in every direction by General Oglethorpe to observe the movements of the enemy and retard any advance in the direction of Frederica, the defences of which were being strengthened as rapidly and as thoroughly as time and the forces at command would permit.

Highland Men and Rangers, and God was pleased to give us such success that we entirely routed the first party, took one Captain prisoner, and killed another, and pursued them two miles to an open Meadow or Savannah, upon the edge of which I posted three Platoons of the Regiment and the Company of Highland foot so as to be covered by the woods from the Enemy who were obliged to pass thro' the Meadow under our fire.* This disposition was very fortunate.† Capt. Antonio Barba and two other Captains with 100 Grenadiers and 200 foot, besides Indians and Negroes, advanced from the Spanish Camp into the Savannah with Huzzah's and fired with great spirit, but not seeing our men by reason of the woods, none of their shot took place, but ours did.‡

* In this charge Oglethorpe encountered one hundred and twenty Spanish Pioneers, forty Yamassee Indians, and an equal number of negroes. So violent was the onslaught that nearly the whole party was either captured or slain. With his own hands the General captured two prisoners. Captain Sanchio commanding this advance, was taken prisoner by Lieut. Scroggs of the Rangers, and Toonahowi, although shot through the right arm by a Spanish officer, drew his pistol with his left and killed his antagonist on the spot.

See Wright's Memoir of Oglethorpe, p. 305.

McCall's History of Georgia, vol. I, p. 181.

† After locating his troops, Oglethorpe hastened back to Frederica to prepare the Rangers and the Marine Company for action at a moments warning.

‡ Captain McCall furnishes the following account of this affair:

Captain Noble Jones, with a detachment of regulars and Indians, being out on a scouting party, fell in with a small detachment in the enemy's advance, who were surprised and made prisoners, not deeming themselves so far in front of the main army. From these prisoners information was received that the whole Spanish army was advancing: this was immediately communicated by an Indian runner to the General who detached Captain Dunbar with a company of grenadiers to join the regulars and Indians, with orders to harrass the enemy on their advance. These detachments having formed a junction, observed at a distance the Spanish army on the march; and taking a favorable position near a marsh, formed an ambuscade. The enemy fortunately halted within a hundred paces of this position, stacked their arms, made fires, and were preparing their kettles for cooking, when a horse observed some of the party in ambuscade, and, frightened at the uniform of the regulars, began to snort, and gave the alarm. The Spaniards ran to their arms, but were shot down in great numbers by Oglethorpe's detatchment, who continued invisible to the enemy; and after repeated attempts to form, in which some of their principal officers fell, they fled with the utmost precipitation, leaving their camp equipage on the field, and never halted until they got under cover of the guns of their battery and ships. General Oglethorpe had detached Major Horton with a reinforcement, who arrived only in time to join in the pursuit. So complete was the surprise of the enemy,

"Some Platoons of ours in the heat of the fight, the air being darkened with the smoak, and a shower of rain falling, retired in disorder.

"I hearing the firing, rode towards it, and at near two miles from the place of Action, met a great many men in disorder who told me that ours were routed and Lieut. Sutherland killed. I ordered them to halt and march back against the Enemy, which orders Capt. Demere and Ensign Gibbon obeyed, but another Officer did not, but made the best of his way to Town. As I heard the fire continue I concluded our Men could not be quite beaten, and that my immediate assistance might preserve them: therefore spurred on and arrived just as the fire was done. I found the Spaniards intirely routed by one Platoon of the Regiment, under the Comand of Lieut. Sutherland, and the Highland Company under the Comand of Lieut. Charles MacKay.

"An Officer whom the Prisoners said was Capt. Don Antonio Barba* was taken Prisoner, but desperately wounded, and two others were prisoners, and a great many dead upon the spot. Lieut. Sutherland, Lieut. Charles MacKay and Sergt. Stuart having distinguished themselves upon this occasion, I appointed Lieut. Sutherland Brigade Major, and Sergt. Stuart second Ensign.

---

that many fled without their arms; others in a rapid retreat discharged their muskets over their shoulders at their pursuers; and many were killed by the loaded arms which were left on the ground; generally the Spaniards fired so much at random that the trees were pruned by the balls from their muskets; their loss in killed, wounded and prisoners, was estimated at five hundred. The loss in Oglethorpe's detachment was very inconsiderable. From the signal victory obtained over the enemy, and the great slaughter amongst the Spanish troops, the scene of action just described has ever since been denominated the *bloody marsh*.†

† History of Georgia, vol. I, pp. 185, 187. Savannah, 1811.

Compare Spalding's Life of Oglethorpe, Collections of the Georgia Historical Society, vol. I. pp. 281–284. Savannah, 1840.

---

* The Spaniards regarded the loss of this officer as more severe than that of a thousand men.

"Capt. Demere and Ensign Gibbon being arrived with the men they had rallied, Lieut. Cadogan with an advanced party of the Regiment, and soon after the whole Regiment, Indians, and Rangers, I marched down to a causeway over a marsh very near the Spanish Camp over which all were obliged to pass, and thereby stopt those who had been dispersed in the fight in the Savannah from getting to the Spanish Camp.* Having passed the night there, the Indian scouts in the morning advanced to the Spanish Camp and discovered they were all retired into the ruins of the Fort and were making Intrenchments under shelter of the cannon of the ships. That they guessed them to be above 4,000 men. I thought it imprudent to attack them defended by Cannon with so small a number but marched back to Frederica† to refresh the soldiers, and sent out Partys of Indians and Rangers to harrass the Enemy. I also ordered into arrest the officers who commanded the Platoons that retired.

"I appointed a General Staff: Lieut. Hugh MacKay and Lieut. Maxwell Aids de Camp, and Lieut. Sutherland Brigade Major.‡ On ye 11th of July the Great Galley and two little ones came up the river towards the Town. We fired at them with the few Guns, so warmly that they retired, and I followed them with our Boats till they got under the cannon of their ships which lay in the sound.

"Having intelligence from the Spanish Camp that they had lost 4 Captains and upwards of 200 men in the last Action, besides a great many killed in the sea-fight, and

* In these two engagements the enemy had sustained a loss of two Captains, one Lieutenant, two Sergeants, two Drummers, and one hundred and sixty privates killed; and one Captain and nineteen men captured.

† This was on the 8th of July.

‡ During the 9th and 10th of July all hands were employed on the works at Frederica, except the scouts and Indians; the latter brought in some scalps and prisoners.

several killed in the night by the Indians even within or near the camp, and that they had held a Council of War in which there were great divisions, insomuch that the Forces of Cuba separated from those of Augustine and the Italick Regiment ——— of Dragoons separated from them both at a distance from the rest near the woods, and that there was a general Terror amongst them, upon which I was resolved to beat up their Quarters in the night and marching down with the largest body of men I could make, I halted within a mile and a half of their camp to form, intending to leave the Troops there till I had well reconitred the Enemy's disposition.

"A French Man who without my knowledge was come down amongst the volunteers fired his Gun and deserted. Our Indians in vain persued and could not take him. Upon this, concluding we were discovered, I divided the Drums in different parts and beat the Grenadiers march for about half an hour, then ceased, and we marched back with silence.

"The next day* I prevailed with a Prisoner, and gave him a sum of money, to carry a letter privately and deliver it to that French Man who had deserted. This Letter was wrote in French as if from a friend of his, telling him he had received the money that he should strive to make the Spaniards believe the English were weak. That he should undertake to pilot up their Boats and Galleys and then bring them under the Woods where he knew the Hidden Batterys were; that if he could bring that about, he should have double the reward he had already received. That the French Deserters should have all that had been promised to them. The Spanish Prisoner got into their

---

* July 13th.

Camp and was immediately carried before their General Don Manuel de Montiano. He was asked how he escaped and whither he had any letters, but denying his having any, was strictly searched and the letter found, and he upon being pardoned, confessed that he had received money to deliver it to the Frenchman, for the letter was not directed. The Frenchman denied his knowing anything of the contents of the Letter or having received any Money or Correspondence with me, notwithstanding which, a Council of War was held and they deemed the French Man to be a double spy, but General Montiano would not suffer him to be executed, having been imployed by him: however, they imbarqued all their Troops,* and halted under Jekyl, they also confined all the French on board and imbarked with such precipitation that they left behind them Cannon, &c., and those dead of their wounds, unburied. The Cuba

---

* St. Simon's town was destroyed by the Spaniards prior to their evacuation of the island. To a writer in the London Magazine for 1745,† who made his observations in the early part of 1743, are we indebted for the following notice of this place:—"At the South Point of this Island of *St. Simon*, are the Ruins of the Town of *St. Simons* destroyed by the *Spaniards* at their Invasion. By the remaining Vestiges it must have been a very uniform Place; and the Situation is quite charming, tho' it now makes one melancholy to see such a Desolation in so new a Country. The only Building they left standing was one House which they had consecrated for a Chapel. How different the Proceedings of the more generous *English* even in their Parts who never leave behind them such direful Remembrances; but here religious Fury goes Hand in Hand with Conquest, resolv'd to ruin whom they can't convert. The Fort has some Remains still, and seems to have been no extraordinary affair; tho' no Place was ever better defended, and the Enemies seem, by their Works and Intrenchments to have thought themselves sure of keeping the Town, but found themselves wofully mistaken. Down the Beach to the westward is a Look-out of Tappy-work which is a very good Mark for standing over the Bar into the Harbour; and on the opposite Point of Jekyl Island is a very remarkable Hammock of Trees much taken notice of by Seamen on the same Account. Somewhat lower and more Northerly is the Plantation call'd Gascoign's which underwent the same Fate with St. Simons. An Officer's Command is station'd at South Point, who disposes his Centries so as to discover Vessels some Leagues at Sea, and upon any such Discovery an Alarm-Gun is fir'd, and an Horseman sent up with Notice to the Head-Quarters which is nine miles from this Place. If they appear to make for the Harbour, a perpendicular mounted Gun is fir'd as a Signal, which, by the Ascent of the Smoke is a Direction to a Ship a long Way in the Offing, and is a most lucky Contrivance. The road from hence to Frederica is cut through the Woods, and through the Marshes rais'd upon a Causeway."

† Page 549.

Squadron stood out to sea to the number of 20 sail: General Montiano with the Augustine Squadron returned to Cumberland Sound, having burnt Captain Horton's houses, &c., on Jekyll. I, with our boats, followed him. I discovered a great many sail under Fort St. Andrew, of which eight appeared to me plain, but being too strong for me to attack, I sent the Scout Boats back.

"I went* with my own Cutter and landed a man on Cumberland who carried a letter from me to Lieut. Stuart at Fort William with orders to defend himself to the last extremity.

"Having discovered our Boats & believing we had landed Indians in the night they set sail with great haste, in so much that not having time to imbarque, they killed 40 horses which they had taken there, and burnt the houses. The Galleys and small Craft to the number of fifteen went thro' the inland Water Passages. They attempted to land near Fort William, but were repulsed by the Rangers; they then attacked it with Cannon and small Arms from the water for three Hours, but the place was so bravely defended by Lieut. Alexander Stuart that they were repulsed and ran out to sea where twelve other sail of Spanish vessells had lain at anchor without the Barr during the Attack without stirring, but the Galleys being chased out, they hoisted all the sails they could and stood to the Southward. I followed them with the Boats to Fort William, and from thence sent out the Rangers and some Boats who followed them to Saint Johns, but they went off rowing and sailing to St. Augustine.

"After the news of their defeat in the Grenadier Savannah arrived at Charles Town, the Men of War and a number of Carolina People raised in a hurry set out

*July 16th.

and came off this Barr after the Spaniards had been chased quite out of this Colony, where they dismissed the Carolina vessels, and Capt. Hardy promised in his Letters to cruise off St. Augustine.

"We have returned thanks to God for our deliverance, have set all the hands I possibly could to work upon the Fortifications, and have sent to the Northward to raise men ready to form another Battalion against His Majesty's Orders shall arrive for that purpose. I have retained Thompson's ship, have sent for Cannon Shott, &c., for Provisions and all kinds of stores since I expect the Enemy, who (tho' greatly terrified) lost but few men in comparison of their great numbers, as soon as they have recovered their fright will attack us with more caution and better discipline.

"I hope His Majesty will approve the measures I have taken, and I must entreat Your Grace to lay my humble request before His Majesty that he would be graciously pleased to order Troops, Artillery and other Necessarys sufficient for the defence of this Frontier and the neighboring Provinces, or give such direction as His Majesty shall think proper, and I do not doubt but with a moderate support not only to be able to defend these Provinces, but also to dislodge the Enemy from St. Augustine if I have but the same numbers they had in this expedition."*

* For further account of this memorable defence, see—

Harris' Complete Collection of Voyages and Travels, vol. II, pp. 340, 342. London, 1748.

McCall's History of Georgia, vol. I., pp. 176, 190. Savannah, 1811.

Hewitt's Historical Account of the Rise and Progress of the Colonies of South Carolina and Georgia, vol. II., pp. 114, 119. London, 1779.

Stevens' History of Georgia, vol. I, pp. 180, 196. New York, 1847.

Harris' Memorials of Oglethorpe, pp. 250, 268. Boston, 1840.

Wright's Memoir of Oglethorpe, pp. 299, 317. London, 1867.

Spalding's Life of Oglethorpe, Collections of the Georgia Historical Society, vol. I, pp. 275, 284. Savannah, 1840.

Ramsay's History of South Carolina, vol. I, pp. 144, 147. Charleston, 1809.

London Magazine, vol. XI, pp. 515, 516, 568.

Gentleman's Magazine for 1742, vol. XII, pp. 494, 496, 550, 561, 693, 694.

Gentleman's Magazine for 1743, vol. XIII, pp. 84, 638, 639.

That a small force of between six and seven hundred men, assisted by a few weak vessels, should have put to flight an army of nearly five thousand Spanish troops, supported by a powerful fleet, and amply equipped for the expedition, seems almost incapable of explanation.* General Oglethorpe's bravery and dash, the timidity of the invaders, coupled with the dissentions which arose in their ranks, and the apprehensions caused by the French letter, furnish the only plausible explanation of the victory. Whitefield's commentary was: "The deliverance of Georgia from the Spaniards is such as cannot be paralleled but by some instances out of the Old Testament." The defeat of so formidable an expedition by such a handful of men was a matter of astonishment to all. Had Don Manuel de Monteano pushed his forces vigorously forward, the stoutest resistance offered along his short line of march and from the walls of the town would have been ineffectual for the salvation of Frederica. Against the contingency of an evacuation of this strong-hold Oglethorpe had provided,

---

* The following estimate was made of the forces engaged:

SPANISH TROOPS.	
One regiment of dismounted Dragoons	400
Havanna Regiment	500
Havanna Militia	1,000
Regiment of Artillery	400
Florida Militia	400
Battalion of Mulattoes	300
Black Regiment	400
Indians	90
Marines	600
Seamen	1,000
Total	5,090
GENERAL OGLETHORPE'S COMMAND.	
His Regiment	472
Company of Rangers	30
Highlanders	50
Armed Militia	40
Indians	60
Total	652

See McCall's History of Georgia, vol I, p. 196. Savannah, 1811.

as best he could, by a concentration of boats in which to transport the garrison to Darien* by way of the cut previously made through General's island. This necessity, however, was fortunately never laid upon him. If the naval forces at Charleston had responded to his requisitions, a considerable portion of the Spanish fleet might have been captured. Oglethorpe's success in his military operations may be explained by the fact that he constantly acted on the offensive. He was never content to grant any peace to an enemy who was within striking distance. The temerity and persistency of his attacks inspired his followers, and impressed his antagonist with the belief that the arm delivering the blow was stronger than it really was.

The memory of this defense of St. Simons island and the southern frontier is one of the proudest in the annals of Georgia. Thus was the existence of the Colony perpetuated. Thus was hurled back in wrath and mortification a powerful army of invasion whose avowed object was to show no quarter,† but crush out of ex-

---

* Of the condition of this town in 1743 we find the following account in the London Magazine for 1745:† "Our first Stage we made *New Inverness*, or the *Darien*, on the Continent near 20 miles from *Frederica;* which is a Settlement of Highlanders living and dressing in their own Country Fashion, very happily and contentedly. There is an Independent Company of Foot of them, consisting of 70 men who have been of good service. The Town is regularly laid ont, and built of Wood mostly, divided into Streets and Squares; before the Town is the Parade, and a Fort not yet finish'd. It is situated upon a very high Bluff, or Point of Land, from whence, with a few cannon, they can scour the River, otherwise it is surrounded by Pine-barrens, and Woods, and there is a Rout by Land to *Savannah* and *Fort Argyle*, which is statedly reconnoitred by a Troop of Highland Rangers who do duty here. The Company and Troop, armed in the Highland manner, make an extreme good appearance under arms. The whole Settlement may be said to be a brave and industrious People; but were more numerous, planted more, and raised more cattle before the Invasion, with which they drove a good Trade to the Southward; but Things seem daily mending with them. They are forc'd to keep a very good Guard in this Place, it lies so open to the Insults of the *French* and *Spanish Indians*, who once or twice have shewn Straglers some very bloody Tricks." † Page 551.

† Samuel Cloake,—who was a prisoner on board the "Pretty Nancy" taken by the Spaniards from the English, and fitted out for the invasion of Georgia,—made oath that during the time they lay off the bar the Spaniards often "whetted their swords and held their knives to this deponent's and other English prisoners' throats, saying they would cut the throats of those they should take at Georgia."

Harris' Complete Collection of Voyages and Travels, pp. 342, 343. London, 1748.

istence the English colonies. Had success attended the demonstration against Frederica, the Enemy would have advanced upon the more northern strong-holds. Appreciating this, and deeply sensible of their great obligations to General Oglethorpe for the deliverance vouchsafed at his hands, the Governors of New York, New Jersey, Pennsylvania, Maryland, Virginia, and North Carolina,* addressed special letters to him "thanking him for the invaluable services he had rendered to the British-American Provinces; congratulating him upon his success and the great renown he had acquired; and expressing their gratitude to the Supreme Governor of Nations for placing the destiny of the southern colonies under the direction of a General so well qualified for the important trust."

Upon the disappearance of the Spanish forces Oglethorpe at once bent his energies to strengthening the fortifications at Frederica and repairing the damages which had been sustained by the southern forts. For a long time he seems to have counted upon a return of the expedition, and could not bring his mind to believe that the enterprise upon which so much preparation and money had been expended would be thus hastily and almost causelessly abandoned. Within a few months the works upon St. Simons, Jekyll, and Cumberland islands were stronger than ever. What those additional defensive works at Frederica were, we shall shortly see. Not content with having repulsed the Spaniards in their effort to crush the colony, General Oglethorpe was soon again engaged in "carrying the war into Africa."

---

* The governor of South Carolina did not unite in these congratulations and thanks; but the people of Port Royal did, much to his chagrin.

Finding the enemy so strong in St. Augustine that they defeated all the parties of Indians he sent against them, ascertaining that a large detachment was marching towards the river St. Mattheo, and concluding that this was a movement to extend their quarters so as to be prepared for the proper location and accommodation of reinforcements expected from Havana in the spring, taking with him a considerable body of Creek warriors, a detachment from the Highland company of Rangers, and a portion of his regiment, Oglethorpe landed by night in Florida in March, 1743, and, moving rapidly, drove the enemy, with loss, within the lines of St. Augustine. Having disposed his command in ambush, the General, with a small party, advanced within sight of the town, intending to skirmish and draw the garrison out. The enemy declined to leave their fortifications;* and the English, being too weak to attack, and having compelled the Spaniards to abandon their advanced posts in Florida, returned, having performed the extraordinary march of ninety-six miles in four days.† This was the last expedition led by the General against the Spaniards.‡

Still persuaded that the attack upon Frederica would be renewed at an early day, he continued to place the

* In the language of General Oglethorpe, "*they were so meek there was no provoking them.*"

† See General Oglethorpe's letters of the 12th and 21st of March, 1743. Collections of the Georgia Historical Society, vol. III, pp. 149, 151. Savannah, 1873.

London Magazine for 1743, vol. XII, pp. 356, 357.

London Gazette, July 9, 1743.

‡ This demonstration had the effect of restraining the Enemy within the lines of St. Augustine; and the active cruizing of the English Guard Schooner and Scout Boats held in check the privateers which were in the habit of annoying the navigation to the southward. "In fine," writes a Charles-Town merchant to his correspondent in London, under date August 10, 1743, "*Georgia* is a Gibraltar to this Province and *North America*, however insignificant some People may make it."

London Magazine for 1743, vol. XII, p. 567.

frontier in the best possible state of defense. Until he left Georgia on the 23d of July, 1743, never again to return, he resided at his cottage on St. Simons island. Of all the places planted and nurtured by him, none so warmly enlisted his energies and engaged his constant solicitude as the fortified town at the mouth of the Alatamaha.

Upon the General's departure, William Stephens was left as Deputy General of the Colony, and Major Horton, as military commander at Frederica. With the civil matters of the province Major Horton had no concern except where his assistance, as commander in chief of the military, was occasionally invoked to enforce the measures of the president and council. In such instances he acted with calmness and humanity, and secured the respect and esteem of the better class of the colonists.

On the 22nd of March, 1743, the magazine at Frederica was blown up, to the general alarm and regret of the inhabitants. Although it contained, at the time, three thousand bombs, so well bedded were they, but little damage occurred. A vagabond Irishman was suspected of having fired the magazine.*

We have two descriptions of Frederica in 1743,—the period of its greatest prosperity and importance,—which we make no apology for transcribing.

The first is from the lips of a captain conversant with the appearance and condition of the town.

Captain John Mac Clellan, who had left Georgia on the 31st of January, 1743, on his arrival in England

* See McCall's Georgia, vol. I, p. 203. Savannah, 1811.
Gentleman's Magazine for 1744, vol. XIV, p. 393.
London Magazine for 1744, vol. XIII, p. 359.

reported the colonists busily engaged in placing themselves in the best posture of defense, in anticipation of a second attack from the Spaniards; that Fort William had been fortified anew with brick work, and that "great numbers of Men were employ'd in compleating the Fortifications at *Frederica*, the Walls whereof are judged strong enough to be Proof against Eighteen-Pound Shot;" that two towers,—one at each corner of the town walls,—capable of holding one hundred men each, and designed to protect the flanks by means of small arms, had been erected; that the men were "full of spirits and unanimous to make a vigorous Defence to the last Drop of Blood;" that General Oglethorpe had been reinforced by two hundred men from Virginia, raised by Major Heron, many of whom were disciplined soldiers from Colonel Gouge's late regiment, and that thirty horsemen were on their way to Georgia to "recruit the Rangers."*

The second is from the pen of an intelligent traveler, who made his observations early in 1743. It reads as follows:

"Frederica, on the Island of St. Simon, the chief Town in the Southernmost Part of the Colony of *Georgia*, is nearly in Lat: 31° 15′ North. It stands on an Eminence, if consider'd with regard to the Marshes before it, upon a Branch of the famous River *Alatamaha*, which washes the West side of this agreeable little Island, and, after several Windings, disembogues itself into the Sea at *Jekyl Sound*. It forms a kind of a Bay before the Town, and is navigable for Vessels of the largest Burden, which may lie along the wharf in a secure and safe Harbour; and may, upon Occasion, haul up to careen and refit, the Bot-

* London Magazine for 1743, vol. XII, p. 305.

tom being a soft oozy Clay, intermix'd with small Sand and Shells. The Town is defended by a pretty strong Fort of Tappy,* which has several 18 Pounders mounted on a Ravelin in its Front, and commands the River both upwards and downwards; and is surrounded by a quadrangular Rampart, with 4 Bastions, of Earth, well stockaded and turfed, and a palisadoed Ditch which include also the King's Storehouses, (in which are kept the Arsenal, the Court of Justice, and Chapel) two large and spacious Buildings of Brick and Timber; On the Rampart are mounted a considerable Quantity of Ordnance of several sizes. The Town is surrounded by a Rampart, with Flankers, of the same Thickness with that round the Fort, in Form of a Pentagon, and a dry Ditch; and since the famous attempt of the Spaniards in *July* 1742,† at the N. E. and S. E. Angles are erected two strong cover'd pentagonal Bastions, capable of containing 100 men each, to scour the Flanks with Small Arms, and defended by a Number of Cannon; At their Tops are Look-outs which command the View of the Country and the River for many miles: The Roofs are shingled,‡ but so contriv'd as to be easily clear'd away, if incommodious in the Defense of the Towers. The whole Circumference of the Town is about a Mile and a Half, including, within the Fortifications, the Camp for General *Oglethorpe's* Regiment, at the North Side of the Town; the Parades on the West, and a small Wood to the South, which is left for Conve-

* A mixture of lime made of Oyster-shells, with Sand, Small Shells, &c., which, when harden'd, is as firm as Stone. I have observ'd prodigious Quantities of Salt Petre to issue from Walls of this Cement.

† See Lond: Mag: 1742, p. 461, 515, 516, 567.

‡ Shingles are split out of many Sorts of Wood, in the shape of Tiles, which, when they have been some Time expos'd to the Weather, appear of the Colour of Slate, and have a very pretty Look; the Houses in America are mostly Shingled.

niency of Fuel and Pasture, and is an excellent Blind to the Enemy in case of an Attack; in it is a small Magazine of Powder. The Town has two Gates, call'd the *Land-port*, and the *Water-port;* next to the latter of which is the Guard-house, and underneath it the Prison for Malefactors, which is an handsome Building of Brick. At the North End are the Barracks, which is an extremely well contriv'd Building in Form of a Square, of Tappy work, in which, at present, are kept the Hospital, and *Spanish* Prisoners of War: Near this was situated the Bomb Magazine which was blown up on March 22, 1744,* with so surprizingly little Damage.†

"The town is situated in a large *Indian* Field. To the East it has a very extensive Savannah (wherein is the Burial Place) thro' which is cut a Road to the other Side of the Island, which is bounded by Woods, save here and there some opening Glades into the Neighboring Savannah's and Marshes, which much elucidate the Pleasure of looking. Down this Road are several very commodious Plantations, particularly the very agreeable one of Capt. *Demery*, and that of Mr. *Hawkins*. Pre-eminently appears Mr. *Oglethorpe's* Settlement, which, at Distance, looks like a neat Country Village, where the consequences of all the various Industries of an *European* Farm are seen. The Master of it has shewn what Application and unbated Diligence may effect in this Country. At the Extremity of the Road is a small Village, call'd the *German* Village, inhabited by several Families of *Saltzburghers*, who plant and fish for their Subsistence. On the River Side

* See Lond. Mag: 1744, p. 359.

† I have been told that in this Explosion near 3,000 Bombs burst, which, had they not been well bedded, would have done much Mischief.

one has the Prospect of a large Circuit of Marshes, terminated by the Woods on the Continent, in Form like an Amphitheatre, and interspers'd with the Meanders of abundance of Creeks, form'd from the aforesaid River. At a Distance may be seen the white Post at *Bachelor's* Redoubt, also on the *Main*, where is kept a good Look-out of Rangers. To the North are Marshes, and a small Wood, at the Western Extremity of which are the Plantations of the late Capt. *Desbrisay*, and some others of less note; together with a Look-out wherein a Corporal's Guard is stationed, and reliev'd weekly, called *Pike's*, on the Bank of the River, from whence they can see Vessels a great way to the Northward. On the South is a Wood, which is, however, so far clear'd as to discover the Approach of an Enemy at a great Distance; within it, to the Eastward, is the Plantation of Capt. *Dunbar;* and to the Westward a Corporal's Look-out. The Town is divided into several spacious Streets, along whose sides are planted Orange Trees,* which, in some Time, will have a very pretty Effect on the View, and will render the Town pleasingly shady. Some Houses are built entirely of Brick, some of Brick and Wood, some few of Tappy-Work, but most of the meaner sort, of Wood only. The Camp is also divided into several Streets, distinguished by the names of the Captains of the several Companies of the Regiment; and the Huts are built generally of Clap-boards and Palmetto's, and are each of them capable to contain a Family, or Half a Dozen Single men. Here

* The Inhabitants begin to plant this charming Fruit very much, and 'tis to be hop'd will banish their numerous Peach Trees to their Country Settlements, which are Nurseries of *Muskettos* and other *Vermin*. The Season I was there, they had Oranges enough of their own Growth for Home Consumption.

these brave Fellows live with the most laudable Œconomy; and tho' most of them when off Duty, practise some Trade or Employment, they make as fine an Appearance upon the Parade, as any Regiment in the King's Service; and their exact Discipline does a great deal of Honour to their Officers; They have a Market every Day; The Inhabitants of the Town may be divided into Officers, Merchants, Store-Keepers, Artisans, and People in the Provincial Service; and there are often, also, many Sojourners from the neighbouring Settlements, and from *New York*, *Philadelphia*, and *Carolina*, on account of Trade. The Civil Government does not seem yet to be quite rightly settled by the Trustees, but is, at present, administered by three Magistrates, or Justices, assisted by a Recorder, Constables, and Tything Men. The Military is regulated as in all Garrison-Towns in the *British* Dominions. In short, the whole Town, and Country adjacent, are quite rurally charming, and the Improvements everywhere around are Footsteps of the greatest Skill and Industry imaginable, considering its late Settlement, and the Rubs it has so often met with; and as it seems so necessary for the Barrier of our Colonies, I am in Hopes of, one Time, seeing it taken more Notice of than it is at present."*

For the ensuing few years, and during the retention of Oglethorpe's regiment on St. Simons island, but little change occurred in the condition of Frederica. It retained its importance as a military post, and was regarded as the safe guard of the Province against Spanish invasion. The expectations, if indeed any were seriously entertained,

* This was written in the beginning of 1743.

See London Magazine for 1745, vol. XIV, pp. 395, 396.

Compare notice in "The North-American and the West-Indian Gazetteer." London, 1778.

of elevating this town into commercial importance, were practically abandoned previous to the withdrawal of the troops. In fact, even before the existing difficulties with Spain were formally accommodated by treaty, and it became manifest that there would in all likelihood occur no further serious demonstrations along the southern frontier, the population of Frederica began to decrease.

The home authorities, however, were loth to acknowledge its manifest tendency to decadence, and for some time, by occasional reports and notices, endeavored to assure the public of the continued prosperity of a town which had attracted such special attention in connection with the progress and perils of the Colony of Georgia.

An article having appeared in the "Daily Gazetteer" giving "a most scandalous and untrue account of the present state of the Colony of Georgia, particularly levelled at the Southern Part thereof (which is the Frontier against the French and Spaniards)" in justice to the public, William Thomson and John Lawrence, Jr., who had been trading with the Colony for some years and who had left Georgia in June, 1747, on business calling them to England, united in a card to the editor of the London Magazine* in which they stated: "That instead of the false Representation in the said Gazetteer 'That only seven Houses were in the Town of *Frederica*,' the said Town has several Streets, in every one of which are many good Houses, some of Brick, some of Tappy (which is a Cement of Lime and Oyster Shells;) That the High Street is planted with Orange Trees and has good Houses on both sides. That the Fort, besides other Buildings has two large Magazines, three Stories high, and sixty Feet long; That there are Bar-

* Volume XVI, p. 484.

racks in the Town, on the North side, ninety Feet Square, built of Tappy, covered with Cypress Shingles, and a handsome Tower over the Gateway of twenty Feet square; That there are two Bastion Towers, of two stories each, in the Hollow of the Bastions, defended on the Outside with thick Earth-works, and capable of lodging great Numbers of Soldiers, the two long Sides being nearly fifty Feet, and the short Sides twenty-five; And that instead of the Inhabitants removing from thence, several Families were come and more coming from *North Carolina* to settle in *Georgia*, who will certainly establish themselves there unless they are prevented by any Fears which may arise from the Reduction of the Rangers and Vessels which have hitherto made that Frontier safe: That before the Barracks were finished, very good Clap-board Huts were built sufficient for the lodging of two Companies who do Duty at *Frederica* (with their Wives and Families) which by an Accident of Fire were lately burnt down; since which others have been made for married Soldiers; and the Soldiers have the Privilege of cutting Timber and building Houses for their Families, which many have done, and thrive very well, and we know the Soldiers are regularly paid and kindly treated. We also certify that there are several Farms which produce not only *Indian* Wheat and Potatoes, but *English* Wheat, Barley, and other Grain. In short, Provisions in general are plentiful, Venison, Beef, Pork, at Two Pence Half-Penny *per* Pound, and sometimes under. Fish extremely cheap."

Upon the confirmation of the Peace of Aix-la-Chapelle in April, 1748, most of the troops were withdrawn from St. Simons island and the fortifications soon began to fall into decay.

The Trustees having surrendered their charter, Captain John Reynolds was, in 1754, appointed by the King, Governor of Georgia, with the title of "Captain General and Commander in Chief of His Majesty's Province of Georgia, and Vice-Admiral of the same." He entered upon his duties in October of that year, and early, the following Spring, made a tour of inspection through the southern portion of the Province. Arriving at Frederica, he found the town "in ruins," the fortifications "decayed," and the "houses falling down." Twenty pieces of cannon were lying dismounted and "spoiled for want of care." The melancholy prospect was presented of "houses without inhabitants, barracks without soldiers, guns without carriages, and streets grown over with weeds."* Fort Frederick was entirely dismantled. Not a gun was mounted, and neither powder nor ball could be found. Among his recommendations for the defense of the Colony, the Governor suggested the construction of a work at Frederica "in the form of half a hexagon, nine hundred and sixty feet each, with two whole and two demi-bastions towards the land, and two demi-bastions and a citadel towards the sea, on which were to be placed fifty cannon manned by three hundred regulars." This fortification was never built, and no effort was made to repair the works then crumbling and abandoned.

This dilapidation and neglect continued without any effort on the part of the Colonial authorities to check their annihilating influences. Frederica had now ceased to be a place of any note. In his report of the condition of the Province of Georgia, submitted to the Earl of Dartmouth on

---

* A destructive fire had consumed nearly all the houses which time had spared. See Stevens' History of Georgia, vol. I, p. 446. New York, 1847.

the 20th of December, 1773, Sir James Wright, then Governor of the Colony, represents Fort Frederick at Frederica as "going to decay very fast." "There is still,"—such is the language of the report,—"some Remains of good Tabby Walls, &c., but there has been no men there since the Independent Company were broke in the Year 1767."*

In March, 1774, William Bartram visited Frederica and St. Simons island and was most hospitably entertained by Mr. James Spalding who was there engaged in an extensive trade with the Indian tribes of East Florida. Following the old highway across the savannah, he devoted a day to exploring the island and was charmed with the magnificent forests of pines and oaks perfumed with the fragrant breath of the white lily and the sweet bay. The venerable live-oaks still overshadowed the spacious avenue leading to the former seat of General Oglethorpe, but that distinguished gentleman was no longer there, and his quiet cottage had passed into the ownership of another. The delights of the woods and waters, the delicious breezes wafted from groves filled with birds of bright plumage and sweet voices, the commingled perfumes of the yellow jasmine, the lonicera, the audromeda and the azalea, and the solemn sound of the incoming surf were, in the recollection of this happy traveller, associated with generous hospitality, a plentiful repast of venison, and an agreeable "drink of honey and water strengthened by the addition of brandy."

Although nature was as balmy, as attractive, and as beautiful as ever, Bartram was oppressed by the indications of desolation which confronted him all over the island. He speaks of "vestiges of plantations, ruins of costly build-

* Collections of the Georgia Historical Society, vol. III, pp. 168, 169. Savannah, 1873.

ings, and highways overgrown with forests." The fort he found entirely dilapidated, and nothing of the town remaining except ruins. From the crumbling walls of the deserted houses peach trees, figs, and pomegranates were growing.* And so this brave town dwindled away into nothingness.

The last detachment of troops stationed there consisted of ten Royal Americans; but even these were withdrawn during the early part of the administration of Governor Wright.

The rupture between Great Britain and her Colonies being imminent, the Council of Safety ordered all guns at Frederica to be secured, and they were used in fortifying other points on the coast deemed of greater importance. During the progress of the expedition projected from Sunbury, by Governor Gwinnett, against Florida, Colonel Elbert, who was in command, on Sunday, the 11th of May, 1777, landed at Frederica "to air" his troops. The following entry occurs in his Order-Book: "Frederica was once a pretty little Town, as appears by the Ruins, having been burned down some years since; the Fort at this place, with a little expence, might be made defensible, and might, if properly garrisoned, be a means of protecting great part of our Southern Frontiers. There are about twelve men that bear arms here; in my opinion all Tories. Their Captain, Ditter, says otherwise of himself, and informed me that about 6 or 8 of the inhabitants had lately gone to Florida for protection."†

By the provisions of the act of the 15th of March, 1758,‡ dividing the Province into eight Parishes, "the

* Travels through North and South Carolina, Georgia, &c., pp. 55–60. London, 1792.

† MS. Order-Book of Col. S. Elbert.

‡ Marbury and Crawford's Digest, p. 151.

town and district of Frederica, including the islands of Great and Little St. Simons and the adjacent islands," were declared a parish and named "St. James." Under the writs of election issued by Sir James Wright, Lachlan McIntosh was returned as member for Frederica.

On the 10th of August, 1777, some boats from a British armed vessel lying in St. Andrews Sound landed on St. Simons island, and their crews captured and carried away Captain Arthur Carney, five citizens, several negroes, and as much household furniture as could be conveyed in the barges. Carney had been appointed to the captaincy of the fourth company in the first Continental Battalion of Georgia troops. After his capture, he espoused the Royal cause and proved himself not only an active Tory but a great cattle thief.*

While General Robert Howe was concentrating his forces on the Southern frontier of Georgia with a view to the invasion of Florida, Colonel Elbert, who was commanding at Fort Howe,—the place of rendezvous,—achieved an exploit which imparts another distinct and gallant memory to the neglected settlements, "Where wild Altama murmurs to their woe."

The details of the affair are thus narrated in a letter to General Howe:

"FREDERICA, April 19th, 1778.

"*Dear General:*

"I have the happiness to inform you that about 10 o'clock this forenoon, the brigantine Hinchinbrooke, the sloop Rebecca, and a prize brig, all struck the British tyrant's colors and surrendered to the American arms.

"Having received intelligence that the above vessels

* See McCall's History of Georgia, vol. I, pp. 131, 132. Savannah, 1811.

were at this place, I put about three hundred men, by detachment from the troops under my command at Fort Howe, on board the three galleys, the Washington—Captain Hardy,—the Lee,—Captain Braddock,—and the Bulloch,—Captain Hutcher;—and a detachment of artillery with two field pieces, under Captain Young, I put on board a boat. With this little army we embarked at Darien, and last evening effected a landing at a bluff about a mile below the town, leaving Colonel White on board the Lee, Captain Melvin on board the Washington, and Lieutenant Petty on board the Bulloch, each with a sufficient party of troops. Immediately on landing I dispatched Lieutenant-Colonel Ray and Major Roberts, with about one hundred men, who marched directly up to the town and made prisoners three marines and two sailors belonging to the Hinchinbrooke.

"It being late, the galleys did not engage until this morning. You must imagine what my feelings were to see our three little men-of-war going on to the attack of these three vessels, who have spread terror on our coast, and who were drawn up in order of battle; but the weight of our metal soon damped the courage of these heroes, who soon took to their boats; and as many as could, abandoned the vessel with everything on board, of which we immediately took possession. What is extraordinary, we have not one man hurt. Captain Ellis, of the Hinchinbrooke, is drowned, and Captain Mowbray, of the Rebecca, made his escape. As soon as I see Colonel White, who has not yet come to us with his prizes, I shall consult with him, the three other officers, and the comanding officers of the galleys, on the expediency of attacking the Galatea now lying at Jekyll."

While Colonel Elbert was preparing to attack her, the Galatea made her escape to sea.* This successful enterprize encouraged the troops at Fort Howe, who were in a very dispirited mood.

Upon his retreat, by water, from Sunbury in December, 1778, Fuser left the regular troops of his expedition at Frederica, with instructions to repair the old military works at that point. These orders were only partially observed, and the force was soon withdrawn.

During the continuance of the Revolutionary war St. Simons island, in common with other isolated localities along the Georgia coast, suffered from privateers and armed parties who pillaged the houses of the inhabitants and led captive negroes and domestic animals. Similar annoyances and losses were encountered during the war of 1812–1815. So ruthless had been the spoliations and devastations by the British troops during the progress of the Revolution, that upon its termination but little remained of Frederica save the sites of burnt houses and heaps of ruin. The town had almost entirely disappeared. Subsequent attempts to revive it were feeble and unsuccessful. Of the State legislation with regard to Frederica, the following synopsis may not be deemed inappropriate :

On the 17th of December, 1792, James Spalding, John Braddock, Raymond Demere, John Palmer, John Burnett, John Piles, Moses Burnett, Samuel Wright, and William Williams were appointed Commissioners of the towns and commons of Frederica and Brunswick. They were directed, after three months' published notice, to

---

* See McCall's History of Georgia, vol. II, pp. 137–139. Savannah, 1811.
Stevens' History of Georgia, vol. II, pp. 161–162. Philadelphia, 1859.
White's Historical Collections of Georgia, p. 468. New York, 1855.

cause surveys to be made of those towns, according to their original plans, and to have the same recorded in the Surveyor General's office, and in the office of the Surveyor of Glynn county. Any vacant lots, except such as were originally reserved for public uses, were then to be sold upon four weeks' public notice; and the proceeds arising from such sales, after deducting the necessary expense of survey, devoted to the building and support of an Academy in Glynn County.*

In February, 1796, special Commissioners were named for the town of Frederica. They were John Cooper, William McIntosh, James Harrison, James Moore, and William Clubbs. It was made their duty to lay off the town, as nearly as practicable, according to its original plan, cause the streets to be opened, the lots to be plainly marked or staked off, the commons to be resurveyed, and an accurate map prepared and recorded in the Surveyor General's office within two months after the passage of the act. The survey of the town having been completed, the Commissioners were required, by notice in one of the public gazettes of the State, to call upon the owners and holders of lots to make due return thereof to the Commissioners within nine months, and pay the sum of one dollar per lot in defrayal of the cost of the survey.

All lots not returned within the prescribed period were, after six weeks public advertisement, to be sold to the highest bidder,—one half of the purchase money to be paid in cash and the remainder in twelve months thereafter;—the deferred payment being secured by bond with mortgage on the premises purchased. The proceeds of such sales,

* Watkins' Digest, p. 470.

after defraying the expences incurred in laying off the town and commons, were to be applied to the support of an academy or seminary of learning in Glynn County.

Any person attempting to run up or appropriate any part of the town common was declared liable to a fine of five hundred dollars, to be recovered in the Superior Court of Glynn County by the Commissioners or any inhabitant or lot owner in the town;—one half the fine to enure to the benefit of the academy, and the other half to go to the party suing for the same.

All surveys previously made, and grants surreptitiously obtained, were declared null and void, and any person in possession by virtue of such survey or grant was liable to the fine above mentioned, to be recovered in the manner indicated.*

In 1801 Frederica is mentioned by Sibbald as "a pleasantly situated town on the island of St. Simons, latitude 31° 15′ North," but he gives no statistics either of its population or commerce.†

By an act assented to November 26th, 1802,‡—the front range of lots in the town of Frederica being "too distant from the water for the convenient storage or shipping of produce, or the landing of goods imported to that place,"—the Commissioners were empowered "to cause a range of lots to be laid off in front of said town, commencing at low water mark, and running back so far as to leave a street eighty feet between the present front range of lots and those to be laid off."

These new lots were to be sold at public outcry upon

* Watkins' Digest, pp. 598, 599.

† "Notes and Observations on the Pine Lands of Georgia," &c. Augusta, 1801.

‡ Clayton's Digest, p. 63.

sixty days' notice, and the moneys realized upon such sale, after defraying the expences of the survey, were to be paid over to the Commissioners of the Academy of Glynn county to be by them expended for the benefit of that institution.

Two correct plans of these water lots were to be prepared and certified by the surveyor, one to be transmitted by the Commissioners to the Surveyor General for record in his office, and the other to be delivered to the County Surveyor of Glynn county to be by him recorded in his office.

On the 18th of November, 1814,* the Commissioners of the towns of Brunswick and Frederica were authorized to levy a tax upon the lots in those towns, whether improved or unimproved, and pay over the moneys thus raised to the Justices of the Inferior Court of Glynn county for the purpose of erecting a Court House and Jail. To the same object was to be applied one-fourth of the future rents of the town commons.

All efforts to revivify the dead town, to perpetuate something like a corporate existence, to realize a revenue by special taxation of abandoned premises, to maintain a semblance of public streets, commons, and private lots, to clothe water fronts with the dignity of commercial wharves, and transmit the physical impressions of the older days, proved utterly futile.† Frederica lost its importance when it ceased to be the strong-hold of the southern frontier. Its mission was accomplished when the Spaniard no longer threatened. Its doom was pronounced in the

* Lamar's Digest, pp. 902, 978.

† Alluding to Frederica, in 1829, Sherwood† says: "The Fort is gone to decay, but there are ten houses in the village."

† Gazetteer of Georgia, p. 111.

hour of its triumph. Upon the withdrawal of Oglethorpe's regiment its decadence began, and ceased not until its fort became a white ruin, its public parade a pasture ground, and its streets and gardens a cotton field.*

Omnia debentur morti.

---

* Frances Anne Kemble, who visited Frederica in the spring of 1839, thus records her impressions of the deserted spot: "This Frederica is a very strange place; it was once a town,—*the* town, the metropolis of the island. The English, when they landed on the coast of Georgia in the war, destroyed this tiny place, and it has never been built up again. Mrs. A.'s and one other house, are the only dwellings that remain in this curious wilderness of dismantled crumbling graywalls compassionately cloaked with a thousand profuse and graceful creepers. These are the only ruins, properly so called, except those of Fort Putnam, that I have ever seen in this land of contemptuous youth. I hailed these picturesque groups and masses with the feelings of a European, to whom ruins are like a sort of relations. In my country, ruins are like a minor chord in music; here they are like a discord; they are not the relics of time, but the results of violence; they recall no valuable memories of a remote past, and are mere encumbrances to the busy present. Evidently they are out of place in America except on St. Simon's island, between this savage selvage of civilization and the great Atlantic deep. These heaps of rubbish and roses would have made the fortune of a sketcher; but I imagine the snakes have it all to themselves here, and are undisturbed by camp-stools, white umbrellas, and ejaculatory young ladies."

Journal of a Residence on a Georgian Plantation, &c., p. 285. New York, 1863.

III.

ABERCORN.

On a creek or branch of the Savannah, distant some three miles from its confluence with that river, and about fifteen miles above the town of Savannah, the village of Abercorn was located in 1733. Its original settlement consisted of ten families. The plan of the town embraced twelve lots, with two trust lots in addition,—one on either extremity. Old Ebenezer was ten miles to the west; and four miles below the mouth of Abercorn creek, was Joseph's Town, where two Scotch gentlemen had selected plantations on the right bank of the Savannah. Journeying towards Savannah, in the early days of the Colony, the visitor would encounter successively Sir Francis Bathurst's plantation, Walter Augustin's settlement, Captain Williams' plantation, Mrs. Matthews' place, the Indian School-house Irene, the Horse Quarter, and the Indian lands reserved just outside the limits of Yamacraw. A strange fatality attended all these early attempts at colonization. Born of the subjugation of the forests, were malarial fevers and fluxes which engendered lassitude and death. Short lived were these little settlements, and it was only upon the introduction of slave labor that these plantations bordering upon the Savannah became permanent and productive. The white men who strove to bring them into a state of cultivation failed in the effort and quickly passed away. Others, who endeavored to complete their labors, encountered similar misfortune and disappointment.

The ten families who were assigned to Abercorn in 1733 were all gone in 1737. That year Mr. John Brodie, with twelve servants, occupied the settlement; but, after three years, he abandoned the place, leaving its improvements to ruin and decay. Most of the thirty servants who cultivated the lands of the Scotch gentlemen at Joseph's Town died, and that plantation lapsed into neglect.

The Saltzburgers who came to Georgia under the conduct of Baron Von Reck and the Rev'd Mr. Bolzius, in passing from Savannah to Old Ebenezer, were sheltered and refreshed at Abercorn. To that place their baggage was brought by water, and for some time all their supplies were delivered at that point whence they were carried, at much pains, up Ebenezer creek and through the woods. Before long, however, a road was cut from Abercorn to Old Ebenezer which facilitated the transportation. While at Abercorn the Saltzburgers suffered much from affections of the bowels.

Various efforts were made by the Trustees to increase the population and ensure the prosperity of Abercorn,—which was regarded as a convenient point for communicating with the Carolina settlements on the Savannah river;—but they all eventuated in disappointment. Such of the colonists as were sent there from time to time grew sick and tired of the abode, took no interest in its advancement, and abandoned it upon the earliest opportunity. The little life which this small place enjoyed was insignificant and without moment in the history of the Colony.

In December, 1739, Mr. Stephens visited the town in company with Mr. Jones, to inspect a large ferry-boat which, in obedience to General Oglethorpe's orders, had been there constructed by one Bunyon,—a boat-builder by trade, and an inhabitant of the town. This boat was capable of transporting nine or ten horses at a time, and was intended to ply between Abercorn and Palachocolas. In perpetuating his impressions of the place Mr. Stephens says: "As there was no Place in the whole Province, of the like Allotment of fifty acres each, which in my eye seemed so desirable, being a most pleasant Situation on the Banks of such a River, with as good Land belonging to each Lot, as is readily to be found in most Parts of the Province; I never saw it but with Regret, that there never yet had been a number of Settlers there deserving it; but generally they happened to be loose, idle People, who after some short Abode, wandered elsewhere and left it: * * * and there are at present five Families only remaining there, nor has there often been more at one Time. As the Trust-Lands seem to be now in some better way of cultivating by their own Servants, than hitherto; I proposed it to Mr. *Jones* to send down a few *German* families to work on the Trust-Lots there; which, by helping to fill the Place, very probably might induce others the sooner to occupy Lands there also: He agreed with me in Opinion, and said he would write of it to the General."*

It is very questionable whether this opinion of Mr. Stephens,—formed during the winter,—of the desirableness of this locality, would have been confirmed by a residence there amid the heats and miasmatic influences of the summer and fall. Some Germans did settle in the neighborhood and cultivate the soil, but all efforts to promote the prosperity of the village and elevate it into the dignity of a town utterly failed. Like Joseph's Town and Westbrook, Abercorn is little more than a name in the history of the Colony. In the end it passed into the hands of two English

* A Journal of the Proceedings in Georgia, &c., vol. II, pp. 215, 216. London, 1742.

gentlemen who converted the village into a plantation cultivated with slave labor. So it continued under various owners until, by the result of the civil war, the negro has been liberated, and the fortunes of this region have become more unpromising than ever before.

After the capture of Savannah in December, 1778, Colonel Campbell advanced a strong force to this place as a convenient base for future operations against the interior of the State; and hence, in 1779, did a British detachment move, crossing over to Purysburg and attempting to surprise General Moultrie at Black-swamp.

The town had so entirely faded from the face of the earth that its location is not indicated on that admirable map of South Carolina and Georgia, published by William Faden at Charing Cross in 1780:—and the only mention made by White is as follows: "Abercorn, sixteen miles from Savannah, was a noted place in the early settlement of Georgia. No memorial of its former condition can now be seen."

Savannah, increasing her borders, practically claims as part of herself the Indian lands opposite the northern end of Hutchinson island. Of the Horse Quarter nothing remains. Joseph's Town long ago lost its identity; and Abercorn, New Ebenezer, Purisburg, and Palachocolas, have, within the recollection of more than one generation, been known simply as boat-landings on the water-highway between Savannah and Augusta.*

---

* For notices of Abercorn, see—

"An Extract of the Journals of Mr. Commissary Von Beck, &c., and of the Reverend Mr. Bolzius," pp. 18, 20, 54, 66, 69. London, 1734.

"An Account Shewing the Progress of the Colony of Georgia, in America," &c., p. 35. London, 1741.

Stephens' "Journal of the Proceedings in Georgia," &c., vol. I, p. 230. Vol. II, pp. 215, 216. London, 1742.

"An Extract of the Rev. Mr. John Wesley's Journal," &c. p. 60. Bristol, n. d.

"A State of the Province of Georgia, attested upon oath," &c., p. 5. London, 1742.

"A True and Historical Narrative of the Colony of Georgia," &c., by Tailfer, Anderson, and Douglas, p. 108. Charles-Town, 1741.

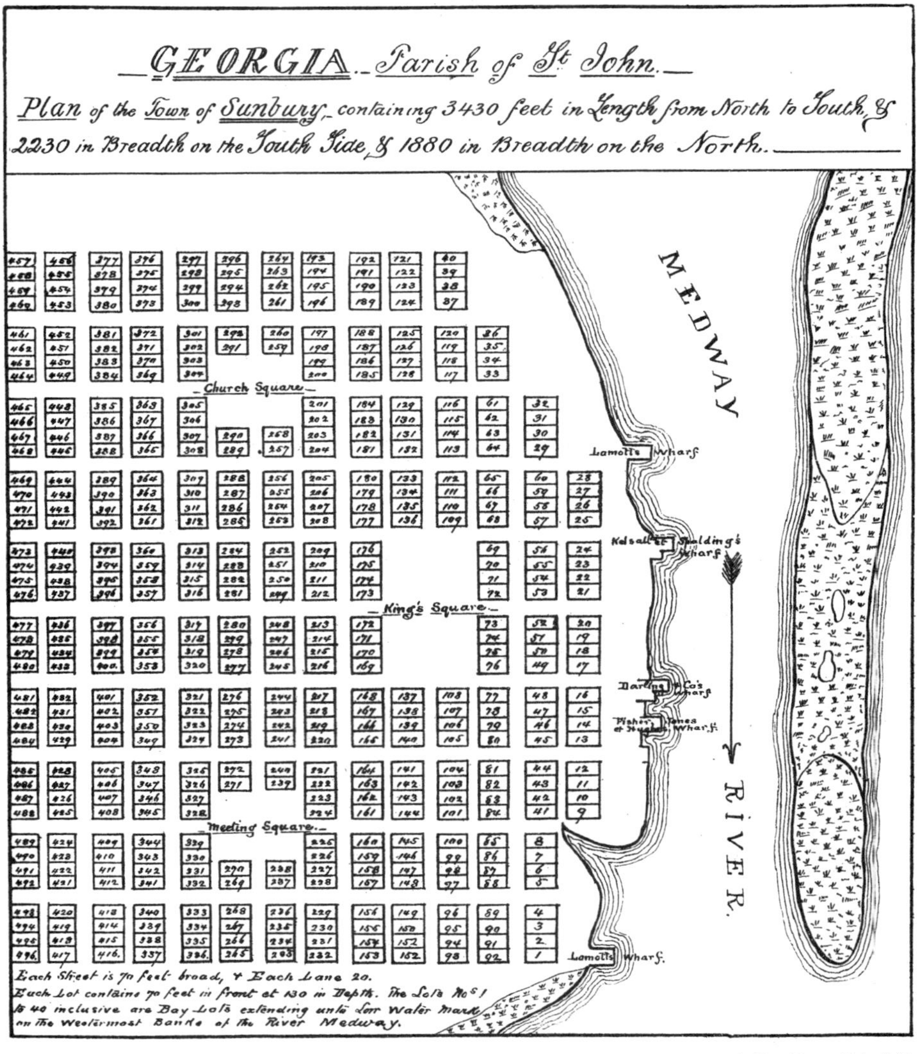

J. Bien Photo. Lith. N.Y.

IV.

SUNBURY.

On the 23rd of January, 1734, Mr. Oglethorpe, accompanied by Captain Ferguson and sixteen attendants,—including two Indians,—set out from Savannah in an open row-boat, followed by a yawl carrying provisions and ammunition, upon an exploratory expedition to the Southern frontiers of Georgia.* His course lay through the inner passages, and was pursued as far as St Simons island. For the protection of the Colony it was then determined to form a military station and settlement near the mouth of the Alatamaha; and,—as an outpost and barrier against Spanish invasion,—to erect a strong fort on the high bluff on the western side of St. Simons island. These sites were shortly afterwards occupied and fortified, and were respectively named New Inverness and Frederica. It was during this reconnoissance that the eyes of the Founder of Georgia first rested upon that bold and beautiful bluff which, overlooking the placid waters of Midway river and the intervening low-lying salt marshes, descries in the distance the green woods of Bermuda island, the dim outline of the southern point of Ossabaw, and, across the sound, the white shores of St. Catherine. Although formal session had been made by the Lower Creeks of all lands along the sea-coast

---

* See Memoir of General James Oglethorpe by Robert Wright, p. 74. London, 1857.

from the Savannah to the Alatamaha river, extending westward as high as the tide flowed, and including all islands except a few which the Indians specially reserved for the purposes of hunting, fishing, and bathing, no English settlements had, at that early day, been formed south of the Great Ogeechee river. Fort Argyle,—garrisoned by Captain McPherson and his troop of Rangers, and commanding the passes by which the Indians during the late wars were accustomed to invade Carolina,—was then the only military post of any consequence in the direction of the Spaniards. From this nameless bluff the Aborigines had not then removed, and their canoes might be seen passing and repassing to and from Hussoope, [Ossabaw], and Cowleggee, [St. Catharine], islands and the main. To the quiet woods and waters of this semi-tropical region the English were strangers. The Bermuda grass which, at a later period, so completely covered Sunbury bluff, did not then appear, but magnificent live oaks, in full grown stature and solemn mien, crowned the high-ground even to the very verge where the tide kissed the shore. Cedars, festooned with vines, over hung the waters. The magnolia grandiflora,—queen of the forest,—excited on every hand the admiration of the early visitor. The sweet-scented myrtle, the tall pine, the odoriferous bay, and other indigenous trees lent their charms to a spot whose primal beauty had encountered no change at the hand of man. The woods were resonant with the songs of birds, whose bright plumage vied in coloring with the native flowers which gladdened the eye and gave gentle odors to the ambient air. Fishes abounded in the waters, and game on the land. Cool sea-breezes tempered the heat of summer, and the rigor of cold was unknown in the depth of winter. It was a gentle, attractive place,—this bold bluff,—as it came from the hand of Nature. Some scene like this did the Poet Waller have in view as he sang:

> "Heav'n sure has kept this spot of earth uncurst,
> To show how all things were created first."

By a certain grant under the great seal of the Province of Georgia, bearing date the 4th of October, 1757, his Majesty George II conveyed to Mark Carr, his heirs and assigns forever, in free and common socage, "All that tract of land containing five hundred acres, situate and being in the District of Midway in the Province of Georgia, bounded on the east by the Midway river, on the west by land of Thomas Carr, on the south by vacant land, and on all other sides by marshes of the said river."

The grantee of these lands, which embraced the site of the future town of Sunbury, had been for some twenty years a man of means and of mark in the Colony of Georgia. In 1741 he had been sent by General Oglethorpe to Virginia to raise recruits for the Colony.* In his last will and testament, dated June 8th, 1767, and proven before his Excellency Sir James Wright on the the 4th of December of the same year, Captain Carr describes himself as being "of the Parish of St. Patrick in the Province of Georgia, Esquire." He owned lots in the town of Frederica, an island on the north side of Midway river, a tract of land on the main fronting that island, which he had purchased from John Cubbage, and "a plantation on the main over against Jekyll island." This was his favorite residence. Here, on the 18th of March, 1741,—despite the presence of a guard of soldiers there stationed

---

* Memoir of General James Oglethorpe, by Robert Wright, pp. 284, 285. London, 1867.

by General Oglethorpe,—the Indians made an attack very early in the morning, killing several of the soldiers and servants, wounding others, "locking down the women and children in the cellar," pillaging the house, and carrying away the booty in a large boat belonging to the plantation.*

The grant of this five hundred acre tract on Midway river to Mark Carr in fee simple, was made under the operation of the rules adopted by the Common Council in May, 1750, which essentially enlarged the tenures of grants already existing, and provided that future alienations should convey "an absolute inheritance to the grantees, their heirs and assigns." It will be remembered that under the regulations at first prescribed by the Trustees, five hundred acre tracts were conveyed only to persons well approved by the Trust;—parties who should at their own expense, and within twelve months from the date of the grant, bring ten able-bodied men servants not younger than twenty years of age, and settle upon the lands.

Former alienations of this magnitude had been coupled with other conditions, among which the following may be enumerated as the most important:

I. The grantee obligated himself to abide in Georgia with his servants for a term of not less than three years, building houses and cultivating the lands.

II. Within ten years from the registry of the grant, at least two hundred of the five hundred acres were to be cleared and cultivated.

III. No alienation of the lands thus granted, either in whole or in part, for a term of years or otherwise, was permitted except by special leave.

---

*See A Journal of the Proceedings in Georgia, &c., by William Stephens, pp. 160, 161. London, MDCCXLII.

IV. After the lapse of eighteen years from the date of the grant, should any part of the five hundred acres remain uncultivated, unplanted, uncleared, and without a worm-fence, or pales six feet high, such portion should revert to the Trust, and the grant, *pro tanto*, was to become void.

V. These grants were in Tail Male.*

On the 20th of June, 1758, Mark Carr conveyed three hundred acres of this five hundred acre tract, including that portion bordering upon Midway river, to "James Maxwell, Kenneth Baillie, John Elliott, Grey Elliott, and John Stevens, of Midway, Esquires," * * * in trust that the same should be laid out as a town by the name of *Sunbury*;—one hundred acres thereof being dedicated as a common, for the use of the future inhabitants;—and in further trust "that they, the said James Maxwell, Kenneth Baillie, John Elliott, Grey Elliott, and John Stevens and their successors, should sell and dispose of all and singular the lots to be laid out in the said town of Sunbury to and for the proper use and behoof of the said Mark Carr."

Captain McCall† suggests that "the town was called Sunbury,—the etymology of which is probably the *residence of the sun*,—from the entire exposure of this place to his beams while he is above the horizon." We believe that this projected village was named for Sunbury, a quiet and beautiful town in Middlesex County, on the left bank of the Thames, only a little way above Hampton Court, and distant some eighteen miles by land from London;—it being a pleasant custom among the colonists to perpetuate

* See An Account Shewing the Progress of the Colony of Georgia in America, &c., pp. 48, 49. London, 1741.

† History of Georgia, vol. I, p. 255. Savannah, 1811.

in their new homes the memories of persons and places dear to them in the mother country.

In ancient records, says Lysons, this place (Sunbury in England) is called *Sunnabyri*, Sunneberie, Suneberie, &c. Sunnabyri is composed of two Saxon words,—sunna, the sun, and *byri*, a town,—and may be supposed to denote a place exposed to the sun, or with a southern aspect.

A name better suited to this locality could scarcely have been suggested. It recalls the peaceful memories of one of the gentle towns of old England, and typifies the genial influences of the "King of Day" as, from early dawn until sunset, he irradiates with floods of light the bold bluff "on the westermost bank of the river Midway."

Two of the Trustees,—John Stevens and John Elliott,—were prominent members of the Midway Congregation. James Maxwell had been for several years a resident of St. John's Parish. He and John Stevens were members of the Provincial Congress which assembled at Tondee's Long-room in Savannah on the 4th of July, 1775.*

Kenneth Baillie and Grey Elliott were active and influential citizens. The latter was subsequently selected by the General Assembly to act as an assistant from the Colony of Georgia to Dr. Benjamin Franklin who had been chosen by several of the Provinces,—Georgia among the number,—and sent on a special mission to England to represent the wants and grievances of the Colonies, remonstrate against such acts of the Crown as were deemed oppressive, and oppose taxation without representation.‡

---

* The following members of that Congress came from the Parish of St. John: James Screven, Nathan Brownson, Daniel Roberts, John Baker, Sr., John Bacon, Sr., James Maxwell, Edward Ball, William Baker, Sr., William Bacon, Jr., John Stevens, and John Winn, Sr.†

† Stevens' History of Georgia, vol. II, p. 106.

‡ See McCall's History of Georgia, vol. II, p. 7. Savannah, 1816.

All the Trustees, therefore, were men of position and character, commanding the respect of the community. Their selection for the trust indicated sound judgment and well-placed confidence on the part of Mark Carr.

The road from Savannah to New Inverness in the Darien settlement which, in 1736, in obedience to Mr. Oglethorpe's orders, was located by Captain Hugh MacKay, Jr., with his company of Rangers, and Indian guides furnished by Tomo-chi-chi, had been completed. Various settlements on the Savannah, Vernon, and Great Ogeechee rivers, and also on St. Simons island and the Alatamaha river having been confirmed, between 1740 and 1750 planters with their families and servants began to move in and occupy desirable localities intermediate the Great Ogeechee and Alatamaha rivers. The sites, at first selected, lay along the line of the Savannah and New Inverness road, and upon high-grounds adjacent thereto bordering upon salt-water streams and swamps emptying into them. Between the Great Ogeechee and South-New Port rivers was formed the Midway settlement.

This district derived its name from its location, which was about *midway* between the rivers Savannah and Alatamaha then constituting the northern and southern boundaries of the colony. It has been suggested, and the belief is current with some, that the true spelling is Medway, and that both the District and the river which permeates it were named for one of the well-known streams of merrie old England.*

* The Medway, in the county of Kent, is a noble stream. Its trunk and branches cover thirty square miles of the surface of the county, and its length is nearly sixty miles,—of which forty are navigable. This river well deserves the name of *Vaga*, by which the Britons described its wanderings. The Saxons added the syllable *Med*, the sign of middle, because the river runs through the centre of the county, and thus gets its present name of *Medway*.

Encyclopædia Britanica, 8th Edition, vol. XIII, Article Kent, p. 65.

See also vol. VIII, p. 716.

On the only plan of Sunbury the writer has been able to procure, and in some of the early records, this river is written *Medway*. It may be fairly stated, however, that while by some the river may have been called Medway, the district was universally known as *Midway*. The time-honored church, which still stands, and its predecessor which so long stood near the intersection of the Savannah and Darien, and the Sunbury roads, are both remembered as the *Midway* and not *Medway* congregational meeting houses. We are persuaded that the river as well as the district were both named *Midway*;—the former being called for the latter.

By an act dividing the several districts and divisions of the Province of Georgia into Parishes, passed the 15th day of March, 1758,* it was provided that "the town of Hardwick and district of Ogechee, on the south side of the river Great Ogechee, extending northwest up the said river so far as the Lower Indian trading path leading from Mount Pleasant, and southward from the town of Hardwick as far as the swamp of James Dunham, including the settlements on the north side of the north branches of the river Midway, with the islands of Ossabaw, and from the head of the said Dunham's Swamp in a north-west line, shall be and forever constitute a parish by the name of 'The Parish of St. Philip': from Sunbury in the district of Midway and Newport from the southern bounds of the parish of St. Philip, extending southward as far as the north line of Samuel Hastings, and from thence southeast to the south branch of Newport, including the islands of St. Katharine and Bermuda, and from the north line of the said Samuel Hastings northwest,

* Marbury and Crawford's Digest, pp. 150 152.

shall be and forever continue a parish by the name of 'The Parish of St. John': the town and district of Darien, extending from the south boundary of the parish of St. John to the river Alatamaha, including the islands of Sapelo and Eastwood, and the sea islands to the north of Egg island northwest up the river Alatamaha to the forks of the said river, shall be and forever continue a parish by the name of 'The Parish of St. Andrew:' and the town and district of Frederica, including the islands of Great and Little St. Simons, and the adjacent islands shall be and forever continue a parish by the name of 'The Parish of St. James.'"

Such were the territorial limits of the four southern parishes of the province, approved by Governor Ellis, and designed to promote the establishment of religious worship according to the rites and ceremonies of the Church of England.*

As the early population of Sunbury was largely drawn from the members of the Midway congregation,—the most pronounced society existing within the limits of St. John's parish at the time of its formation,—a brief sketch of that congregation and its establishment in Georgia, may not be deemed irrelevant.

Early in 1697 a body of Puritans from the Towns of Dorchester, Roxbury, and Milton, in Massachusetts, taking with them their pastor,—the Reverend Joseph Lord,—and proclaiming as a leading object the encouragement of churches and the promotion of religion in the Southern plantations, removed with their families and personal effects

---

*Under the writs of election issued by Sir James Wright in 1761, Thomas Carter, Parmenus Way and John Winn were returned as members from Midway and Sunbury in St. John's Parish.†

† McCall's Georgia, vol. I, p. 286.

and formed a new home at Dorchester, in the province of South Carolina. The church which they there established was the first Congregational or Independent Church within the confines of that Colony. All the other religious societies belonged to the established Church of England.

After a residence of more than fifty years, finding their lands impoverished and insufficient for the rising generation,—Dorchester and Beach-Hill proving very unhealthy,—the good reports of the lands in Georgia having been confirmed upon the personal inspection of certain members of the Society who had been sent for that purpose, and a grant of 22,400 acres of land having been secured from the authorities in Georgia,—which grant was subsequently enlarged by the addition of 9,950 acres,—the members of the Dorchester Society commenced moving in 1752 into what is now the swamp region of Liberty County. The settlement lay between Mount Hope Swamp,—the head of Midway river,—on the North, and Bull-Town Swamp on the South. At first, however, it was not so comprehensive. It extended neither to the pine barrens on the West, nor to the salt water on the East. This immigration, begun in 1752, was continued until 1771, when it ceased.* According to the records of the Society, there were forty-four removals in all, of which one family came from Charlestown, four from Pon-Pon, and the remaining thirty-nine from Dorchester and Beach-Hill. These re-

---

*DeBrahm says: "The Beach-Hill Congregation settled upon the Heads of the two Newport Rivers early in the year 1752, when they left Carolina in a great Body, they continued drawing their Effects and Cattle after settling all other Concerns in their native Province until 1755, many rich Carolina Planters followed the Example of that Congregation, and came with all their Families and Negroes to settle in Georgia in 1752; the Spirit of Emigration out of South Carolina into Georgia became so universal that year, that this and the following year near one thousand Negroes was brought in Georgia, where in 1751 were scarce above three dozen."†

†History of the Province of Georgia, &c., p. 21. Wormsloe, 1849.

movals were most numerous during the years 1754, 1755, and 1756. These immigrants brought their negroes with them, and it appears probable, from the best lights before us, that the population of this colony, after its full establishment, consisted of about 350 whites, and 1500 negro slaves.

The region into which the Dorchester Congregation immigrated was already known as the *Midway District.* To the General Assembly which convened in Savannah in 1751, Audley Maxwell, Esquire, was sent as a delegate;—its population then entitling it to such representation. It would appear that a number of families residing in the Midway District previous to the arrival of the Dorchester Congregation, united with that Society after it was regularly domiciled in its new home. The Dorchester Colony did not immigrate, in its entirety, to Georgia. Some families continued to dwell at Dorchester and Beach-Hill, where their descendants may yet be found. Others removed elsewhere. With the formation of the new settlement in St. John's parish, however, the old Dorchester colony in South Carolina lost its integrity and distinctive characteristics.

In locating their plantations amid the swamps of St. John's parish, the following plan was adopted: After laying by their crops in Carolina in the fall of the year, the planters came with able-bodied hands, and, during the winter, cleared land and built houses. In a season or two having thus sufficiently prepared the way, they brought their families and servants in the early spring, and at once entered upon the cultivation of the soil. Thus was the removal rendered as safe and comfortable as the nature of the case permitted.

Strange to say, their dwellings and plantation quarters

were invariably located on the edges of the swamps, in utter disregard of the manifest laws of health. In such malarial situations was the entire year passed. Their houses at first were built of wood, one story high, with dormer windows in the roofs, small in size, without lights, with no inside linings, and with chimneys of clay. The negro-houses were made either of clay or poles. For market, rice was the only article cultivated. While corn was planted on the upland, chief attention was bestowed upon the clearing, ditching, and drainage of the swamps. A miasmatic soil was thus exposed to the action of the sun, at their very doors. The consequence of such injudicious location, and of a general inattention to domestic comfort, was violent sickness and considerable mortality. So frequent were the deaths among children that they seldom arrived at puberty. Those who attained the age of manhood and womanhood possessed feeble constitutions. According to the register kept by the Society, from 1752 to 1772,—the period during which this settlement was being formed,—193 births and 134 deaths occurred. The mortality was greatest during the months of September, October, and November. April, May, June, and August appear to have been the healthiest months:—June particularly so. Bilious fevers in the fall, and pleurisies in the winter and spring, were the diseases which proved most fatal. It used to be said of such as survived a severe attack of bilious fever in the fall, that they would certainly die of pleurisy in the winter or spring.

The Indians being in the vicinity, and at times indulging in acts of hostility, some of the houses of these early settlers were made of hewn cypress logs after the fashion of block houses, and were bullet proof.

The style of agriculture in vogue was of the most primitive sort. The ground was tilled with hoes only. Ploughs were not in use. All rails for fencing were carried on the heads and shoulders of the negroes, and in the same manner was rice transported from the fields. This grain was not only threshed but also beaten by hand : and thus was the crop prepared for market. At first some of the planters sold their crops in Savannah. A trip to that place was the event of the year, and the anticipated journey was talked of in the neighborhood for some time before it was undertaken. Horses were specially fed and carefully attended for a week or more preparatory to the jaunt. Ordinary journeys to church, and of a social character, were performed on horseback. Hence horse-blocks were to be seen at every door. When he would a-wooing go, the gallant appeared mounted upon his finest steed and in his best attire, followed by a servant on another horse, conveying his master's valise behind him.

Shortly after the Revolutionary war stick-back gigs were introduced. If a woman were in the vehicle and unattended, the waiting man rode another horse, keeping along side of the shaft horse and holding the check rein in his left hand. When his master held the lines, the servant rode behind. Men often went armed to church for fear of the Indians.

The country was filled with game. Ducks and wild geese in innumerable quantities frequented the rice-fields. Wild turkeys and deer abounded. Bears and beavers were found in the swamps, and buffalo herds wandered at no great remove to the southward and northward. There was no lack of squirrels, raccoons, opossums, rabbits, snipe, wood-cock, and quail. Wildcats and hawks were the pest of the region, while the cougar was sometimes heard and seen in the depths of the vine-clad swamps. The waters which they held were alive with fishes, alligators, terrapins, and snakes.

Such, in a few words, was the condition of the swamp region of the Midway District when the town of Sunbury was located. Responding to the trust reposed in them by the conveyance from Mark Carr, Messrs. James Maxwell, Kenneth Baillie, John Elliott, Grey Elliott, and John Stevens, with due dispatch set about laying off the town upon the "westermost bank" of Midway river. The plan, as matured and carried out by them, embraced three public squares,—known respectively as *King's*, *Church*, and *Meeting*,—and four hundred and ninety-six lots. These lots had a uniform front of seventy feet, and were one hundred and thirty feet in depth. Lots numbers one to forty, inclusive, fronting on the river, were denominated *Bay Lots*, and carried with them the ownership of the shore to low-water mark. Four lots constituted a block, bounded on three sides by streets, and on the fourth by a lane. The streets were seventy-five feet broad, and the lanes twenty feet wide. The plan of the town was entirely regular. The streets in one direction ran at right angles to the river, and were, at right angles, intersected by the cross streets and lanes. From north to south the length of Sunbury, as thus laid out, was 3430 feet. Its breadth on the south side was 2230 feet, and on the north, 1880 feet.

Within a short time substantial wharves were constructed, the most marked of which were subsequently owned and used by the following merchants: Kelsell & Spalding, Fisher, Jones & Hughes, Darling & Co., and Lamott.

That Sunbury must rapidly have attracted the notice of

the colonists and quickly secured a population by no means insignificant or destitute of influence in that day of small things, is evidenced by the fact that as early as 1761 the Governor, by and with the advice and consent of his council, established and declared it to be a port of entry, and appointed Thomas Carr, Collector, John Martin, Naval Officer, and Francis Lee, Searcher. These appointments were confirmed by the Commissioners of his Majesty's Customs.*

By deed prepared by Thomas Bosomworth, Malatche Opiya, Mico, Emperor of the Upper and Lower Creeks, in consideration of ten pieces of stroud, twelve pieces of duffles, two hundred weight of powder, two hundred weight of lead, twenty guns, twelve pairs of pistols, and one hundred weight of vermilion, on the 14th day of December, 1749, conveyed to Thomas and Mary Bosomworth [formerly Musgrove] Hussoope or Ossabaw island, Cowleggee or St. Catherine island,† and Sapelo, with their appurtenances, warranting the same to them, their heirs, and assigns, so long as the sun should shine, or the waters flow in the rivers.‡ This claim to the ownership of these valuable islands proved a very annoying one to the colonists. After years of litigation, the dispute was finally

---

* See Stevens' History of Georgia, vol. II, p. 21. Philadelphia, 1859.

In his letter to Lord Halifax, written in 1763, Sir James Wright says: "I judged it necessary for his Majesty's service that Sunbury,—a well settled place, having an exceeding good harbour and inlet from the sea,—should be made a Port of Entry; and I have appointed Thomas Carr, Collector, and John Martin, Naval Officer for the same. There are eighty dwelling houses in the place: three considerable merchant stores for supplying the town and planters in the neighborhood with all kinds of necessary goods; and around it for about fifteen miles is one of the best settled parts of the country."

† When visited by an English traveller in 1743, this island was inhabited by eight or ten families of Indians, who had considerable tracts of open land, and were largely engaged in the cultivation of corn. It abounded with game, "on which," says the writer, "the good *Indians* regaled us, and for Grëens boiled us the Tops of China Briars, which eat almost as well as Asparagus."*

* London Magazine for 1745, pp. 551, 552.

‡ McCall's History of Georgia, vol. I, pp. 214, 215. Savannah, 1811.

settled in 1759, by Royal command, by admitting a demand of Mrs. Bosomworth for £450 for goods alleged to have been expended by her in his Majesty's service during the years 1747 and 1748, by allowing her a back salary at the rate of £100 per annum for sixteen years and a half, during which she had acted in the capacity of government agent and interpreter, and by confirming to her and her designing husband full right and title to St. Catherine island, in consideration of the fact that they had fixed their residence and planted there.*

St. Catherine island was the home of the Bosomworths when Sunbury was settled. Some fourteen years afterwards it formed the residence of the honorable Button Gwinnett, who, having disposed of his stock of merchandise in Charleston, South Carolina, with the proceeds purchased some negroes and a tract of land on St. Catherine, where he devoted himself to agricultural pursuits until, on the outbreak of the Revolutionary war, he was summoned from his retirement by the voice of his fellow-citizens.†

Captain McCall, in alluding to the early history of Sunbury, says: "Soon after its settlement and organization as a town, it rose into considerable commercial importance; emigrants came from different quarters to this healthy maritime port, particularly from Bermuda: about seventy came from that island, but unfortunately for them and the reputation of the town, a mortal epidemic broke out and carried off about fifty of their number the first year: it is highly probable they brought the seeds of the disease with them. Of the remainder, as many

---

* See Stevens' History of Georgia, vol. I, pp. 453, 454.

† See Sanderson's Biography of the Signers, vol. III, p. 120. Philadelphia, 1823.

as were able, returned to their native country. This circumstance, however, did not very much retard the growing state of this eligible spot: a lucrative trade was carried on with various parts of the West Indies in lumber, rice, indigo, corn, &c. Seven square-rigged vessels have been known to enter the port of Sunbury in one day, and about the years 1769 and 1770 it was thought by many, in point of commercial importance, to rival Savannah. In this prosperous state it continued with very little interruption until the war commenced between Great Britain and America."*

In his report on the condition of the Province of Georgia, dated the 20th of September, 1773, Sir James Wright mentions Savannah and Sunbury as being the only ports in the Province. The inlet to the latter he describes as "very good; and, although the river is not more than twenty two miles in length, fifteen feet of water may be carried up to the town distant twelve miles from the sea." From the same source we learn that during the year 1772 fifty-six vessels of various sorts were entered and cleared at the custom house in the port of Sunbury.† The collector of the port at this time was James Kitchen, with a salary of £65 stg, and fees of office amounting to £90. The comptroller and searcher was Isaac Antrobus: salary £60: fees of office amounting to a like sum.

Sunbury soon commanded the rice crop from the adjacent swamp regions. Indigo was planted on the island just below, then called Bermuda, and now known as the Colonel's Island. The principal trade was with the West

* McCall's History of Georgia, vol, I, pp. 255, 256. Savannah, 1811.

† See Collections of the Georgia Historical Society, vol. III, p. 161, et seq. Savannah, 1873.

Indies and with the Northern Colonies. From the former, supplies of rum and sugar were obtained, and from the latter rum, flour, biscuits, and provisions. To the West Indies were shipped rice, corn, peas, indigo, lumber, shingles, live stock, and barreled beef and pork. Governor Wright regarded the trade with the Northern Colonies as injurious to the Province of Georgia, because, says he, "they take of but little of our produce, and drain us of every trifle of Gold and Silver that is brought here, by giving a price for Guineas, Moidores, Johannes's Pistols and Dollars far above their real and intrinsic value, so that we can never keep any amongst us." So anxious was Sunbury to concentrate all the trade of the interior, that at one time it was proposed to connect Midway and North Newport rivers by a canal running between Bermuda island and the main. This project, however, was never consummated. Occasionally vessels arrived from English ports bringing manufactured goods, but such generally sought Savannah as the port of entry and discharge. The purchases of the Sunbury merchants were largely made in or through Savannah, and were thence conveyed in coasting sloops and schooners through the inland passages. Below the town, and on the road to the Colonel's island, is a locality to this day known as the *stave landing*, whence, in these early days, constant shipments of staves and shingles were made. On the eastern side of that island, the site of the old shipyard is still pointed out where vessels were repaired and new ones built. It was here that the British landed during the Revolutionary war, when, under Lieut. Col. Fuser, they attempted the reduction of Sunbury.

The health of Sunbury from the time of its settlement until, and even after the Revolutionary war, was good. It became a pleasant residence for the families of many planters whose plantations were located in the swamp regions.

The following is a "list of the Proprietors of the Town of Sunbury in Georgia," and of the Lots owned by them or their representatives about the period of the war of the Revolution :

Lot No. 1.—Mark Carr.
" " 2. Arthur Carnaby.
" " 3. Grey Elliott.
" " 4. Do.
" " 5. Francis Arthur.
" " 6. William Graves.
" " 7. Francis Arthur.
" " 8. John Cubbidge.
" " 9. James Maxwell.
" " 10. Mary Spry.
" " 11. Samuel Bennerworth.
" " 12. Stephen Dickinson.
" " 13. James Fisher. Schmidt & Mölich.
" " 14. Do. Do.
" " 15. Swinton & Co.
" " 16. Darling & Munro.
" " 17. Francis Arthur.
" " 18. James Derwell.
" " 19. Swinton & Co.
" " 20. Thomas Peacock.
" " 21. Andrew Darling.
" " 22. Thomas Young.
" " 23. Do.
" " 24. Roger Kelsall.
" " 25. John James.

Lot No. 26.—Joseph Bacon.
" " 27. John Stewart, Sen'r.
" " 28. John Lupton.
" " 29. Dunbar, Young & Co.
" " 30. Do.
" " 31. John Elliott.
" " 32. James Dunham.
" " 33. Lyman Hall.
" " 34. Do.
" " 35. Samuel Miller.
" " 36. Kenneth Baillie, Sen'r.
" " 37. Samuel Bennerworth.
" " 38. Do.
" " 39. William Sererson.
" " 40. Do.
" " 41. Mark Carr.
" " 42. Tabitha Bacon.
" " 43. Do.
" " 44. John Winn.
" " 45. David Jervey.
" " 46. Do.
" " 47. Francis Arthur.
" " 48. Francis Lee.
" " 49. John Quarterman, Jr.
" " 50. James Dowell.
" " 51. John Irvine.
" " 52. Jeremiah Irvine.
" " 53. Darling & Co.
" " 54. Matthew Smallwood.
" " 55. William Peacock.
" " 56. Isaac Lines.
" " 57. John Osgood.

Lot No. 58.—Rebecca Way.

" " 59. John Stewart, Sr.

" " 60. John Lupton.

" " 61. James Dunham.

" " 62. John Shave.

" " 63. Jacob Lockerman.

" " 64. Paynter Dickinson.

" " 65. John Lawson.

" " 66. Do.

" " 67. Thomas Ralph.

" " 68. John Quarterman, Sr.

" " 69. Thomas Gouldsmith.

" " 70. James Houstoun.

" " 71. John Stevens.

" " 72. Mark Carr.

" " 73. Hugh Clark.

" " 74. Do.

" " 75. Kenneth Baillie, Sr.

" " 76. Do.

" " 77. Paris Way.

" " 78. Nathaniel Yates.

" " 79. William Dunham.

" " 80. Charles West.

" " 81. Daniel Slade.

" " 82. Jacob Lockerman.

" " 83. Samuel West.

" " 84. Thomas Carter, P. Schmidt.

" " 85. John Elliott.

" " 86. Do.

" " 87. William Baker.

" " 88. Do.

" " 89. Audley Maxwell.

Lot No. 90.—Elizabeth Simmons.
" " 91. John Graves.
" " 92. Do.
" " 93. Robert Bolton.
" " 94. John Baker.
" " 95. John Humphreys.
" " 96. James Fisher, Francis Guilland.
" " 97. John Lupton.
" " 98. Do
" " 99. Henry Saltus.
" " 100. Donald McKay.
" " 101. Stephen Dickinson.
" " 102. Do.
" " 103. William Clark.
" " 104. Thomas Christie.
" " 105. Samuel Jeanes.
" " 106. Moses Way.
" " 107. William David.
" " 108. Paynter Dickinson.
" " 109. Francis Lee.
" " 110. Do.
" " 111. James Harley.
" " 112. Samuel Bacon.
" " 113. Tabitha Bacon.
" " 114. John Stewart, Snr.
" " 115. Do.
" " 116. Do.
" " 117. Stephen Dickinson.
" " 118. Do.
" " 119. John Elliott.
" " 120. Do.
" " 121. Benjamin Stevens.

Lot No. 122.—John Lynn.
" " 123. Do.
" " 125. John Sutherland.
" " 126. Do.
" " 127. Samuel Jeanes.
" " 128. Do.
" " 129. Joseph Tickener.
" " 130. William Miller.
" " 131. Richard Mills.
" " 132. Do.
" " 133. Peter McKay.
" " 134. James Miller.
" " 135. Do.
" " 136. David Jervey.
" " 137. William Davis.
" " 138. Do.
" " 139. Joseph Serjeant.
" " 140. John Jones.
" " 141. Strong Ashmore.
" " 142. Francis Arthur.
" " 143. Donald McKay.
" " 144. Do.
" " 145. Andrew Way.
" " 146. James Fisher.
" " 147. George Monis.
" " 148. Thomas Way.
" " 149. James Hatcher.
" " 150. Do.
" " 151. Francis Arthur.
" " 152. Do.
" " 153. Do.
" " 154. Do.

Lot No.	155.—	John Perkins.	
" "	156.	Do.	
" "	157.	William Lowe.	
" "	158.	Do.	
" "	159.	Charles West.	Schmidt & Mölich.
" "	160.	Do.	Do.
" "	161.	Do.	
" "	162.	Do.	
" "	163.	William Peacock.	
" "	164.	Do.	
" "	165.	Charles West.	
" "	166.	Do.	
" "	167.	William Davis.	
" "	168.	Do.	
" "	169.	Francis Lee.	
" "	170.	Do.	
" "	171.	Thomas Vincent.	
" "	172.	Benjamin Baker.	
" "	173.	Grey Elliott.	
" "	174.	Do.	
" "	175.	Do.	
" "	176.	Do.	
" "	177.	John Lupton.	
" "	178.	Do.	
" "	179.	Do.	
" "	180.	Do.	
" "	181.	T. Quarterman.	
" "	182.	Joseph Bacon.	
" "	185.	Susannah Jones.	
" "	186.	Do.	
" "	189.	Barnard Romans.	
" "	190.	Do.	

Lot No. 191.—Barnard Romans.
" " 192. Do.
" " 200. John K. Zubley.
" " 205. Edward Way.
" " 206. Do.
" " 207. James Fisher.
" " 208. Do.
" " 209. Edward Maham.
" " 210. Do.
" " 211. Richard Spencer.
" " 212. Do.
" " 213. William Swinton.
" " 214. Do.
" " 215. Do.
" " 216. Do.
" " 217. Samuel Jeanes.
" " 218. Do.
" " 219. Do.
" " 220. Henry Saltus.
" " 221. James Read.
" " 222. Do.
" " 223. Charles West.
" " 224. Do.
" " 225. John Shave.
" " 226. Do.
" " 227. Richard Baker.
" " 228. Do.
" " 229. Marn'k Perry.
" " 230. Do.
" " 231. Thomas Dunbar
" " 232. Joshua Snowden.
" " 233. Samuel Burnley. Schmidt & Mölich.

Lot No. 234.—Samuel Burnley. Schmidt & Mölich.
" " 235. Do.
" " 236. Do.
" " 237. John Milchett.
" " 238. Do.
" " 239. James Andrew.
" " 240. Do.
" " 241. William Dunham.
" " 242. Do.
" " 243. Samuel Jeanes.
" " 244. Winw'd McIntosh.
" " 245. David Jervey.
" " 246. Do.
" " 247. Francis Lee.
" " 248. Samuel Morecock.
" " 249. Mark Carr.
" " 250. Do.
" " 251. George Bodington.
" " 252. Mary Bateman.
" " 253. John Goff.
" " 257. Robert Bolton.
" " 258. Do.
" " 265. Mark Carr.
" " 266. Do.
" " 267. John Bryan.
" " 268. Do.
" " 269. Patrick M. Kay.
" " 270. Do.
" " 271. Benjamin Andrew.
" " 272. Do.
" " 273. Morgan Tabb.
" " 274. Do.

Lot No. 275.—Morgan Tabb.
" " 276. Do.
" " 277. James Watcher.
" " 278. Do.
" " 279. Francis Arthur.
" " 280. Do.
" " 281. John Bryan.
" " 282. Samuel Richardson.
" " 283. John Gaspar Stirkey.
" " 284. Do.
" " 285. John Jones (mulatto.)
" " 289. Thomas Carter.
" " 290. Do.
" " 305. Do.
" " 306. Do.
" " 307. Do.
" " 308. Do.
" " 309. Do.
" " 313. Samuel Tomlinson.
" " 314. Do.
" " 315. Do.
" " 317. William Swinton.
" " 318. Do.
" " 319. Do.
" " 320. Do.
" " 340. Peter McKay.
" " 341. Do.
" " 342. Do.
" " 343. Do.
" " 344. Do.
" " 345. Do.
" " 346. Do.

Lot No. 347.—Peter McKay.
" " 348. Do.
" " 349. Do.
" " 350. Do.
" " 351. Do.
" " 352. Thomas Quarterman.
" " 353. Barrack Norman.
" " 354. Do.
" " 355. Do.
" " 356. Tarah, Senior.
" " 357. Francis Arthur.
" " 358. Do.
" " 359. Frederick Hobrendorff.
" " 360. Do.
" " 361. Joseph Richardson.
" " 362. Do.
" " 373. John Ford.
" " 403. Thomas Christie.
" " 404. Do.
" " 431. Marmaduke Gerry.
" " 432. Do.
" " 433. Do.
" " 434. Robert Smallwood.
" " 435. Do.
" " 436. John Winn.
" " 437. Francis Arthur.
" " 438. Do.
" " 473. Do.
" " 474. Do.
" " 475. Do.
" " 476. Do.
" " 477. Do.

Lot No. 478.—Samuel Bacon.
" " 479. Francis Lee.
" " 480. John Tutes.

In the Spring of 1773 William Bartram, at the request of Dr. Fothergill of London, set out "to explore the vegetable kingdom," and search the Floridas and the western portions of Carolina and Georgia "for the discovery of rare and useful productions of nature." In his charming narrative of travels and observations, he presents us with this glimpse of our lost town: "After resting, and a little recreation for a few days in Savanna, and having in the meantime purchased a good horse, and equipped myself for a journey southward, I sat off early in the morning for Sunbury, a sea-port town beautifully situated on the main between Medway and Newport rivers, about fifteen miles south of great Ogeeche river. The town and harbour are defended from the fury of the seas by the north and south points of St. Helena and South Catharine's islands; between which is the bar and entrance into the sound: the harbor is capacious and safe, and has water enough for ships of great burthen. I arrived here in the evening in company with a gentleman, one of the inhabitants, who politely introduced me to one of the principal families, where I supped and spent the evening in a circle of genteel and polite ladies and gentlemen."*

The following day was occupied in exploring Bermuda [now Colonel's] island, whose soil, plantations of indigo, corn, and potatoes, Indian tumuli of earth and shell, flora and fauna, greatly interested and delighted him.

"On the morrow," continues Mr. Bartram, "obedient to the admonitions of my attendant spirit, curiosity, as well

* Travels Through North and South Carolina, Georgia, &c., p. 5. London, 1792.

as to gratify the expectations of my worthy patron, I again sat off on my southern excursion and left Sunbury in company with several of its polite inhabitants who were going to Medway meeting, a very large and well constructed place of worship, in St. John's parish, where I associated with them in religious exercise and heard a very excellent sermon delivered by their pious and truly venerable pastor, the Rev. —— Osgood. This respectable congregation is independent, and consists chiefly of families and proselytes to a flock which this pious man led, about forty years ago,* from South Carolina, and settled in this fruitful district. It is about nine miles from Sunbury to Medway meeting-house, which stands on the high road opposite the Sunbury road. As soon as the congregation broke up I re-assumed my travels, proceeding down the high-road towards Fort Barrington, on the Alatamaha, passing through a level country well watered by large streams, branches of Medway and Newport rivers, coursing from extensive swamps and marshes, their sources: these swamps are daily clearing and improving into large fruitful rice plantations, aggrandizing the well inhabited and rich district of St. John's parish."†

In the absence of records it is impossible to specify, with any degree of accuracy, the ratio of increase which characterized the population of Sunbury during the first twenty years of its existence. That at an early period it became a favorite resort not only for commercial purposes but also for health, admits of no doubt. The probability is that this town culminated in prosperity, population, and importance, about the beginning of the Revolutionary war, when its in-

* His Observations were published in 1792.

† Idem, pp. 9, 10.

habitants, white and black, numbered, we should say, between eight hundred and a thousand. That, until the retarding influences of the Revolutionary struggle were encountered, Sunbury had steadily, although slowly, advanced in material wealth, influence, and population, may be safely asserted. Bermuda island, too, was comfortably settled by agriculturists, on small plantations, busied chiefly with the production of indigo. Sunken spaces, indicating where the old vats were located, may be seen to this day. A rich and by no means inconsiderable back country was entirely tributary to Sunbury. Rice, cattle, lumber, shingles, staves, and other articles of commerce, brought from the furthest practicable distances, were here concentrated for sale and shipment; and quite an extensive territory drew its supplies from the store-houses and shops of the Sunbury merchants. On one or two occasions cargoes of Africans were landed and sold in this port. The houses, although of wood, were some of them large, and even imposing. The wharves were faced with palmetto and live oak logs, and filled in with oyster shells, sand, and stone-ballast. Among the residents were not a few of gentle birth, refinement, and education. As a rule, the inhabitants led easy, comfortable, simple lives, and were much given to hospitality. No one was ever in a hurry, and the mornings and afternoons, among the better class, were largely devoted to amusements, such as fishing, sailing, riding, and hunting. The evenings were spent in visiting and in social intercourse. It was a good, easy life that these planters, even at that early day, began to lead upon the Georgia coast. It became more striking, abundant, and attractive after the Revolution; but the delightful germs of the most pleasing existence this country has ever known were then present. No aid seems to have been invoked from the Colonial Council in either supporting the town or indicating the manner in which it should be governed. We find no public resolutions or acts on the subject prior to the legislation of 1791. In all likelihood a Magistrate's Court, and the concurrent views of a few of the prominent citizens, invoked on an emergency, sufficed for the preservation of order and the maintenance of peace.

The general council, however, from time to time, appointed packers, inspectors, and "cullers of lumber" for the port.

By an act passed the 26th of March, 1767, it was made obligatory upon the inhabitants to "clear and keep clear the several squares, streets, lanes, and common" within the town. In consideration of such service they were declared exempt from road duty in the parish of St. John.* By the constitution, adopted in convention at Savannah on the 5th day of February, 1777, the parishes of St. John, St. Andrew, and St. James, were consolidated into one county called LIBERTY. The counties then named and defined within the limits of Georgia were eight in all:—Wilkes, Richmond, Burke, Effingham, Chatham, Liberty, Glynn, and Camden. While to each of the other counties was accorded a representation of ten members, fourteen were allowed to Liberty in consideration of its extent and importance. Sunbury was permitted two special and additional members to represent the trade of the place; and, for like purpose, Savannah was empowered to send four.

At the outbreak of the Revolutionary war the parish of St. John possessed nearly one-third the wealth of the entire

* See Watkins' Digest, p. 144.

province; and its inhabitants were remarkable for their upright and independent character.* Three hundred and seventeen of the four hundred and ninety-six lots into which the town of Sunbury was divided, had been sold, and were, many of them at least, occupied by their respective proprietors and their tenants. Among the prominent citizens was Dr. Lyman Hall, a native of Connecticut and a member of the Midway congregation. Although owning and cultivating a rice plantation situated on the Savannah and Darien road a few miles beyond Midway meeting house in the direction of Savannah, he was the proprietor of and resided upon two of the most desirable lots in Sunbury, numbered 33 and 34 on the plan of that town, and fronting upon the river. He was the leading physician not only of the place but also of the adjacent country for many miles. It was mainly through his influence that the parish of St. John acted independently and in advance of the Republican party in Georgia. In acknowledgment of the decided stand then assumed by him, he was, on the 21st of March, 1775, unanimously elected as a delegate to represent the parish in the next general Congress.† On the 13th of May following, upon the production of his credentials, he was unanimously admitted to a seat in Congress "*as a delegate from the parish of St. John in the Colony of Georgia*, subject to such regulations as the Congress should determine relative to his voting." He carried with him from Sunbury, as a present to the suffering Republicans in Massachusetts, one hundred and sixty barrels of rice, and fifty pounds sterling.

It was not until the 15th of July, 1775, that the

* See Stevens' History of Georgia, vol. II, p. 92. Philadelphia, 1859.

† See Sanderson's Biography of the Signers, vol. III, p. 55. Philadelphia, 1823. McCall's Georgia, vol. II, p. 41. Savannah, 1816.

Convention of Georgia acknowledged complete allegiance to the general Confederacy, and appointed Archibald Bulloch, John Houstoun, the Rev'd Dr. Zubly, Noble W. Jones, and Lyman Hall as delegates to the Provincial Congress.

Intermediately between the time when Dr. Hall took his seat in Congress as a delegate from the parish of St. John, and this action of the Convention, as he represented only a portion of the Colony of Georgia, he declined voting upon questions which were to be decided by a vote of Colonies. He, however, participated in the debates, advocated the necessity and value of the present Congress, recorded his opinion in all cases except such as required an expression of sentiment by Colonies, and declared his earnest desire and conviction "that the example which had been shown by the parish which he represented would be speedily followed, and that the representation of Georgia would soon be complete."

When the Declaration of Independence was signed, of the three members from Georgia whose names were affixed to that memorable document, two—Lyman Hall and Button Gwinnett,—were from St. John's parish: and we may add, from the town of Sunbury:—for, although Gwinnett then resided on St. Catharine island, his home was within sight of that flourishing seaport, all his public and much of his private business was there transacted, he was constantly seen in its streets, was known and honored of its citizens, and in very truth constituted one of them. Two Signers of the Declaration of Independence from one little town in St. John's parish! and that town clean gone from the face of that beautiful, lonely, and bermuda-covered bluff! It is in perpetuating acts and names like these that memory stays the engulfing waves of oblivion, and administers signal rebuke to "time which antiquates antiquities and hath an art to make dust of all things."* Did the limits of this sketch permit, it would be interesting to detail the efforts made by the parish of St. John to persuade positive resistance to English rule and inaugurate steps contemplating an absolute separation from the mother country when the greater part of Georgia was not persuaded of the expediency of such action and was actually opposed to the proceedings of the Continental Congress. So determined and independent was the rebel spirit in Sunbury, throughout the Midway settlement, and at Darien, that it actually brought about, for the time being, a voluntary political separation from the other parishes of the Colony. So annoyed were the citizens of St. John's parish by the temporizing policy which characterized the Savannah Convention, that on the 9th of February, 1775, they applied to the Committee of Correspondence in Charleston "requesting permission to form an alliance with them and to conduct trade and commerce according to the act of non-importation to which they had already acceded." It was strongly urged that having detached themselves from the other parishes in Georgia which hesitated to participate in the movement, they ought to be considered and received as a "separate body comprehended within the spirit and equitable meaning of the Continental Association."†

While admiring the patriotism of the parish, and entreating its citizens to "persevere in their laudable exer-

* Sir Thomas Browne's Hydriotaphia.

† See Letter of the 9th of February, 1775, signed by Lyman Hall, Chairman. White's Historical Collections of Georgia, pp. 520, 521. New York, 1855. Sanderson's Biography of the Signers, vol. III, p. 54. Philadelphia, 1823.

tions," the Carolinians conceived it improper, and "a violation of the Continental Association to remove the prohibition in favor of any *part* of a province."

Disappointed, and yet not despairing, the inhabitants of the parish of St. John "resolved to prosecute their claims to an equality with the Confederated Colonies." Having adopted certain resolutions by which they obligated themselves to hold no commerce with Savannah, or elsewhere, except under the supervision of a Committee, and then only for the absolute necessaries of life, they appointed Dr. Hall, as we have already seen, an independent delegate to represent the parish in the general congress of provinces.

The patriotic spirit of its inhabitants, and this independent action of St. John's parish in advance of the other parishes of Georgia, were afterwards acknowledged when all the parishes were in accord in the Revolutionary movement. As a tribute of praise, and in token of general admiration, by special act of the Legislature the name of LIBERTY COUNTY was conferred upon the consolidated parishes of St. John, St. Andrew, and St. James. Sir James Wright was not far from the mark when he located the head of the rebellion in St. John's parish, and advised the Earl of Dartmouth that the rebel measures there inaugurated were to be mainly referred to the influence of the "descendants of New England people of the Puritan Independent sect" who, retaining "a strong tincture of Republican or Oliverian principles, have entered into an agreement amongst themselves to adopt both the resolutions and association of the Continental Congress." On the altars erected within the Midway district were the fires of resistance to the dominion of England earliest kindled;

and Lyman Hall, of all the dwellers there, by his counsel, exhortations, and determined spirit, added stoutest fuel to the flames. Between the immigrants from Dorchester and the distressed Bostonians existed not only the ties of a common parentage, but also sympathies born of the same religious, moral, social, and political education. Hence we derive an explanation of the reason why the Midway settlement declared so early for the Revolutionists. The Puritan element cherishing and proclaiming intolerance of established church and the divine right of Kings, impatient of restraint, accustomed to independent thought and action, and without associations which encouraged tender memories of and love for the mother country, asserted its hatreds, its affiliations, and its hopes with no uncertain utterance, and appears to have controlled the action of the entire parish.*

When it became evident that England was resolved to coerce her Colonies, the inhabitants of Sunbury and of St. John's parish determined to place themselves in the best possible condition for effective resistance. While some of the citizens joined the State militia and the regularly

---

* The apparent tardiness and hesitancy on the part of the Colony of Georgia in casting her lot with her Sister Colonies at the inception of those movements which culminated in a declaration of independence, may be excused or accounted for when we remember that she was the youngest and the least prepared of all the Colonies, and recall the fact that Schovilites, leagued with Indians, were scourging her borders and awakening in the breasts even of the most patriotic and daring, gravest apprehensions for the safety of their wives and children. "The charge of inactivity vanishes," says Captain McCall, "when the sword and hatchet are held over the heads of the actors to compel them to lie still."†

During the progress of the Revolution the term Schovilite which, at first, was used to designate not only the bandit follower of Schovil, but also every adherent of the Crown in the Southern provinces, was dropped, and that of Loyalist and Tory substituted. The Revolutionists were known as Whigs, Rebels, and Patriots. Many Loyalists who had fled from the Carolinas and Georgia secured a retreat in East Florida whence, having associated with themselves parties of Indians, under the name of Florida Rangers, they indulged in predatory incursions into Georgia to the great loss and disquietude of the southern portions of the Province.

† History of Georgia, vol. II, p. 4. Savannah, 1816.

constituted Colonial forces, others formed themselves into an infantry company, and a troop of horse, for local defense. The latter was commanded by Captain John Baker, who afterwards attained the rank of Colonel, and, in association with Colonels Cooper and Andrew Maybank, and Major Charles West, rendered signal service in the partisan warfare which ensued.

For the immediate protection of Sunbury a fort was built just below the town upon the point where the high ground ended and the wide impracticable marshes between the main and Bermuda island commenced.

A small defensive work may have existed here at an earlier date. The Record Book of Midway Church discloses the fact that in 1756 a letter was received from the honorable Jonathan Bryan,—one of his Majesty's council for the Colony,—conveying the intelligence that the Indians were much incensed at several of their people having been killed by some settlers on the Great Ogeechee river in a dispute about cattle, and advising the Midway congregation, with expedition, to construct a fort for their protection. "People," continues the Journal, "are very much alarmed with the news, and consultations were immediately had about the *building and place for a fort, and it was determined by a majority that it should be at Captain Mark Carr's, low down, and upon the river near the sound, at about seven or eight miles distance from the nearest of the settlement of the Society, which accordingly was begun on the* 20*th September*, 1756."*

On the 11th of July following, apprehending an attack from a French privateer, the Midway people were summoned to Sunbury, where they "raised a couple of batteries

* See White's Historical Collections of Georgia, pp. 517, 518. New York, 1855.

and made carriages for eight small cannon which were at the place." These were probably nothing more than field works thrown up on the bluff just in front of the town. It is to these little forts that Governor Ellis alluded when, upon his second tour of inspection through the southern portion of the Province, he "was pleased to observe that the inhabitants of the Midway District had enclosed their church within a defence, *and had erected a battery of eight guns at Sunbury in a position to command the river.*"*

The State of Georgia being under consideration, it was resolved by Congress, on the 5th of July, 1776, to raise two battalions (one of them to consist of riflemen) to serve in Georgia; that blank commissions be sent to the Convention of Georgia to be filled up with the names of such persons as the Convention should deem proper; that the Legislatures of Virginia, North Carolina. and South Carolina be recommended to allow recruits for these battalions to be enlisted in their several States; that four galleys be built for the defense of the sea-coast, and that two artillery companies, of fifty men each, be enlisted *to garrison two forts which the State was to erect at Savannah and Sunbury.*†

It may, we presume, be safely asserted that the heavy earthwork on Midway river, just south of Sunbury, was laid out and erected about the period of the commencement of the Revolutionary war. If any prior defense there existed, it was so modified and enlarged as completely to lose its identity.

---

*Stevens' History of Georgia, vol. I, pp. 445, 446. New York, 1847.

† Journal of Congress, vol. I, p. 375.

Stevens' History of Georgia, vol. II, p. 151. Philadelphia, 1859.

Three days afterwards Congress appropriated $60,000 for the support of the battalions thus ordered to be raised.

The names of those who were specially charged with the construction of this fort have not been perpetuated, but it lives in tradition that the planters of Bermuda island and of the Midway District, and the citizens of Sunbury contributed mainly to its erection. It was built chiefly by slave labor, and was armed with such cannon as could be procured on the spot, or obtained elsewhere.* That its armament was by no means inconsiderable will be conceded when it is remembered that twenty-five pieces of ordnance were surrendered by Major Lane when he yielded the ownership of this work to Colonel A. Prevost. These guns, however, were small, consisting of 4, 6, 9, 12, and 18-pounders, with perhaps one or two 24-pounders. It was called by the Americans, FORT MORRIS;† but, upon its capture by Colonel Prevost, its name was by him changed to FORT GEORGE.

At the inception of the Revolutionary war the coast defenses of Georgia were in a most pitiable and dilapidated condition. All her forts were in ruins, or nearly so. On the 20th of September, 1773, Sir James Wright,—who makes no mention of any defensive work at Sunbury,—reports Fort George on Cockspur island, which was built in 1762 of mud walls faced with palmetto logs, with a caponiere inside to serve for officers' apartments, as "almost in ruins, and garrisoned only by an officer and three men, just to make signals, &c." Fort Halifax, within the town of Savannah, constructed in 1759 and 1760, and made of plank filled in with earth, with the exception of two of its caponieres, was totally down and unfit for use. Fort

* It is not improbable that some of these guns may have been brought from Frederica; for the Council of Safety had ordered all warlike stores at that place to be secured.

† In compliment to Captain Morris, commanding a company of Continental Artillery raised for coast defence. By this company was the fort garrisoned upon its completion.

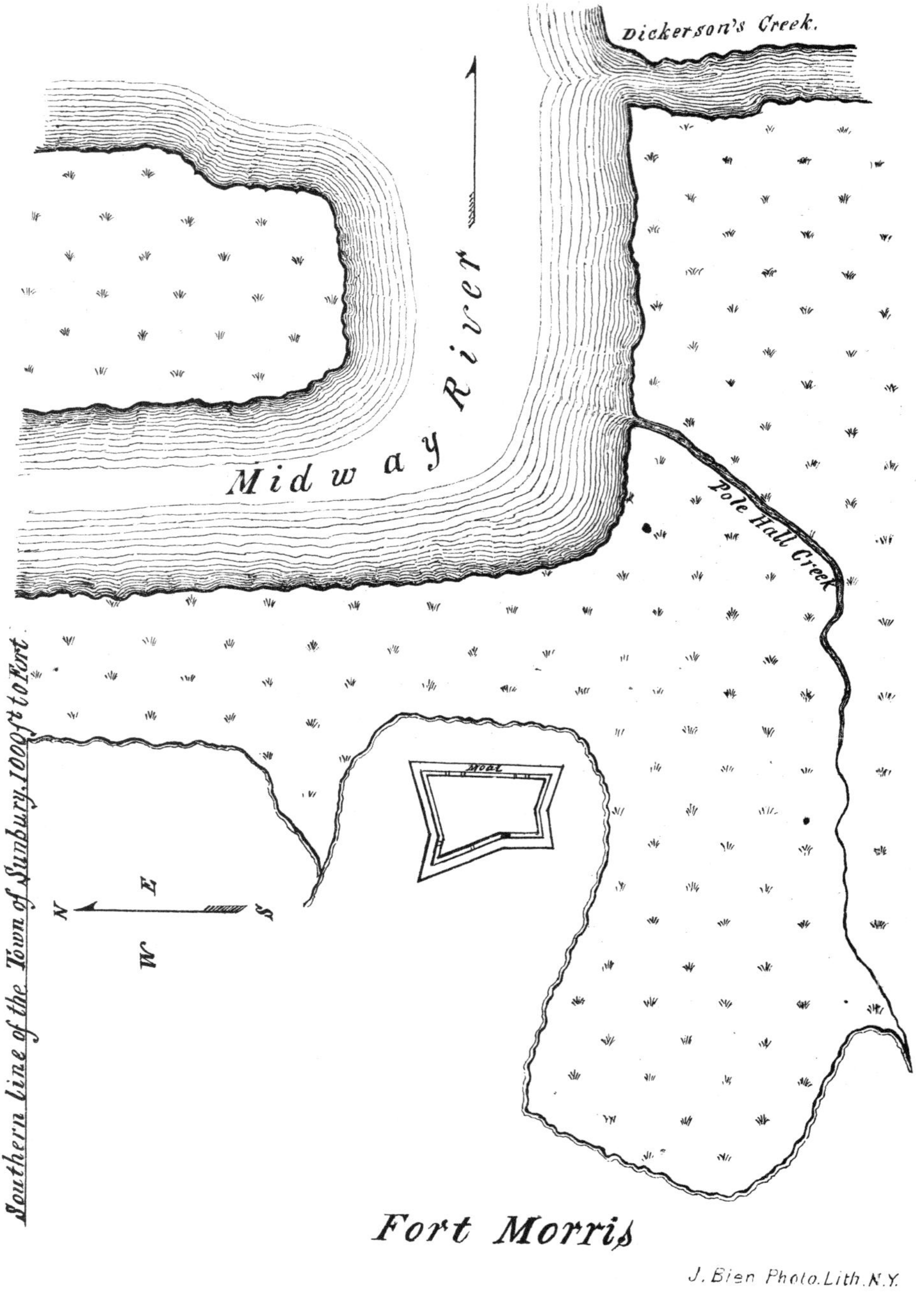

Fort Morris

J. Bien Photo. Lith. N.Y.

Frederick, at Frederica, erected by General Oglethorpe when his regiment was stationed there, had been without a garrison for upwards of eight years, and although some of its tabby walls remained, the entire structure was fast passing into decay. Fort Augusta, in the town of Augusta, made of three-inch plank, had been neglected since 1767 and was rotten in every part. Fort Barrington on the Alatamaha river was in like condition. Of the fort at New Ebenezer, of Fort William on the southern extremity of Cumberland island, of Fort Argyle, and of the other minor defenses erected in the early days of the Colony, scarce a vestige remained.

Located some three hundred and fifty yards due south of Sunbury, and occupying the bluff where it first confronts Midway river as, trending inward from the sound, it bends to the north, Fort Morris was intended to cover not only the direct water approach to the town, but also the back river by means of which that place might be passed and taken in reverse. Its position was well chosen for defensive purposes. To the south stretched a widespread and impracticable marsh permeated by Pole-haul and Dickerson creeks,—two tributaries of Midway river,—whose mouths were commanded by the guns of the fort. This marsh also extended in front of the work, constituting a narrow and yet substantial protection against landing parties, and gradually contracting as it approached the southern boundary of Sunbury. This fortification was an enclosed earth-work, substantially constructed. Its walls embraced a parade about an acre in extent. The eastern face, confronting the river, was two hundred and seventy-five feet in length. Here the heaviest guns were mounted. The northern and southern faces were respectively one hundred and ninety-one, and one hundred and forty feet in length, while the curtain, looking to the west, was two hundred and forty-one feet long. Although quadrangular, the work was somewhat irregular in shape. From the southern face and the curtain, no guns could be brought to bear upon the river. Those there mounted served only for defense against a land attack. The armament of the northern face could be opposed to ships which succeeded in passing the fort, until they ascended the river so far as to get beyond range. It also commanded the town and the intervening space. The guns were mounted *en barbette*, without traverses. Seven embrasures may still be seen, each about five feet wide. The parapet, ten feet wide, rises six feet above the parade of the fort, and its superior slope is about twenty-five feet above the level of the river at high tide. Surrounding the work is a moat at present ten feet deep, ten feet wide at the bottom, and twice that width at the top. Near the middle of the curtain may be seen traces of a sally-port or gateway, fifteen feet wide. Such is the appearance of this abandoned work as ascertained by recent survey. Completely overgrown by cedars, myrtles, and vines, its presence would not be suspected, even at a short remove, by those unacquainted with the locality. Two iron cannon are now lying half buried in the loose soil of the parade, and a third will be found in the old field about midway between the fort and the site of the town. During the recent war between the States, two 6-pounder guns were removed from this fort and carried to Riceboro. No use, however, was made of them. Two more, of similar calibre, of iron, and very heavily reinforced at the breech, were taken by Captain C. A. L. Lamar,—whose company was then stationed at Sunbury,—and temporarily mounted on the bluff to serve as signal guns. Despite their age and the exposure to which they had so long been subjected, these pieces were in such excellent condition that they attracted the notice of the Ordnance department, and were soon transported to Savannah. There they were cleaned, mounted upon siege carriages, and assigned to Fort Bartow, where they remained, constituting a part of the armament of that work, until upon the evacuation of Savannah and its dependent forts by the Confederate forces in December, 1864, they passed into the hands of the Federal army.*

Sunbury was occupied by the Revolutionists as a military post, and its fort garrisoned at a very early period in the Colonial struggle for independence.† In 1776 when Gen. Charles Lee, after full conference with the venerable Jonathan Bryan, projected a plan of operations against St. Augustine for the relief of the southern frontier of Georgia, which had been constantly and sorely vexed by raiding bands from Florida, and to destroy what promised to be

* For the accompanying plan of Fort Morris, I am indebted to a recent survey made at my suggestion by Sam'l L. Fleming, Esq., of Liberty County.

† The following orders were issued by Colonel S. Elbert, for the fuller instruction of the Artillerists stationed at Sunbury: ¶

¶ See MS. Order Book of Col. Elbert.

"HEADQUARTERS SAVANNAH, 5th Dec'r, 1777.

"ORDERS TO CAPTAIN DEFATT OF THE ARTILLERY.

"You are to proceed immediately to the Town of Sunbury, in this State, where are a corps of Continental Artillery posted, which you are constantly to be employed in teaching the perfect use of Artillery, particularly in the Field. Both Officers and Men are hereby strictly ordered to attend on you for the above purpose, at such times, and in such places as you may direct; and the Commanding Officer of the Troops in that place on your shewing him these Orders, will furnish Men to do the necessary duty in the Town & Fort; so that there will be nothing to prevent Captain Morris and his Company from being perfected in the Business for which they were raised. Such pieces of Artillery as you approve of, have mounted on Field-Carriages; and for this purpose you are empowered to employ the necessary Workmen, and procure Materials. Your drafts on me for every necessary Expense, accompanying the Vouchers, will be duly honored.

"I am, Sir, your most Obdt Servt,

"S. ELBERT, Col. Commd'g."

a stronghold for the English, the Virginia and North Carolina troops who were in the expedition were ordered to rendezvous at Sunbury. It being the sickly season of the year, and the men being unaccustomed to the climate, much suffering was encountered from fevers. The mortality became so great,—from ten to fifteen dying in a single day,—that the soldiers were removed to the sea-islands in the vicinity for health.*

As we all know, through the failure of General Lee to concentrate the requisite men and munitions, the contemplated movement from which so much was anticipated never took place; and when, on the 20th of September, he went North to assume the command to which he had been appointed, he ordered the troops in the neighborhood of Sunbury to follow him.

This project was renewed by General Robert Howe, who advanced as far as Fort Tonyn. There, however, a council of war decided a further prosecution of the enterprise unadvisable. The sick and convalescent,—of whom there was a considerable number,—in gallies and such boats as could be procured were, under the command of Colonel C. C. Pinckney, conducted by the inland passage to Sunbury where, for a time, they were allowed to rest and recruit. They were subsequently transferred to Charleston by the way of Port Royal.† Colonel John McIntosh was left in command of Sunbury with one hundred and twenty-seven men. The remnants of Elbert's and White's regiments proceeded to Savannah.‡ So far, Sunbury had suffered no molestation at the hands of the King's forces.

* McCall's Georgia, vol. II, p. 96. Savannah, 1816.

† See McCall's Georgia, vol. II, p. 153. Savannah, 1816.

‡ During the year 1777 American privateers were busy off the Georgia coast and among the inland passages. They cruised as far south as St. Augustine and made frequent captures. In his communication of the 8th of October, Sir James Wright informs Lord

Lord George Germain's plan for the Southern campaign in 1778 was prepared with "minuteness of detail." The reduction of Savannah was resolved upon. As a diversion, and with a view to distracting the attention of General Howe and the American forces concentrated for the protection of the then capital of Georgia, General Augustine Prevost was ordered to dispatch from St. Augustine two expeditions, one, by sea, to operate directly against Sunbury, and the other, by land, to march through and harrass the lower portions of Georgia, and, at Sunbury, form a junction with the former.

Responding to his instructions, that officer sent by water a detachment of infantry and light artillery under the command of Lieutenant Colonel Fuser for the capture of Sunbury. Lieutenant Colonel Mark Prevost was charged with the conduct of the expedition by land. He took with him one hundred British regulars. At Fort Howe, on the Alatamaha, he was joined by the notorious McGirth, with three hundred refugees and Indians. On the 19th of November this force entered the Georgia settlements, taking captive all men found on their plantations, and plundering the inhabitants of every article of value capable of transportation. At the point where the Savannah and Darien road crosses Bulltown swamp, Prevost was confronted by Colonel John Baker, who had hastily collected some mounted militia to dispute his advance. After a short skirmish the Americans retreated. Colonel Baker,

---

George Germain that a short time previous a privateer from Sunbury, mounting ten guns, had taken five prizes ; two of which were safely carried in. He urges upon the Secretary of War the expediency of stationing a twenty-gun ship or a frigate at Cockspur, two sloops of war in the Savannah river, and one at Sunbury.†

From Sunbury, on the 1st of May, 1777, did Col. Elbert embark in transports his troops destined for the expedition against Florida undertaken at the instance of Governor Button Gwinnett.

† Collections of the Georgia Historical Society, vol. III, pp. 246, 248. Savannah, 1873.

Captain Cooper, and William Goulding were wounded. At North Newport Bridge, [afterwards called Riceborough Bridge,] further resistance was encountered at the hands of the Patriots, but it was too feeble to materially retard the progress of the invading forces. Meanwhile, Colonel John White,* having concentrated about one hundred Continentals and militia, with two pieces of light artillery, took post at Midway Meeting House and constructed a slight breastwork across the road at the head of the causeway over which the enemy must advance. His hope was that he might here keep Prevost in check until reinforcements could arrive from Savannah. An express was sent to Colonel Elbert to advise him of the hostile invasion, and Major William Baker, with a party of mounted militia, was detached to skirmish with the enemy and, at every possible point, interrupt his progress. On the morning of the 24th Colonel White was joined by General Screven with twenty militiamen. It was resolved to abandon the present and occupy a new position a mile and a half the other side of Midway Meeting House where the road was skirted by a thick wood in which it was thought an ambuscade might be advantageously laid. McGirth being well acquainted with the country, and knowing the ground held by Colonel White, suggested to Prevost the expediency of placing a party in ambush at the very point selected by the Americans for a similar purpose. It was further proposed, by an attack and feigned retreat, to draw Colonel White out of his works and into the snare. The contending parties arrived upon the ground almost

*He had been for some time stationed at Sunbury, and commanded not only the Continental troops there concentrated, but also all detached companies operating to the southward. Captain Morris' artillery company constituted the permanent garrison of the Fort.

simultaneously, and firing immediately commenced. Early in the action the gallant General Screven, renowned for his patriotism and beloved for his virtues, received a severe wound, fell into the hands of the enemy, and was by them killed while a prisoner and suffering from a mortal hurt. A shot from one of the field pieces passed through the neck of Prevost's horse, and both animal and rider fell. Major Roman, commanding the artillery, supposing that the British commander had been killed, quickly advanced his two field pieces to take advantage of the confusion which ensued, and Major James Jackson, thinking the enemy was retreating, shouted *victory*. Prevost however soon appeared remounted, and advanced in force. Finding himself overborne by numbers, Colonel White retreated upon Midway Meeting House, breaking down the bridges across the swamp as he retired, and keeping out small parties to annoy the enemy's flanks. Compelled to withdraw still further, and desiring by strategem to retard the advance of the enemy, Colonel White "prepared a letter as though it had been written to himself by Colonel Elbert, directing him to retreat in order to draw the British as far as possible, and informing him that a large body of cavalry had crossed over Ogechee river with orders to gain the rear of the enemy, by which their whole force would be captured." This letter was so dropped as in the end to find its way into Colonel Prevost's hands, who seems to have considered it genuine. It is believed that it exerted much influence in retarding his advance, which was pushed not more than six or seven miles beyond Midway Meeting House in the direction of Savannah. Meanwhile, McGirth, with a strong party, reconnoitering in the direction of Sunbury, ascertained the fact that the expedition under Lieutenant Colonel Fuser had not arrived. This circumstance, in connection with the concentration of the forces of Colonels Elbert and White at Ogeechee ferry, where a breastwork was thrown up and preparation made vigorously to dispute his further progress, determined Prevost to abandon his enterprise and return to St. Augustine. Treating the population as rebels against a lawful sovereign, and utterly refusing to stipulate for the security of the country, Prevost, upon his retreat, burnt Midway Meeting House, and all dwellings, negro-quarters, rice-barns, and improvements within reach. The entire region was ruthlessly plundered;—the track of his retreating army being marked by smoking ruins. His soldiers, unrestrained, indulged in indiscriminate pillage, appropriating plate, bedding, wearing apparel, and everything of value capable of easy transportation. The inhabitants were subjected to insult and indignities. The region suffered terribly, and the patriotism of the people was sorely tried.* The scene was such as was subsequently repeated when General Augustine Prevost in 1779 raided through the richest plantations of South Carolina,†

* The following lines descriptive of the desolations wrought by this invading force, are extracted from a quaint old-fashioned poem composed by John Baker, a son of Colonel John Baker, and found among the MSS of the latter:

"Where'er they march, the buildings burn,
Large stacks of rice to ashes turn:
And me [Midway] a pile of ruin made
Before their hellish malice staid.

"Nor did their boundless fury spare
The house devote to God and prayer:
Brick, coal, and ashes shew the place
Which once that sacred house did grace.

"The churchyard, too, no better sped,
The rabble so against the dead
Transported were with direful fumes,
They tore up and uncover'd tombs."

† Bancroft's History of the United States, vol. x, p. 294. Boston, 1874.

or when the Federal cavalry under General Kilpatrick, in the winter of 1864–1865, over-ran, occupied, and plundered Liberty county, converting a well ordered and abundantly supplied region into an abode of poverty, lawlessness, and desolation.

Delayed by head winds, Colonel Fuser did not arrive in front of Sunbury until Prevost had entered upon his retreat and was beyond the reach of communication. Late in November, 1778, his vessels, bearing some five hundred men, battering cannon, light artillery, and mortars, anchored off the Colonel's island. A landing was effected at the ship yard. Thence, the land forces with field pieces, moving by the main road, marched upon Sunbury. The armed vessels sailed up Midway river in concert, and took position in front of the fort and in the back river opposite the town, simultaneously with its investment on the land side by the infantry and artillery. Colonel John McIntosh, with one hundred and twenty-seven Continental troops, and some militia and citizens from Sunbury,—numbering less than two hundred men in all,—held Fort Morris. The town was otherwise unprotected. Having completed his dispositions, Fuser made the following demand upon Colonel McIntosh for the surrender of the fort:

"Sir,

"You cannot be ignorant that four armies are in motion to reduce this Province. One is already under the guns of your fort, and may be joined, when I think proper, by Colonel Prevost who is now at the Medway meeting-house. The resistance you can, or intend to make, will only bring destruction upon this country. On the contrary, if you will deliver me the fort which you command, lay down your arms and remain neuter until the fate of

America is determined, you shall, as well as all of the inhabitants of this parish, remain in peaceable possession of your property. Your answer, which I expect in an hour's time, will determine the fate of this country, whether it is to be laid in ashes, or remain as above proposed.

"I am Sir,

"Your most obedient, &c.,

"L. V. FUSER,

"Colonel 60th Regiment and Commander of his Majesty's
"Troops in Georgia, on his Majesty's Service."

"P. S.

"Since this letter was closed, some of your people have been firing scattering shot about the line. I am to inform you, that if a stop is not put to such irregular proceedings, I shall burn a house for every shot so fired."

To this demand the following brave response was promptly returned by Col. McIntosh: *

"FORT MORRIS, Nov. 25, 1778.

"SIR,

"We acknowledge we are not ignorant that your army is in motion to endeavour to reduce this State. We believe

* Mr. John Couper, in a letter dated St. Simon's, 16th April, 1842, and written when he was eighty-three years of age, gives the following anecdote of the famous and eccentric Captain Rory McIntosh who, at the time, had attached himself in a volunteer capacity to the infantry company commanded by Captain Murray, forming part of the 4th Battalion of the 60th Regiment. Captain Murray's company was in the lines which Colonel Fuser had developed around Sunbury and its Fort. "Early one morning," writes Mr. Couper, "when Rory had made rather free with the 'mountain dew,' he insisted on sallying out to summons the fort to surrender. His friends could not restrain him, so out he strutted, claymore in hand, followed by his faithful slave Jim, and approached the fort, roaring out, 'Surrender, you miscreants! How dare you presume to resist his Majesty's arms?" Captain McIntosh knew him, and, seeing his situation, forbid any one firing, threw open the gate, and said "Walk in, Mr. McIntosh, and take possession." "No," said Rory, "I will not trust myself among such vermin; but I order you to surrender." A rifle was fired, the ball from which passed through his face, sideways, under his eyes. He stumbled and fell backwards, but immediately recovered and retreated backwards, flourishing his sword. Several dropping shots followed. Jim called out, "Run, massa—de kill you." "Run, poor slave," says Rory. "Thou mayest run, but I am of a race that never runs." In rising from the ground, Jim stated to me, his master, first putting his hand to one cheek, looked at his bloody hand, and then raising it to the other, perceived it also covered with blood. He backed safely into the lines." †

† White's Historical Collections of Georgia, p. 472. New York, 1855.

it entirely chimerical that Colonel Prevost is at the Meeting-House: but should it be so, we are in no degree apprehensive of danger from a junction of his army with yours. We have no property compared with the object we contend for that we value a rush:—and would rather perish in a vigorous defence than accept of your proposals. We Sir, are fighting the battles of America, and therefore disdain to remain neutral till its fate is determined. As to surrendering the fort, receive this laconic reply: COME AND TAKE IT.* Major Lane, whom I send with this letter, is directed to satisfy you with respect to the irregular, loose firing mentioned on the back of your letter.

"I have the honor to be Sir,

"Your most obedient Servant,

"JOHN McINTOSH,

"Colonel of Continental Troops."

In delivering this reply Major Lane informed Colonel Fuser that the irregular firing of which he complained was maintained to prevent the English troops from entering and plundering Sunbury. With regard to the threat that a house should be burned for every shot fired, Major Lane stated that if Col. Fuser sanctioned a course so inhuman, and so totally at variance with the rules of civilized warfare, he would assure him that Colonel McIntosh, so far from being intimidated by the menace, would apply the torch at his end of the town, whenever Colonel Fuser fired the town on his side, "and let the flames meet in mutual conflagration."†

---

* The Legislature of Georgia, in acknowledgment of the conspicuous gallantry of Colonel McIntosh on this occasion, voted him a sword with the words *Come and take it*, engraven thereon.

† See White's Historical Collections of Georgia, pp. 523, 524. New York, 1855.
McCall's Georgia, vol. II, pp. 155, 161. Savannah, 1816.
Moultrie's Memoirs of the American Revolution, &c., vol. I, p. 189. New York, 1802.

Instead of assaulting, Fuser hesitated and awaited a report from scouts whom he had sent into the country to ascertain the precise movements of Prevost and learn when his junction might be expected. That officer, as we have seen, unwilling, after the affair near Midway Meeting House, to hazard an engagement with the Continental forces supposed to be advancing from the Great Ogeechee, and surprised at the non-appearance of Fuser before Sunbury, had already commenced his retreat and was beyond the reach of easy communication. Surprised and chagrined at the intelligence, Fuser raised the siege, re-embarked his troops, and returned to the St. Johns river, where he met the returned forces of Prevost. Mutual recriminations ensued between these officers, each charging upon the other the responsibility of the failure of the respective expeditions. Remembering the superior forces at command, it cannot be doubted that either singly or in conjunction Prevost and Fuser could have speedily occupied Sunbury and compelled a surrender of Fort Morris, had their operations been vigorously pressed. When we consider the paucity of Continental troops and militia offering resistance to the invading column of the one, and the slender garrison opposed to the investing forces of the other, the small space and the short time to be overcome in accomplishing a junction, and the further fact that they both must have been aware of the near approach to Savannah of Colonel Campbell's expedition from which these advances from Florida were distinctly intended to distract the attention of the Revolutionists, we cannot but be surprised that Colonels Fuser and Prevost should thus have abandoned their enterprise when a consummation was manifestly within easy grasp. Upon his retreat from Sunbury Colonel Fuser landed his British regulars at Frederica with instructions to repair and place in good defensive condition the military works which General Oglethorpe had planned and erected at that point.

Having collected his forces, Gen. Robert Howe marched to Sunbury. During his short stay there he did little more than point out and condemn the defenseless condition of the works, and memorialize Congress upon the dangers which threatened the Georgia coast, the lack of men and munitions of war, and the disorganization existing in his scattered army. He was one of those unfortunate officers who, lacking the energy and the ability to make the most of the resources at command, and harping upon the existence of defects and wants which inhered in the very nature of things, constantly clamored for the unattainable, indulged in frequent complaints, neglected careful organization, discipline and dispositions, and, on important occasions, became involved in unnecessary perplexities and loss.

Although relieved from the presence of the enemy, heavy shadows rested upon the inhabitants of St. John's parish.* Desolation and ruin were on every hand. The gathered crops having been burnt, many were without sufficient means of subsistence, and not a few were compelled to look elsewhere for support. These tribulations, however,

---

*The inhabitants of Sunbury seem, at times, to have been considerably annoyed by the lawless conduct of the troops quartered in their midst. So marked were these violations of good order, that General Howe on the 16th of January, 1778, deemed it proper to call attention to them in a General Order, from which we make the following extract:

"Complaints have been made to the General that some of the Soldiers have injured the Buildings in the Town; and his own observation convinces him that these complaints are but too well founded. Actions like these disgrace an army, and render it hateful. Any Soldier who either offers Insult or does Injury to the Persons or Property of the Inhabitants will be punished in the severest manner. And officers of every degree are injoined to exert themselves to prevent such Enormities for the future if possible, or to detect those who may commit them, that they may receive that punishment which such Actions so richly deserve. Officers of Companies are to take particular care that their men are made acquainted with this Order."

were but an earnest of sadder ones soon to follow,—trials so grievous that patriotic hearts were well-nigh overborne at thought and apprehension of distresses almost beyond human endurance. These peoples,—the first of the Colony to declare for freedom,—were on the eve of passing under a yoke far more oppressive than that from which not three years before they had sought to escape, and their homes were to become so desolate that expatriation would be found preferable to a perplexing residence and distressful life in the region where they had garnered up present possessions and future hopes.*

The year 1778 closed gloomily upon the patriots in Georgia. Its capital fell before the advance of Colonel Campbell. General Howe's army, retiring in confusion and with much loss, crossed the Savannah river at Sister's and Zubly's ferries and rendezvoused in South Carolina, leaving the newly born State entirely open to the enemy. While at Cherokee Hill, on his .retreat, General Howe dispatched Lieutenant Tennill with orders to Major Joseph Lane commanding at Sunbury to evacuate that post, and, retiring up the south side of Great Ogeechee river, to join the main army at Zubly's ferry. This order was received in ample

---

*If we may credit a contemporary writer, the population of the Midway settlement was considerably demoralized.

"Fields once her [Midway's] glory and her pride,
Weeds, grass, and briars now do hide.
And worst of villains make their home
Where flames had happen'd not to come.

"Instead of preaching, prayers, and praises,
Now on the Gospel holy days
They race, and fight, and swear and game,
Without regard to law or shame.

"They arm'd, disguis'd, with faces blacked,
Do many villainies transact;
The few, few honest that are here,
Do often rob and put in fear."

MS. Diary of Benj'n Baker.

time, if promptly obeyed, to have ensured the salvation of the garrison; but Major Lane, moved by the persuasions of Captain Dollar,—commanding a company of artillery,—and the entreaties of the citizens of Sunbury, resolved to disregard the instructions of his General, and assumed the responsibility of remaining and defending the fort and town.* The account of the reduction of Fort Morris and the fall of Sunbury we give in the language of Captain McCall:

"On the first notice of the arrival of the transports [conveying Colonel Campbell's command,] off the coast of Georgia, General Prevost [then in Florida] marched; and embarked in boats, two thousand men, consisting of artillery, infantry, loyalists, and Indians. On the 6th of January, [1779] that part of his army which moved by water was landed on Colonel's island, seven miles south of Sunbury, about ten o'clock in the morning; and Prevost with the light infantry, marched and took possession of the town early on the ensuing day. Two American gallies and an armed sloop cannonaded the enemy, but with little effect. The following day the main body of the enemy arrived. Every exertion was made to prevent the landing of the cannon and mortars near the town, by the fire from the gallies and the fort. On the night of the 8th they took advantage of the low tide to pass behind a marsh island† opposite to the fort, with a few of their boats containing cannon, howitzers, and mortars, and landed them above the town and placed them on batteries previously prepared.

---

* For this disobedience of orders Major Lane was subsequently tried by a Court Martial and dismissed the service.

McCall's Georgia, vol. II, p. 177. Savannah, 1816.

† This island lying in front of Sunbury, divides Midway river into two channels known respectively as the front and back rivers.

On the morning of the 9th Prevost summoned the fort to surrender unconditionally, accompanied by a statement of his force and the weight of his metal. Major Lane replied that his duty; inclination, and means pointed to the propriety of defending the post against any force however superior it might be. The British batteries of cannon and mortars were opened on the fort and replied to. Lane soon discovered that his fortress would not be long tenable, and began to repent his disobedience of orders. He parlied to obtain better terms than unconditional surrender, but no other would be allowed him: and the time having elapsed for his acceptance or refusal, hostilities recommenced. He parlied again and requested until eight o'clock the next morning to consider of the conditions offered to him, which being peremptorily refused, he assented to them and surrendered the fort containing twenty-four pieces of artillery, ammunition, and provisions, and the garrison consisting of seventeen commissioned officers and one hundred and ninety-five non-commissioned officers and privates, including Continental troops and militia. The American loss was one Captain and three privates killed, and seven wounded. The British loss was one private killed and three wounded.

"The Washington and Bulloch gallies were taken to Ossabaw island, stranded on the beach, and burned by their crews, who took passage on board of Captain Salter's sloop and sailed for Charleston, but were captured by a British tender and taken to Savannah. Captain John Lawson, of the sloop Rebecca, of sixteen guns, put to sea and got safe to Charleston."*

* McCall's History of Georgia, vol. II, pp. 177, 179. Savannah, 1816.

General Moultrie,* then at Purysburg, before the news of the surrender of Sunbury and its fort had reached him, wrote to Colonel Pinckney: "I fear we have lost Sunberry and the two gallies that took shelter under that battery, last Thursday or Friday, as we heard

After the fall of Sunbury the Continental officers captured at Savannah were sent to that place on parole.

When General Prevost, after the junction of his forces with those under Colonel Campbell, moved from the coast into the interior for the complete subjugation of Georgia, the command of Savannah and the adjacent country was confided to Lieutenant Colonel Alexander Innes. Proclamations of the most stringent character were issued by him, by Colonel Campbell, and by Sir Hyde Parker. The inhabitants were enjoined to collect their arms and accoutrements of every description, and surrender them to the military storekeeper. Should these have been concealed or buried, as was not infrequently the case, they were to be uncovered and brought in under pain of rigid search, exposing the delinquent to punishment as an enemy to the King. Special places were designated for the arrival and departure of boats and trading vessels; and permits were required from the superintendents of such ports for the receipt or conveyance of property of any description. An infringement of these regulations worked confiscation of the goods, and punishment of the crews engaged. Peace, freedom, and protection were offered to all who would at once return to their allegiance and join the Royal standard. Three months were allowed for the incoming of the disaffected and deserters, and Savannah was designated as the place where the oath of allegiance would be administered. The proclamation of the 11th of January, 1779, was even more onerous. A reward of two guineas was

a very heavy cannonade from that quarter. The officer commanding had about 120 Continentals and some inhabitants within the fort,—refused to evacuate the post; notwithstanding his receiving positive orders for that purpose he, Don Quixote-like, thought he was strong enough to withstand the whole force the British had in Georgia, for which, I think, he deserved to be hanged."

*Memoirs of the American Revolution, &c., vol. I, p. 259. New York, 1802.

offered for the apprehension of every citizen still adhering to the Rebel cause, and ten guineas were promised upon the surrender of a Committee or Assembly man to any commanding officer of the King's garrisons. Prices were prescribed for all articles of merchandise and country produce. Any deviation from this scale of prices was punished by the confiscation of the articles exposed for sale. Only to those who had resumed their allegiance to the Crown were permits to trade granted, and a fine of one hundred pounds sterling was collectible against any merchant dealing with one not an acknowledged and loyal subject of the King. No produce could be exported except under a certificate of the superintendent of the port that it was not wanted for the use of the Royal troops. To the families of those who maintained their devotion to the Rebel cause no mercy was shown. Stripped of property,—their homes rendered desolate,—often without food and clothing,—they were thrown upon the charity of an impoverished neighborhood. The entire coast region of Georgia was now open, and the enemy overran and exacted the most stringent tribute. Many fled from St. John's parish and from Sunbury upon the first approach of Prevost.

Writing from Purysburg on the 10th of January, 1779, to Colonel C. C. Pinckney, General Moultrie mentions the fact that thousands of poor women, children, and negroes were fleeing from Georgia,—they knew not whither;—"sad spectacle that moved the hearts of his soldiers."*

For the time being the parish of St. John was in a deplorable condition. Multitudes of the inhabitants, unable to sustain themselves in the midst of the utter destitution which there prevailed, set out for Carolina, where they sub-

* Memoirs of the American Revolution, &c., vol. I, p. 259. New York, 1802.

sisted upon the charity of others until the opening spring afforded an opportunity for planting crops in their new homes. Others, possessing the means of subsistence, were so oppressed by the operation of Royal proclamations and restrictions, that they abandoned the region, seeking refuge in other quarters. Sunbury suffered a material diminution of population, and never recovered from the shock then experienced.

Although in the enemy's possession, and paralyzed by the onerous exactions then imposed, Southern Georgia did not wholly cease from offering resistance. Colonels Twiggs, Few, and Jones, closely watched the British outposts, cutting off supplies, and harrassing the garrisons whenever opportunity occurred. Along the sea-coast were found private armed vessels, in the service of the Revolutionists, engaged in the removal of Rebel property in the interest of the owners, and in capturing craft in the employ of the King.

Ascertaining that some British officers had accepted an invitation from Mr. Thomas Young to dine with him at Belfast on the 4th of June, 1779, Captain Spencer, commanding an American privateer, determined to surprise and capture the party. For this purpose, proceeding up Midway river in the evening, he landed between eight and nine o'clock at night, and, with twelve of his men, entering the house, made Colonel Cruger and the English officers at the table prisoners of war. Intending to carry off some negroes, Captain Spencer kept his prisoners under guard until morning when, having taken their paroles, he permitted them to return to Sunbury. Colonel Cruger was soon after exchanged for Colonel McIntosh who had been captured at Briar Creek.

On the 28th of the same month Major Baker, advancing toward Sunbury, attacked and defeated a company of mounted recruits under Captain Goldsmith at the White-house. Several of the enemy were killed and wounded. Among the former was Lieutenant Gray, whose head was almost severed from his body by a sabre cut delivered by Robert Sallett. Major Baker entered Sunbury without opposition.*

It was by these, and kindred partizan exploits, that the British troops at various detached posts were held in partial check, and the drooping spirits of the oppressed inhabitants from time to time revived.

Upon the appearance of Count D'Estaing's fleet off the coast of Georgia, General Augustine Prevost concentrated as rapidly as he could within the lines around Savannah the various detachments on duty in the vicinity. That under Lieutenant Colonel Cruger, at Sunbury, was ordered in and reached Savannah on the 10th of September, just two days prior to the landing of the French troops at Beaulieu.

It does not lie within the compass of this sketch to recount the operations of the allied armies under Count D'Estaing and General Lincoln which culminated in that bloody and disastrous repulse on the morning of the 9th of October, 1779. Suffice it to say that Sunbury had her patriotic representatives among the troops commanded by General Lachlan McIntosh, both during the progress of the siege and in the final assault. Two of them at least attested with their lives their supreme devotion to the patriot cause:—Major John Jones who had been for some years a resident of Sunbury, and who was at the time an aid

* McCall's History of Georgia, vol. II, pp. 235, 237. Savannah, 1816.

to General McIntosh; and Charles Price, formerly a practising Attorney at Sunbury, and a young gentleman of promise in his profession.*

Upon the repulse of the allied armies, and after the departure of Count D'Estaing, and the retreat of General Lincoln into Carolina, the condition of the sea-coast of Georgia was more pitiable than ever. Exasperated by the formidable demonstration, and rendered more arrogant and exacting, the Loyalists sět out in every direction upon missions of insult, pillage, and inhumanity. Plundering banditti roved about unrestrained, seizing negroes, stock, furniture, wearing apparel, plate, jewels, and anything they coveted. Children were severely beaten to compel a revelation of the places where valuable property and money were concealed. In the language of Captain McCall,† "The militia who had been under the protection of the British, not allowing themselves to doubt of the success of the allied forces, cheerfully participated in a measure which promised the recovery of the State to the union. Future protection was not to be expected, and nothing remained for them but the halter and confiscation from the British or exile for themselves, and poverty and ill-treatment by an insolent enemy for their wives and children who were ordered forthwith to depart the country without the means for travelling or any other means but a reliance on charity for subsistence on their way.

"The obscene language which was used, and personal insults which were offered to the tender sex, soon rendered a residence in the country insupportable. Having neither funds nor means of conveyance for themselves and children,

* McCall's Georgia, vol. II, pp. 270 and 271. Savannah, 1816.
White's Historical Collections of Georgia, pp. 533, 537. New York, 1855.

† History of Georgia, vol. II, p. 283, et seq. Savannah, 1816.

they were obliged to abandon the country under the most deplorable circumstances and seek a dependent residence in the adjoining States at the most inclement season of the year. Numbers whose former condition enabled them to make their neighboring visits in carriages, were obliged to travel on foot; many of them without shoes, through muddy roads and deep swamps."

Prominent among these raiding Tories was the renegade McGirth.

Under such depressing influences some portions of Liberty county were almost depopulated. Deprived of a support from the back-country, and with nothing to sustain commerce from abroad, Sunbury languished. Its decline, inaugurated when Prevost and Cruger demonstrated the insecurity of the position, and confirmed when Major Lane surrendered Fort Morris, was now day by day accelerated. All who could possibly get away fled the place, and those who remained led lives of disquietude, and penury. In the face of these difficulties, however, Commodore Oliver Bowen, Captains Spencer, Howell, Maxwell, Pray, Hardy, Lawson, Stiles, and others owning private armed vessels, made frequent voyages along the coast, capturing parties who were engaged in collecting provisions for the British troops in Savannah and transporting them through the inland passages, removing the property of the Whigs from the down-trodden districts, and occasionally executing summary vengeance upon the crews of such craft as were known to be enployed upon missions of arson, robbery, and murder. Sometimes sharply contested naval engagements occurred, such as that between Captain Braddock with his two American gallies, and the brigantine, Dunmore, Captain Caldeleugh, mounting twelve guns. The

Dunmore had sailed from Sunbury for Jamaica, and was attacked so soon as she crossed St. Catharine bar, on the 18th of September, 1779.

On the 4th of June of this year Captain Howell entered the inlet of Sunbury, and learned from a negro that he had been sent out to catch fish for Mr. Kitchins, the Collector of the port, with whom a party of British officers, both civil and military, were to dine that day,—it being the King's birthday. Although Mr. Kitchins' house was within four hundred yards of the fort,—now no longer called fort Morris, but named by its captors fort George in honor of his majesty, King George III,—presuming that the assembled guests on this festive occasion would indulge freely and be found entirely off their guard, Captain Howell resolved upon their capture. Ascending the river with muffled oars, and under cover of the night, the Captain with twelve men passed the fort without attracting its notice, and, landing at Sunbury, surrounded the house about eleven o'clock and took the entire party, numbering twelve persons, prisoners. Among the captured was Colonel Roger Kelsall, who had insulted and ill-treated Captain Howell while he was a prisoner of war. Incensed at the recollection of these indignities, Captain Howell was on the eve of taking him out and drowning him in the river, when the prayers of the lady of the house induced him to spare his life. Having exacted from his captives a pledge that they would not again take up arms until regularly exchanged, Captain Howell returned, without loss or molestation, to his privateer.

Upon the transfer of active operations to the Carolinas, Sunbury seems to have been but feebly garrisoned by the enemy. At times, and for a considerable portion of the year 1780, it appears doubtful whether any British force was there stationed. The Royal army in Georgia was then so much reduced that the garrison at Savannah did not exceed five hundred men.*

The truth is, the available forces of the State had been so largely withdrawn for service elsewhere, the entire coast region was so thoroughly impoverished, and so many of the Whig families had moved away, that there was scarcely any necessity for maintaining this post except as a matter of convenience in keeping open the land communication between Savannah and St. Augustine.

In this exhausted and comparatively quiet condition did matters remain until the close of the war. We are not aware that any events occurred in Sunbury, during the residue of the struggle, worthy of special mention or calculated to rouse the inhabitants from that quietude born of want and oppression, feebleness and present despair.

The successes of General Greene in Carolina enabled him to inaugurate such measures for the relief of Georgia that, in order to escape from the advancing and investing columns under General Wayne and Colonel Jackson, the British garrison embarked on the 11th of July, 1783, and Savannah, after having been more than four years and a half in the possession of the enemy, was formally surrendered to the Patriots who had already virtually achieved the independence of the thirteen Confederated States.

Colonel James Jackson was designated by General Wayne as the officer to receive the surrender of the town;—a compliment well merited in view of the patriotism and gallantry which had distinguished him during the whole

* See letter of Sir James Wright to Lord George Germain, under date Savannah, 20th August, 1780.

Collections of the Georgia Historical Society, vol. III, p. 314. Savannah, 1873.

war, and in recognition of the recent active and hazardous service performed by his command while operating in advance of the army of occupation.

Georgia's losses, particularly along her south-eastern borders, had been very great. Her slave population, although quiet during the struggle, was essentially demoralized and reduced. It is estimated that between the 12th and 25th of July, 1783, not less than five thousand negroes made their escape from Savannah in sailing vessels. Upon the cessation of hostilities the agricultural and commercial interests of the State were in a most disastrous situation. Particularly was this the case in Liberty county where negroes and property of every description had been, from time to time during the continuance of the struggle, carried off, patriotic citizens driven into exile, plantations burned and converted into waste places, and the seeds of poverty and distress sown broadcast.

On the first Monday in August, 1783, Governor Martin convened the Legislature in Savannah. Courts of Justice were re-established, commissioners of confiscated estates appointed, and measures adopted for the rehabilitation of the State. It was not, however, until the assembling of the Constitutional Convention on the first Monday in January, 1784, when Lyman Hall was appointed Governor, George Walton, Chief Justice; Samuel Stirk, Attorney General; John Milton, Secretary of State; John Martin, Treasurer, and Richard Call, Surveyor General, that the machinery of reconstruction was fully set in motion.

With the incoming of peace many who had been absent in the army, and others who had sought, in South Carolina and elsewhere, temporary refuge from the devastations of the war, returned to their former homes in Sunbury and on the adjacent plantations, and entered with becoming spirit and energy upon the labor of rebuilding and repeopling the desolated region. For a season it seemed as if the prosperity of this seaport would be revived. Not a few of its inhabitants, however, having, during the continuance of hostilities, formed settlements elsewhere, determined to remain where they were, and so the ante bellum population was by no means regained. Others had died, and others still in their places of retreat found themselves so impoverished that they could not command the means requisite for a removal.

The first session of the Superior Court of Liberty county was held at Sunbury on the 18th of November, 1783,—their Honors, Chief Justice George Walton, and Assistant Judge Benjamin Andrew, Senior, presiding. On the 20th, the Grand Jury being empanneled and sworn, the Chief Justice delivered a charge in which,—having alluded to the fact that good order and subordination had everywhere characterized the courts presided over by him on this his first riding since the close of the war, and assured them that nothing could so much contribute to confirm the blessings of peace as an observance of the laws which had for their sole object the general happiness of the people,—he spoke as follows: "I congratulate you, gentlemen, on the news of a definitive treaty of peace by which our freedom, sovereignty, and independence are secured. The war which produced it was one of necessity on our part. That we were enabled to prosecute it with firmness and perseverance to so glorious an issue, should be ascribed to the protecting influence of the Great Disposer of events, and be a subject of grateful praise and adoration. While the result of the contest is so honourable and advantageous to us and to posterity, it is to be lamented that those moral and religious duties so essential to the order of society and the permanent happiness of mankind, have been too much neglected. To recover them into practice, the life and conduct of every good man should be a constant example. Your temples, which the profane instruments of a tyrant laid in ashes, should be built again: for nothing tends to harmonize the rude and unlearned organs of man more than frequent meetings in the places of holy worship. Let the monument of your brave and virtuous soldier and citizen,* which was ordered by Congress to his memory, be erected on the same ground, that his virtues and the cause in which he sacrificed his life may be seen together by your children and remembered through distant ages.†

"In the course of the conflict with an enemy whose conduct was generally marked with cruelty, the whole State has suffered undoubtedly more than any in the Confederacy. The citizens of Liberty County, with others, have drunk deep in the stream of distress. Remembering these things, we should not lose sight of the value of the prize we have obtained. And now that we are in full possession of our freedom, we should all unite in our endeavours to benefit and perpetuate the system, that we may always be happy at home and forever freed from the insults of petty tyrants commissioned from abroad."‡

The grand jurors to whom this charge was delivered, were Joseph Law, William Baker, Senior, James Maxwell, James Jeffries, John Mitchell, Junior, Palmer Goulding,

---

* General James Screven, who fell in the skirmish near Midway Meeting House.

† This monument has never been reared. The obligation is as binding now as when thus solemnly recognized.

‡ Quoted in White's Historical Collections of Georgia, p. 530. New York, 1855.

John Elliott, John Whitehead, William West, Thomas Bradwell, William Peacock, Senior, Nathan Taylor, John Hardy, William Baker, Junior, Nathaniel Saxton, James Powell, William Way, John Myers, Senior, John Way, John Winn, Edward Way, Joseph Way, and William Quarterman.

By an act approved the 26th of February, 1784, Sunbury was designated as the place for holding the Superior and Inferior Courts of Liberty County. They were there held until, by the act of 1797, Riceborough was made the county seat.*

On the 10th of February, 1787, John Baker, John Hardy, and Alexander McIver were, by the Legislature, appointed Commissioners for the port of Sunbury, and were invested with powers similar to those conferred in and by the law regulating the pilotage of Savannah.

For the better encouragement of trade, the Governor was authorized to draw on the treasurer of the State in favor of the Commissioners for the port of Sunbury for £100. The act further appointed a harbor and tonnage master, and provided for the collection of tonnage duties, and an additional sixpence to be levied and set apart for erecting lighthouses and supporting pilots.

Commerce revived to a considerable extent, but the trade of Sunbury did not reach that activity or volume which existed at the inception of the Revolutionary war.

The Indians were still troublesome on occasions, coming from beyond the Alatamaha in predatory bands and making short but sometimes cruel inroads into the white settlements On the 24th of October, 1787, a man was scalped within eighteen miles of Sunbury, and on the 9th of the following January, Rogers, Queeling, and Bennett were killed and

* See Watkins' Digest, pp. 298, 618.

scalped within the limits of the Midway settlement, by a party of Indians. During this year skirmishes occurred with the Indians at Phinholloway creek and at Shepherd's plantation. On the first of May the savages attacked Mr. Girardeau's plantation, carrying off some of his negroes, and wounding a young man named Smallwood. Seven days afterwards they appeared at Colonel Maybank's plantation and captured a number of his slaves. At Sapelo a young man was killed by them while milking his cow. On the 6th of June, on the plantation of John Houstoun, Esq., McCormick was killed by the Indians, his son scalped, and three of his daughters and a little boy carried into captivity. In September, thirteen negroes were stolen by them from Mr. Quarterman's plantation. Captain Sumner and Lieutenant Burnley pursued and overtook them in a swamp on Taylor's creek. The Indians fled and the negroes were recovered.*

The militia of the county was constantly on duty to repel these incursions, and the citizens generally went armed to church to guard against surprises. To assist the militia, the inhabitants of Liberty County, at their own charge, placed and maintained in service for three months "a company of Horsemen" under the command of Captain Elijah Lewis. This troop acted as scouts. In September, 1788, a "Body of Light Horse,"—consisting of a captain, two lieutenants, two sergeants, and forty privates,—was raised for the defense of the county, and supported by the voluntary subscriptions of the inhabitants. It was commanded by Captain Rudolph, and subsequently by Lieutenant Whitehead. This company was paid off and disbanded at Newport Bridge [afterwards called Riceborough] on the

* See White's Historical Collections of Georgia, p. 528. New York, 1855.

28th of March, 1789 :—six privates and one sergeant being retained in service to act as scouts.*

In these matters of home defense, and in the subsequent military service which, rendered necessary in 1793, was continued until, by the treaty of Colerain, a peace was concluded with the Indians, the citizens of Sunbury bore their full part.

On the 8th of December, 1791, an act was adopted entitled "An act for the better regulating of the town of Sunbury."† Until its passage no legislative provision had been made for the incorporation or government of this town, then in the thirty-third year of its existence.

The general provisions of that act were as follows: On the second Monday in January next ensuing, and on the second Monday in January in every third year thereafter, all proprietors of lots or houses in the town of Sunbury, of full age, were required to meet at the place of holding the courts in said town and, under the direction of two or more justices of the peace for the county of Liberty, proceed to ballot for five persons,—each of whom should be the proprietor of a house or lot in Sunbury, and an inhabitant thereof, and of full age,—who should be styled "Commissioners of the Town of Sunbury."

On the Monday next following such election it was made the duty of these Commissioners, or a majority of them, to assemble and appoint a clerk and such other officers as they might regard as proper and necessary for the execution of the provisions of the act.

Full power was lodged with these Commissioners to

---

*See Historical Address before the Liberty Independent Troop by the Rev. Dr. Charles Colcock Jones, pp. 10, 11. Savannah, 1856.

†See Watkins' Digest, p. 431.

Marbury and Crawford's Digest, pp. 128, 129.

make such by-laws and regulations, and impose such pains, penalties, and forfeitures as they might deem conducive to the good order and government of the town, provided the same were not repugnant to the constitution and laws of the State, and did not extend to life or member.

By the third section the Commissioners, or a majority of them, were required "yearly and every year to make, lay, and assess a rate or assessment upon all and every person or persons who do or shall inhabit, hold, use, occupy, possess, or enjoy any lot, ground, house, building, tenement, or hereditament within the limits of the town of Sunbury, for raising such sum or sums of money as the said Commissioners or a majority of them shall judge necessary for and towards carrying this act into execution: and in case of a refusal or neglect to pay such rate or assessment, the same shall be levied and recovered by warrant of distress and sale of the offender's goods, under the hands and seals of the said Commissioners or a majority of them, or under the hand and seal of any justice of the peace for the County of Liberty."

The concluding section appointed such Commissioners superintendents of pilotage for the port of Sunbury, and invested them with the power and authority of Justices "so far as to keep the peace and preserve good order in the said town."

By the act of December 12th, 1804,* it was provided that the election of Commissioners should occur annually on the first Monday of August, and be held in the Sunbury Academy.

The Justices of the Peace of Liberty County having "neglected to hold an election for Commissioners for the

* Clayton's Digest, p. 213.

town of Sunbury, to the great injury of said town," the Legislature on the 2d of December, 1805,* directed the Justices of the Inferior Court of Liberty County "to call an election for that purpose, giving ten days notice of the same at the most public place in the town."

In case of failure, at any time thereafter, to elect Commissioners on the day appointed, it was made the duty of the Inferior Court, when notified of the fact, to advertise an election.

This is all the legislation appearing on the Statute books with reference to the government of the town of Sunbury. These Commissioners continued to hold office in a quiet way,—looking after the police and order of the town,—until about the year 1825, when elections went by default, and such of the citizens as remained, by common consent managed their premises each after his own fashion, having the taller weeds in the streets and along the Bay "chopped down" at irregular intervals, and permitting the cows and the Bermuda grass to strive for the mastery in the lanes and upon the common.

In 1801 Sunbury was described as "a seaport in Liberty County, favoured with a safe and convenient harbour," as being "a very pleasant, healthy place," and promising without doubt to become "a port of commercial consequence." "It is resorted to," says Sibbald, "by many persons during the Summer months; it has an Academy under an able instructor."†

The most famous institution of learning in Southern Georgia, for many years, was the SUNBURY ACADEMY. It was established by an act of the Legislature assented to

---

* Clayton's Digest, p. 243.

† "Notes and Observations on the Pine Lands of Georgia," &c., p. 65. Augusta, 1801.

the first of February, 1788.* Abiel Holmes, James Dunwody, John Elliott, Gideon Dowse, and Peter Winn were nominated in the act as Commissioners. To them, or a majority of them, was authority given to sell at public sale, and upon previous notice of thirty days in one of the gazettes of the State, any confiscated property within the county of Liberty to the amount of £1,000. This sum, when realized, was to be by them expended in the construction of a building suitable for the purposes of the Academy. Each Commissioner was required to execute a bond, in favor of the Governor of Georgia, in the penalty of £1,000, conditioned for the faithful performance of the trust. In 1803 the number of Commissioners was increased to seven, but two years afterwards the Legislature directed a return to the original number, which was five.†

As late as December 4th, 1811, the Legislature directed a grant and conveyance to the Commissioners of Sunbury Academy, for the sole use and benefit of that institution, of one-third of a tract of land adjoining Sunbury, known as the Distillery Tract; the same having been confiscated as the estate of Roger Kellsall, and being then the property of the State.

The administration of the affairs of this academy during the long course of its valuable existence appears at all times to have been conducted by its trustees with prudence and skill. Certain it is that until the marked decadence of Sunbury this institution maintained an enviable reputation, and attracted scholars in no inconsiderable numbers from various portions of the State, and even from sister States. The teacher whose name is for

* Watkins' Digest, p. 380.

† Clayton's Digest, pp. 115, 246.

the longest period and most notably associated with the management of this Academy, and who did more than all others to establish a standard of scholarship and maintain rules of study and discipline unusual in that period and among these peoples, was the Reverend Dr. William McWhir. Great was the obligation conferred upon the youths of Southern Georgia, for certainly two generations, by this competent instructor and rigid disciplinarian. A native of Ireland, a graduate of Belfast College, and licensed to preach by the Presbytery of that city, he came to America in 1783 and settled in Alexandria, Virginia. There, for ten years he was the Principal of the Academy of which General Washington was a trustee. He was frequently a guest at Mount Vernon, enjoying the hospitality of that noted mansion. On one occasion while he was dining with the family, General Washington, as his custom was, asked the usual blessing. Mrs. Washington, somewhat surprised that Mr. McWhir had not been invited to do this, remarked to General Washington, "You forgot that we had a clergyman at table with us to-day." "No, madam," he replied, "I did not forget. I desire clergymen, as well as all others, to see that I am not a graceless man."

About 1793 he removed to Sunbury where he became the Principal of the Academy and, for nearly thirty years, made it the leading institution of learning in this entire region. A thorough Greek, Latin, and English scholar, an uncompromising observer of prescribed regulations, and a firm believer in the virtue of the birch as freely applied in those days in the English and Irish schools in which he had received his training, he was a terror to all dolts and delinquents. To the studious and the ambitious, he always proved himself a generous instructor, full of suggestion and encouragement. The higher branches of mathematics were also taught; and, as a preparatory school, this institution, under his guidance, had no superior within the limits of the State. The average attendance was about seventy. Pupils were attracted not only from Liberty, but also from the adjacent counties of Chatham, Bryan, McIntosh, and Glynn. Some came from even greater distances. Two generations sat at the feet of this venerable preceptor. Fathers and sons in turn responded to his nod, and feared his frown. Although

"A man severe he was, and stern to view,"

so impartial was he in the support of whatever was just and of good report, and so competent and thorough as a teacher, that for more than a quarter of a century his numerous pupils found in him, above all others, their mentor, guide, and helper in the thorny paths of knowledge. Strongly did he impress his character and influence upon the generations in which he lived, and his name and acts are even now well remembered. The evening of his days was spent, as inclination prompted, at the residences of his old scholars, by whom a cordial welcome was always extended. That welcome was recognized by him as peculiarly genuine and agreeable when accompanied by a generous supply of buttermilk and a good glass of wine. The latter might be dispensed with: a failure to provide the former was, in his eyes, an unpardonable breach of hospitality, and materially impaired the comfort of his sojourn, and the tranquility of the venerable guest.

Among the other teachers at this Academy may be mentioned Mr. James E. Morris, the Rev. Mr. Lewis, the Rev. Mr. Shannon, the Rev. Mr. Thomas Goulding, Uriah Wilcox, Rev. Mr. John Boggs, Captain William Hughes, Mr.

C. G. Lee, Rev. A. T. Holmes, Rev. S. G. Hillyer, Major John Winn, Mr. W. T. Feay, and Mr. Oliver W. Stevens. The building—a large two story and a half double wooden house, about sixty feet square and located in King's Square,—was pulled down and sold some time about the year 1842.

As early as 1797 it being manifest that the population of the town was steadily decreasing, and that its commercial importance could not be reëstablished, it was resolved by a large majority of the citizens of Liberty that Sunbury,—the then seat of justice,—was inconveniently situated for conducting the public business, and that North New Port Bridge was the most eligible location for the Court House and Jail. Matthew McAllister, Esq. had very generously offered to convey in fee simple, for public uses, a piece of ground two hundred and thirty feet in length and one hundred and fifty feet in width, situated near "the Bridge," without "price or consideration other than a wish on his part to promote the growth of the town of Riceborough and benefit the inhabitants thereof." The middle and upper portions of the county had by this time the controlling vote in public matters, and the Legislature was memorialized, in opposition to the feebler will of the residents of Sunbury and its vicinity, to authorize a removal of the seat of justice. Accordingly, on the 1st of February, 1797, an act was passed appointing Thomas Stevens, Daniel Stewart, Peter Winn, Joel Walker, and Henry Wood, Commissioners to superintend the admeasurement of the land offered by Mr. McAllister, receive the titles therefor, and erect thereon and keep in repair a Court House and Jail for the County of Liberty. The act further provided that after its passage "all courts and elections heretofore held, and all public business heretofore transacted at said town of Sunbury, should be held and transacted at the said town of Riceborough," to which place the County offices and records were to be removed.*

Riceborough was a more convenient point for shipping to Savannah the rice, cotton, and agricultural products of the County, and was much more central for the facile convocation of the citizens and the transaction of public business. Sunbury, however, still remained the favorite resort of the wealthier planters during the summer months, and maintained a permanent population of perhaps four hundred. The hurricane of 1804, with its wild devastations, begat a sense of insecurity in the minds of not a few dwellers on the coast, and to some extent diminished the population of the town. Soon afterwards, Bermuda grass began to overspread the bluff and cover, with its deep mat, the streets and lanes. With its importation the health of the place became sensibly affected. Chills and high grades of billious fever grew frequent in the fall of the year, and from time to time removals occurred to healthier localities. Many citizens still clung to their old homes rendered so pleasant by the refreshing sea-breezes and the never-failing stores of the waters and the orchards, and Sunbury for many years continued to be the abode of culture, hospitality, and ease. Then came the hurricane of 1824 blowing down out-houses, bearing away fences, bringing in the sea in great masses, and carrying fear to many, and even death to some who resided at exposed points. The wild indigo disappeared more rapidly than ever, and the dark Bermuda grass asserted its dominion on every hand. From the numerous cattle accustomed to feed upon its common and wander through its streets and lanes, and from the refuse

*See Watkins' Digest, p. 618.

of the town, now no longer new, the original sandy soil became saturated with fertilizing matter, and grew rich. Thence, under the heat of autumnal suns, year by year rose exhalations annually more and more prejudicial to health. Chills and fevers were more frequent, and Sunbury proved less and less attractive as a summer resort. In 1829 Sherwood describes the town as having "a flourishing academy, a house of worship for the Baptists, twenty dwelling houses, two stores, three offices, and a population of one hundred and fifty."*

Ten years before, the Sunbury Female Asylum had been incorporated by the Legislature of Georgia.† Supported by the generous charities of kind hearted women, it never enjoyed a vigorous existence, and after some years suffered a languishing death.

Although by resolutions adopted on the 18th of November, 1812, and the 12th of November, 1813, the Legislature provided for stationing troops in the counties of Bryan, Liberty, McIntosh, Glynn, and Camden, for the protection of the sea-coast of Georgia, it does not appear that any permanent detail was made for Sunbury. The fort, however, was again placed in tolerable condition, the planters furnishing the labor requisite for cleaning out the ditch, strengthening the parapet, and mounting such guns as there remained and were deemed trustworthy. A few light pieces were obtained from Savannah and added to the armament. Such gun-carriages as were manufactured in the county were made by Jonathan Goulding, of Taylor's Creek. Not a shot, however, was fired from the fort during the war of 1812–1815.

Although British vessels of war were constantly upon

* Gazetteer of the State of Georgia. Philadelphia, 1829.

† Lamar's Digest, p. 84.

the coast, and the smoke of merchantmen captured, robbed, and burnt by them was on several occasions seen from Sunbury, the enemy never ascended Midway river. A company composed of the citizens of the town and its vicinity, numbering some forty men and commanded by the honorable John A. Cuthbert, and another company consisting of the larger boys then students at the Sunbury Academy, and under the command of Captain [afterwards Brigadier General] Charles Floyd, were formed for local defense, drilled at regular intervals, and held themselves in readiness to act as occasion might require.

Besides these, there were then three volunteer companies in Liberty County: the Liberty Independent Troop,—Captain Joseph Jones,—and two infantry companies, commanded respectively by Captains Robert Quarterman and John Winn. "The Guards," under Captain Winn, were at one time stationed at Hardwick, in Bryan County.

After his defeat at Point Peter, Captain Jones' cavalry company and the Rifle company of Captain Quarterman were ordered to the relief of Major Messias. They were for some time on duty at Darien.

The militia of the County being well organized and efficiently officered, was largely engaged in maintaining a careful watch along the coast. In this service assistance was rendered by barges and cutters from the American Navy, which patrolled Midway river and the adjacent inlets, and not infrequently established their headquarters at Sunbury. The "Committee of Safety" for Liberty County, during the war, consisted of General Daniel Stewart, William Fleming, John Winn, John Stacy, John Elliott, John Stevens, and Joseph Law. These gentlemen were authorized to take general charge of the local defense, and to call upon the citizens of the County for such labor as appeared necessary. In case of a refusal on the part of any one to respond to the requisition, they were instructed to advertise the name of such delinquent in the most frequented places, that he might be held up to public contempt "for having disgraced the character of the citizen and the patriot."

This Committee assured General C. C. Pinckney of their ability and willingness to repair and garrison the Fort at Sunbury, and made requisition upon him for two 18-pounder guns and a suitable supply of ammunition. In its remodeled condition, the fortification at Sunbury received at the hands of the Committee of Safety a new name,—"Fort Defence." As being more easily defended, and requiring a smaller garrison, General Pinckney suggested the erection of a tower for the protection of Sunbury. This project, however, was never consummated.

The last vessel of any moment, which visited the town, was a Swedish brig which, in 1814, came in and conveyed away a load of cotton. Mr. James Holmes was the last Collector of the port; and for many years prior to his death the office was a mere sinecure. Subsequently a Surveyor was appointed by the General Government whose principal duty was to sign blank reports and draw his quarterly salary. The last person who held this office was the genial Colonel William Maxwell.

Until 1833, the Liberty Independent Troop,—the oldest volunteer military organization within the limits of Georgia except the Chatham Artillery,—celebrated the fourth of July each year at Sunbury. This company was then the guest of the town, and the recipient of every welcome and hospitality. The morning was spent in military exercises, in contentions at the head, ring, and target, and the afternoon was crowned with a public dinner replete with good cheer and patriotic speeches. This annual parade was the event of the year in that quiet community. On such occasions the U. S. Revenue Cutters stationed on the coast would generally come up to the town by special invitation, and participate in the festivities.

The summer retreats established at Jonesville, Flemington, Hinesville, and Dorchester, compassed the depopulation of the old town. Without trade, destitute of communications, and visited more and more each season with fevers, Sunbury, for nearly thirty years, has ceased to exist save in name. Its squares, lots, streets, and lanes have been converted into a corn field. Even the bricks of the ancient chimneys have been carted away. No sails whiten the blue waters of Midway river save those of a miserable little craft employed by its owner in conveying terrapins to Savannah. The old cemetery is so overgrown with trees and brambles that the graves of the dead can scarcely be located after the most diligent search. Fort Morris is enveloped in a wild growth of cedars and myrtle. Academy, churches, market, billiard room, wharves, store-houses, residences, all gone; only the bold Bermuda covered bluff and the beautiful river with the green island slumbering in its embrace to remind us of this lost town. A stranger pausing here would find no trace of the past once full of life and importance, but now existent only in the skeleton memories which redeem place and name from that oblivion which sooner or later is the common lot of all things human. The same bold bluff,—the same broad expanse of marshes stretching onward to the confines of the broad Atlantic,—the same blue outlines of Colonel's island and the Bryan shore,—the same sea-washed beach of St. Catherine,—the same green island dividing the river as it ebbs and flows with ever restless tide,—the same soft sea-breezes,—the same bright skies,—the same sweet voices and tranquil scene which nature gave and still perpetuates,—but all else how changed! Truly "oblivion is not to be hired." Blindly scattering her poppy she deals with places as with men, and they become as though they had not been. Strange that a town of such repute, and within the confines of a young and prosperous commonwealth, should have so utterly faded from the face of the earth!

> "The garden with its arbor—gone,
> And gone the orchard green;
> A shattered chimney stands alone,
> Possessor of the scene."

It is with pleasurable sadness and filial reverence that we have brought together these fragmentary memories of a place once the abode of so much refinement, intelligence, hospitality and patriotism,—the home of Lyman Hall and Button Gwinnett,—signers of the Declaration of Independence,—of John Elliott and Alfred Cuthbert,—United States Senators from Georgia,—and of John A. Cuthbert, member of Congress,—the birth-place of William Law,—the accomplished lawyer, upright judge, and courtly gentleman,—and of John E. Ward,—the eloquent advocate, speaker of the House of Representatives, president of the Georgia Senate, and United States Minister to China,—for some years the residence of Richard Howley and Nathan Brownson, Governors of Georgia,—claiming intimate association with the Reverend Moses Allen, Benjamin Baker, Colonels William and John Baker, General Daniel Stewart, Colonel John McIntosh, and Major John Jones, patriots all, who risked fortune and life in support of the primal struggle for independence,—the scene of the professional labors of Doctors Dunwoody, Alexander, and West,—and numbering among its citizens clergymen, teachers, physicians, lawyers, merchants, and planters, whose influence was appreciated in their day and generation, and whose names, if here repeated, would challenge respect and veneration.

Nature survives, but nearly all the rest is shadow. In this humid soil so fecund with vegetation, neglected gravestones,—covered with brambles and overturned by envious forest trees,—"tell truth scarce forty years."

V.

HARDWICK.

During his tour of inspection in 1755, Governor Reynolds was so much pleased with the natural advantages of the Great Ogeechee river, that he selected a bluff upon its right bank, some fourteen miles from the sea, as a location for a new town, which, in honor of his relative the Lord High Chancellor of England, he named HARDWICK. In his letter to the Board of Trade he says: "Hardwicke has a charming situation, the winding of the river making it a peninsula; and it is the only fit place for the capital.* There are many objections to this town of Savannah being so, besides its being situated at the extremity of the province, the shoalness of the river, and the great height of the land, which is very inconvenient in the loading and unloading of ships. Many lots have already been granted in Hardwicke, but only one house is yet built there; and as the province is unable to be at the expence of erecting the necessary public buildings, and the annual sum of £500 allowed for erecting and repairing public works, entertain-

* To Mr. G. W. J. DeRenne are we indebted for the following memoranda from H. M. Public Record Office, Georgia, Vol. 35, B. T., touching the primal settlement, and naming of *Hardwick:*

"May 13, 1754.—The Neck of Land called the Elbow on Great Ogeechee River—which (on the 10th Day of this Month) they had named George-Town."

"4 Feb., 1755.—His Excellency was pleased (with the approbation of the Board) to name the Town lately laid out at a Place commonly called the Elbow on Great Ogeechee River, Hardwick."

"*Minutes of the Proceedings of the Governor in Council.*"

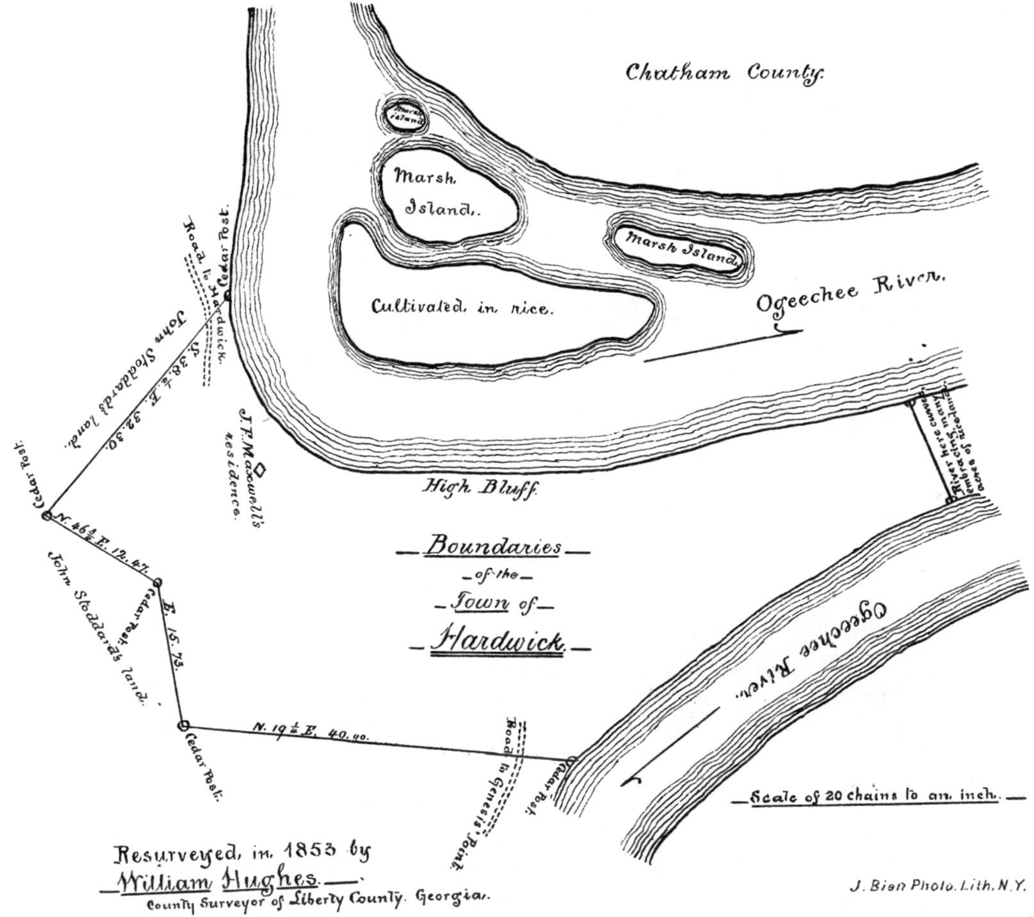
Chatham County
Marsh Island
Marsh Island
Marsh Island
Cultivated in rice.
Ogeechee River.
River here curves embracing many acres of riceland.
High Bluff
Boundaries
of the
Town of
Hardwick
Ogeechee River.
Cedar Post.
Road to Hardwick.
S. 38¼ E. 32.30.
John Stoddard's land.
J. F. Maxwell's residence.
Cedar Post.
N. 46¾ E. 12.47.
Cedar Post.
John Stoddard's land.
E. 15.73.
Cedar Post.
N. 19¼ E. 40.40.
Road to Genesis' Point.
Cedar Post.
Scale of 20 chains to an inch.
Resurveyed in 1853 by
William Hughes.
County Surveyor of Liberty County, Georgia.
J. Bien Photo. Lith. N.Y.

ing Indians, and other incidental expenses being insufficient for all those purposes, I am in hopes your Lordships will think proper to get a sufficient sum allowed for erecting a Court-House, an Assembly-House, a Church, and a Prison at Hardwick; which will be such an encouragement to private people to build there as will soon make it fit for the seat of government to the universal benefit of the province."*

Upon the agitation of this project to transfer the capital of the colony from Savannah to the Great Ogeechee,† twenty-seven lots were quickly taken up in the town of Hardwick, and twenty-one thousand acres of land in its vicinity were granted to various parties who favored and promised to develop the enterprize. DeBrahm proposed that the place should be fortified by the erection of three polygons, six hundred feet each, and three detached bastions, to be armed with twenty-five cannon; and suggested a garrison of one hundred and fifty men.‡

The Home Government neglecting to furnish the necessary funds, and Governor Reynolds being without the means requisite to compass the contemplated change, his scheme of transferring the seat of government to Hardwick was never consummated, and the town, deprived of its anticipated dignity and importance, developed simply into a little trading village adapted to the convenience of

---

* Board of Trade. V. 167.

Stevens' History of Georgia, vol. I, pp. 405, 406. New York, 1847.

White's Historical Collections of Georgia, p. 183. New York, 1855.

† This river was then called the GREAT HOGOHECHIE, which responds more nearly to its original Indian name than the appellation subsequently adopted.

‡ See Plans and Elevations of the Forts necessary in Georgia, forwarded with Governor Reynolds' letter of the 5th of January, 1756, and now of file in the Public Record Office, London; Maps B. T., vol. XIII, No. 14.

the few who there located and cultivated lands in the vicinity.¶

By DeBrahm* it was reckoned among the five sea-port towns of the province. Although for many years a port of entry, its commerce was wholly domestic and coastwise, being chiefly confined to the conveyance of the products of the region, in small vessels, to Savannah, and the transportation, in return, of such articles and supplies as were needed by the planters.

By the act of the 15th of March, 1758,† dividing Georgia into eight parishes, "the town of Hardwick and district of Ogechee on the south side of the river Great Ogechee, extending north west up the said river as far as the lower Indian trading path leading from Mount Pleasant, and southward from the town of Hardwick as far as the swamp of James Dunham, including the settlements on the north side of the north branches of the river Midway, with the islands of Ossabaw, and

¶ The design of transferring the Capital of the Colony from Savannah to Hardwick, conceived by Governor Reynolds, was adhered to by his successor, Governor Ellis. "The depth of water in the river, its more central position, its greater distance from Charleston—the proximity to which, he argued, restricted the commerce of Savannah—the convenience of its harbour as a naval station, and the fertility of its adjacent lands, were the principal motives which operated with him to enforce the plan suggested by his predecessor. As a consequence of clinging to this scheme of removal, Governor Reynolds had neglected repairing the public buildings of Savannah, and its inhabitants had ceased enlarging and beautifying a town so soon to be deserted. The Filature was out of repair, the Church was so decayed that it was only kept from falling down by surrounding it with props, and the prison 'was shocking to humanity.'

"The removal of the Seat of Government to Hardwicke, which had received the favorable notice of former Governors, was discouraged by Sir James Wright, who argued that if the object of a removal was to obtain a more central position, Hardwicke was too near; while, on the other hand, a removal there would be very disadvantageous to the present capital which was conveniently settled for intercourse with the Indians and for trade with South Carolina. The project was therefore abandoned, and the attention of the Assembly was directed to enlarging and strengthening the City which Oglethorpe had founded."

Stevens' History of Georgia, vol. I, p. 433. Vol. II, p. 19.

* History of the Province of Georgia, &c., p. 25. Wormsloe, 1849.

† Marbury and Crawford's Digest, p. 151.

from the head of the said Dunham's swamp in a north west line," were declared a parish by the name of St. Philip.

In 1786* regulations were prescribed for the inspection of Tobacco at a warehouse to be erected at Hardwick.

By an Act, assented to on the 19th of December, 1793,† a new County was laid off from Chatham, and, in honor of a venerable patriot,‡ was called Bryan.

The legislature which passed this Act constituted John Wereat, Robert Holmes, James McGillivray, William Clark, Simmons Maxwell, Thomas Collier, and Joseph Stiles, Commissioners for the town and commons of Hardwick, with power, upon three months' notice published in the Georgia Gazette, to cause a survey to be made, as nearly as possible, in conformity to the original plan of the place. This survey they were required to record in the office of the Surveyor of Bryan County; and also in the office of the Surveyor General of the State.§

By the second section of the Act these Commissioners were directed to sell at public vendue, to the highest bidder, at such time and place as they should deem best, and after published notice of six weeks in the Georgia Gazette, any vacant lots in the town, and any lots which should have become vested in the State of Georgia, reserving such only as might be proper for public uses. The proceeds arising from these sales were to be primarily applied to the erection of a Court House and Jail; and, if any balance remained in the hands of the Commissioners, it was to be expended in building an Academy. Within three months after

* Watkin's Digest, p. 339.

† Marbury and Crawford's Digest, p. 167.

‡ Jonathan Bryan.

§ Careful search fails to disclose a map of this survey either among the records of Bryan County, or in the State Archives.

the completion of such sales these Commissioners were to make full return to the State Treasurer of the number of lots sold, the price which each brought, and of the application of the funds realized.

On the 23rd of December, 1791,* Hardwick was again designated, by special legislative enactment, as one of the points in Georgia for the erection of a public ware-house, and the inspection and shipment of tobacco.

Eight years afterwards† the Justices of the Inferior Court of Bryan County were authorized to lease, from time to time, and for a term not exceeding seven years, the common of Hardwick and the glebe lands of the County, and apply the rents and profits therefrom arising to the repair and improvement of the County roads and bridges.

Although the Act of 1793 appointed Commissioners and provided for the erection of a County Court House and Jail at Hardwick, it does not appear that the contemplated buildings were ever constructed. But few terms of the Superior Court were held at this place. As early as 1797 the General Assembly of Georgia‡ authorized the Justices of the Inferior Court of Bryan County to make permanent seat of the public buildings "at the Cross-Roads about two miles from Ogechee bridge, or at any other place within half a mile of the said Cross-Roads." For this purpose they were empowered to purchase land not exceeding two acres in extent.

There the public business was transacted, until, in 1814, the Legislature§ was induced to sanction the selection of

* Marbury and Crawford's Digest, pp. 544, 546.
† Idem., p. 160.
‡ Marbury and Crawford's Digest, p. 174.
§ Lamar's Digest, p. 211.

a new site more central in its location and more convenient of access to the inhabitants who had multiplied in the upper portion of the County. Godhilf Smith, Henry Sherman, James Martin, Zachariah Wells, and Luke Man were designated as Commissioners to sell the old lot and buildings at the cross-roads, and purchase in behalf of the County a parcel of ground at the new site to be chosen at or near Mansfield, on the Canouchee river, and superintend the erection thereon of new public buildings.

Thus, instead of becoming the Capital of Georgia, Hardwick soon ceased to be even the County-town of Bryan County.

In Sibbald's "Notes and Observations on the Pine Lands of Georgia,"* &c., written in 1801, we find the following notice of this village: "Hardwick, situated near the mouth of Ogeechee river in Bryan County,—the navigation being good, and having an extensive river running through a fertile country,—bids fair to arrive at some considerable degree of Importance." This promise was never fulfilled.

From the best information we can obtain we are persuaded that the population of Hardwick probably, at no time, exceeded one hundred souls. In 1824 Mr. Alexander Netherclift was the only resident; and Sherwood, in his Gazetteer of the State of Georgia for 1829,† speaks of Hardwick simply as "a cluster of houses in Bryan." Among those who, from time to time, were inhabitants of the place, may be mentioned Mr. Clark, Dr. Ward, Mr. Mifflen, Dr. John Jenkins, Dr. Anthony Benezet, Dr. T. J. Charlton, Dr. Louis Turner, and Mr. William Savage. The

---

* Page 65. Augusta, 1801.

† Page 116.

commerce of Hardwick was never large, and was conducted by means of small craft plying between it and Savannah. Sloops and schooners sufficed, with occasional trips, to convey to a market the agricultural products of the neighborhood, and in return to bring back plantation supplies.

After the removal of the public buildings from the Cross-Roads, and upon the completion of the causeway through the swamp and of the bridge over the Great Ogeechee river,—thereby establishing immediate and convenient communication by land with Savannah,—the trade of Hardwick declined, and its small stores,—abandoned of their keepers,—lapsed into decay.

The bluff upon which the town was located rises about fourteen feet above the level of the Great Ogeechee, and is distant some two miles from Genesis' Point, to which Fort McAllister gave such heroic memories during the Confederate struggle for independence. In front, stretching to the north, is a point of land or peninsula. On the west the fresh waters of the Great Ogeechee river lave the Hardwick bluff, and then treading northward, and at right angles to the general course of the stream, by a graceful bend to the east embrace the northern extremity of the peninsula. Again turning to the south, the river reaches the eastern bluff of the town, where, curving gently, it pursues its course, emptying through Ossabaw sound into the Atlantic Ocean. This peninsula in front of the town constitutes a dividing line between the fresh and brackish waters of the river. At the point where it springs from the bluff it is less than a quarter of a mile wide, although a journey of several miles is requisite to complete its circuit by water.

From the bluff, backward toward the south, extends a high and dry plain adapted for the location of a town. The surroundings, however, were unhealthy during the Summer and Fall months, and there was nothing to encourage population, or ensure the continuance and prosperity of the settlement.

In 1866 a feeble effort was made to revive the town of Hardwick; and the Georgia Legislature on the 21st of March of that year passed an act the leading provisions of which are as follows:

After reciting the fact that the Commissioners of Hardwick had long ago departed this life, that the site of the town and its common had been regranted by the State to private individuals, and suggesting the advisability that Hardwick should be reëstablished for the better advancement of the industrial resources of the State, the Act appointed Jacob M. Middleton, Thomas C. Arnold, William Patterson, Henry E. Smith, and John W. Magill, Commissioners, and authorized them to acquire by cession or purchase the town of Hardwick and its common "not to exceed one hundred and fifty acres in extent." Having obtained proper titles to the land, these Commissioners, or a majority of them, were directed to have the town of Hardwick surveyed and laid out into lots of such form and dimensions as they should deem fit. Plans of the town were to be by them filed in the office of the Clerk of the Superior Court of Bryan County, and in the office of the Surveyor General of the State.

Full power was vested in them to sell the town lots, except such as they might determine to reserve for public uses. Upon completion of the survey, and upon filing plans of the town in accordance with the requirements of the Act, the Commissioners were authorized to select one of their number as an Intendant. Thereupon they were declared incorporated by the name and style of the "Intendant and Commissioners of the town of Hardwicke," with power to make such by-laws and regulations for its good order and government as were not repugnant to the constitution and laws of Georgia, and of the United States.

Although fortified by this legislation, no action was taken by the Commissioners, three of whom are now dead.

Hardwick exists only in name, and will probably never be vitalized into a municipal entity.

VI.

PETERSBURG, JACKSONBOROUGH, FRANCISVILLE, &C., &C.

Near the close of a spring day in 1776 Mr. William Bartram, who, at the request of Dr. Fothergill, of London, had been for some time carefully studying the flora of Carolina, Georgia, and Florida, forded Broad river just above its confluence with the Savannah, and became the guest of the commanding officer at Fort James. This fort,—which he describes as "a four-square stockade with saliant bastions at each angle, mounted with a block-house, where are some swivel guns, one story higher than the curtains which are pierced with loop-holes, breast-high, and defended by small arms,"—was situated on an eminence in the forks of the Savannah and Broad, equidistant from those rivers and from the extreme point of land formed by their union.

Fort Charlotta was located about a mile below on the left bank of the Savannah.

The stockade of Fort James was an acre in extent. Within this enclosure were a substantial house for the commandant, officers' quarters, and barracks for the garrison, consisting of fifty rangers well mounted, and armed each with a rifle, two dragoon pistols, a hanger, a powder horn, a shot pouch, and a tomahawk.*

For a distance of two miles the peninsula above the fort was laid out for a town called *Dartmouth* in honor of the Earl who had exerted his influence in procuring from the

* Travels through North and South Carolina, Georgia, &c., pp. 321, 322. London, 1792.

King a grant and special privileges in favor of the *Indian Trading Company of Georgia.* For the defense of the territory known as the *New Purchase,* had this fort been erected and maintained.

Dartmouth never realized the expectations which, in its infancy, had been formed for it. After a short and feeble existence it gave place to Petersburg which, during the tobacco culture in Georgia, attracted to itself a considerable population and was regarded as a place of no little commercial importance.

For the convenience of the early settlers of Eastern-Middle Georgia, Dionysius Oliver was, on the 3rd of February, 1786, authorized by the Legislature* to erect a warehouse on his land, lying in the fork between the Savannah and Broad rivers, for the inspection and storage of tobacco. With the location of this warehouse dates the commencement of the town of PETERSBURG.

The cultivation of tobacco was then enlisting the attention of many planters. In the lower counties of the State the production of silk had ceased to be remunerative, and the tillage and manipulation of indigo had not yielded the profits anticipated.

Cotton was little grown. Many of the early inhabitants of the present counties of Elbert, Lincoln, Wilkes, and Oglethorpe, came from Virginia and brought with them not only a love for the weed, but a high appreciation of tobacco as an article of prime commercial value. The virgin lands of this region were found well adapted to its cultivation: and, as a consequence, this plant grew rapidly into general favor and proved the staple commodity or market crop of the farmers. As the existing laws of the State forbade

---

* Watkins' Digest, p. 325.

its exportation without previous inspection and the payment of specified fees, it became necessary to establish public warehouses at convenient points where the inspection and storage of this article could be had. No hogshead or cask of tobacco could be shipped which did not bear the stamp of some "lawful inspector."* These inspectors were required to give bond for the faithful performance of their duties, and it was made obligatory upon them to attend continuously at their respective warehouses from the first of October to the first of August in each year. It was their duty carefully to inspect, weigh, receipt for, and stamp each hogshead delivered at the warehouse. The hogshead or cask was "not to exceed forty-nine inches in length, and thirty-one inches in the raising head." Its weight, when packed, was to be not less than nine hundred and fifty pounds nett. It was not customary in those primitive days to transport these hogsheads upon wagons. Vehicles of all sorts were scarce. The hogshead or cask being made strong and tight, and having been stoutly coopered, was furnished with a temporary axle and shaft, to which a horse was attached. By this means was it trundled to market or to the public warehouse. Water courses also were freely taken advantage of for the conveyance of tobacco. The location of this public warehouse at the confluence of the Broad and Savannah rivers proved most acceptable to the tillers of the soil in this rich region, and speedily attracted merchants who, there fixing their homes, became purchasers of the tobacco when inspected, and in return sold to the planters such supplies as they needed.

Petersburg soon assumed the proportions of a respectable village. It was regularly laid off in town lots, with conve-

* See Watkins' Digest, p. 444.

nient streets intersecting each other at right angles. The tobacco warehouses and shops were located as near the point formed by the confluence of the rivers as the nature of the ground and the liability to overflow would permit. The residences were situated above, and occupied lots, each about three quarters of an acre in extent.

In 1797 William Watkins secured from the Legislature* the right to establish upon his lots,—35 and 37,—in the town of Petersburg, an extensive warehouse for the inspection and storage of tobacco.

By an act† of the General Assembly assented to November 26th, 1802, eighteen of the principal citizens of the town were incorporated into a society "under the name and style of the Petersburg Union Society." The avowed objects of this association were the diffusion of knowledge and the alleviation of want. It maintained an active existence for some years and exerted a marked influence for good.

On the first of December, 1802,‡ Robert Thompson, Leroy Pope, Richard Easter, Samuel Watkins, and John Ragland were appointed Commissioners of the town of Petersburg, and were charged with its "better regulation and government." They were to hold office until the first Monday in January, 1804. Then, and on the first Monday in every January thereafter, the citizens entitled to vote for members of the General Assembly were required to choose by ballot five persons to act as Commissioners of the town. These Commissioners were invested "with full power and authority to make such by-laws and regulations, and to inflict or impose such pains, penalties, and

*Watkins' Digest, p. 658.
†Clayton's Digest, p. 58.
‡Clayton's Digest, p. 92.

forfeitures as in their judgment should be conducive to the good order and government of the said town of Petersburg:" provided such by-laws and regulations were not repugnant to the constitution and laws of Georgia, and that the pains and penalties contemplated did not extend to life or member.

Two years afterwards * the powers of these Commissioners were materially enlarged, and they were directed to have a correct plat of the town and commons made by the County Surveyor and recorded in the office of the Clerk of the Superior Court of Elbert County.

Speaking of Petersburg in 1800, Mr. George Sibbald says:† "In point of situation and commercial consequence it is second only to Augusta. * * It is a handsome, well built Town, and presents to the view of the astonished traveller, a Town which has risen out of the Woods in a few years as if by enchantment: It has two Warehouses for the Inspection of Tobacco."

So long as the cultivation of tobacco engrossed the attention of the planters in the circumjacent region, Petersburg continued to be a place of considerable commercial importance. In the zenith of its prosperity it contained a distributing post-office, a market place, a town-hall, several churches, and not less than forty stores and warehouses. Its population then has been estimated at between seven and eight hundred souls. During the early part of the present century its trade was greater than that of Augusta. It is claimed that goods of a superior quality were then there sold, and in greater quantities, and at cheaper rates. A large and lucrative business was transacted by the Peters-

* Clayton's Digest, p. 182.

† "Notes and Observations on the Pine Lands of Georgia," &c., pp. 62, 63. Augusta, 1801.

burg boats, which, along the line of the Savannah river, constituted the favorite common carriers of passengers and goods. The existence of the town was due to the concentration at this point of the tobacco crop of a considerable area. The necessity for a rigid inspection of this product forced the planters to bring it here. With Petersburg the presence of this plant was emphatically the cause of population and the parent of trade. After inspection, most of it was purchased on the spot by merchants and speculators, who, from their full stores, supplied every need of the producers. Thence was it shipped to Augusta and Savannah. So soon, however, as the cotton plant began to assert its ascendency, the fortunes of the town commenced to wane. Requiring no inspection, and capable of easy shipment from any convenient point, the cotton bales were sent to various bluffs along the river for transmission to the coast; and thus it came to pass that with the discontinuance of the tobacco culture Petersburg dwindled away and died. Sickness, and the attractions of new and fertile fields in Alabama hastened its ruin :—and now sunken wells and the mounds of fallen chimneys are all that attest the former existence of the town. Its corporate limits are wholly included within the confines of one well-ordered plantation; and extensive fields of corn and cotton have obliterated all traces of warehouse, shop, town-hall, church, and dwelling.

Beneath the conserving shadows of tall trees which mark the outlines of the old cemetery on the left bank of Broad river may still be seen numerous graves, fresh and green when the town was replete with life, but neglected and overgrown with brambles now that the village too is dead.

A few sleepy houses mark the spot where LISBON,* with envious eye, in former years viewed across Broad river the rising fortunes of Petersburg; and, beyond the Savannah, narrowly scanned the efforts made by Vienna to participate in the lucrative tobacco trade.

FEDERAL-TOWN, in Washington County, on the east bank of the Oconee, was another of these Tobacco villages. It perished so soon as the cultivation of cotton became general in the region, and its fort was no longer required as a protection against the incursions of the Creeks.

Deprived of the vitalizing influence of the tobacco trade, Harrisburgh, Edinborough, and other small towns designated as sites for the inspection of this crop, speedily lapsed into disuse and decay.

Not infrequently a change in the location of public buildings dealt a death-blow to villages of moderate size and feeble support. Take, for example, the old town of JACKSONBOROUGH, confirmed as the county seat of Screven county on the 15th of February, 1799.† As late as the 20th of December, 1823, an act‡ of the Legislature, passed for its incorporation, designated the Court House as the centre of the town, and extended the corporate limits a half mile in every direction. Five years afterwards the "Jacksonborough Methodist Episcopal Church" was incorporated.§ The business of the county was, for some forty years and more, mainly transacted at this place. Here, too, for some

---

* The original name of this village was the *Town of Lincoln*. See Sibbald's "Notes and Observations on the Pine Lands of Georgia," &c., p. 63. Augusta, 1801.

† Marbury and Crawford's Digest, p. 177.

‡ Dawson's Digest, p. 450.

§ Dawson's Digest, p. 109.

time, resided Mr. John Abbot, whose work upon the Lepidopterous Insects of Georgia is still highly prized by the students of Natural History. Upon the removal of the public buildings to Sylvania in 1847, this place was robbed of all importance. It was speedily abandoned; and now a few sherds of common pottery scattered over the surface of the ground are all that is left to remind the visitor that the tide of life was once here.

For more than a quarter of a century HARTFORD was a thriving town and the capital of Pulaski county.* When in 1837† the Court House and jail were transferred to Hawkinsville, ruin and decay overtook the place, and at present there is little else save silence, desolation, and sea-shells on the abandoned Ocmulgee bluff.

Alarmed at the murders committed by the Cherokees, the Friends forsook their neat abodes above Augusta; and, for quite a century, no memory of that primal settlement has been perpetuated in the neighborhood except by the "QUAKER-SPRING."

Military posts, maintained for temporary purposes, eventually fall into disuse and live only in history. We have already seen how the fortifications, erected for the protection of the southern frontier of the Colony, when the Spanish war-cloud had vanished returned to the dust from which they sprang. Rendered unnecessary by the overleaping tide of population some were transferred to the outer verge,

* Clayton's Digest, p. 606.

† Pamphlet Laws of 1836, p. 103.

and these in turn were abandoned upon the assured occupancy of the disputed territory.

Fort Barrington,—its mission ended,—long ago crumbled into nothingness beside the yellow waters of the Alatamaha. By DeBrahm's plan and local memories is it preserved from utter oblivion. *Forts Early, Gaines, Hawkins, James, Lawrence, Perry, Scott, Wayne,* and *Wilkinson,*—and others, once potent for protection, and important in the military operations of the State,—deserted alike by soldier and Indian have utterly perished, and the tillers of the soil run their peaceful furrows over areas once swept by their guns.

What subsequently became the site of the little town of FRANCISVILLE, in Crawford County, was at first selected and used by Colonel Benjamin Hawkins as a convenient locality for the transaction of the important duties confided to him by Mr. Jefferson. Here, upon the left bank of the Flint river, and on the line of what was afterwards the established route between Macon and Columbus, he resided for a number of years: devoting his energies to the execution of the trust devolved upon him as United States Agent to the Creek Indians, striving to ameliorate their condition, and by his judicious influence and management perpetuating amicable relations between them and the whites. During his occupancy of the *Old Agency,* as it came to be known, this place gave manifest indications of thrift and activity. A considerable plantation was formed, with residence, mills, work-shops, store-houses, and appurtenances requisite for comfort, security, and the conduct of the business connected with this advanced post. Hither the Indians repaired for supplies at stated intervals. With them an extensive traffic was maintained. Aside from the performance of his official duties, Colonel Hawkins devoted much attention to rearing cattle and hogs. So extensive became his herd that at one time he is said to have possessed not less than five hundred calves. The care of these animals, and the details of the agency furnished employment for many subordinates. The Flint river was utilized as a convenient dividing line to separate the grown kine from their young. Across this stream a substantial bridge was constructed, with a gate at either end. This large stock of cattle and swine enabled him to entertain the Indians,—who constantly visited him,—with abundant although primitive hospitality, and materially assisted in perpetuating the kindly and wide-spread influence which he exerted over them. While he lived, his cattle brand was rigidly respected by the Red men; although, soon after his death, if report be true, the Creeks,—oblivious of former obligations,—stole numbers of these cows and hogs. Colonel Hawkins was a man of decided mark. To him does the State of Georgia owe a debt of special gratitude. His Sketch of the Creek Country* is a most valuable and interesting contribution. The French General Moreau who, while in exile, was for some time his guest, was so much impressed with his character and labors that he pronounced him one of the most remarkable men he had met in America. "Under the faithful proconsular sway of Col. Hawkins," says Mr. Chappell,† "the Creek Indians enjoyed for sixteen years, unbroken peace among themselves and with their neighbors, and also whatsoever other blessings were possible to the savage state, which it was his study

* Collections of the Georgia Historical Society, vol. III, part I. Savannah, 1848.

† Miscellanies of Georgia, part I, p. 67. Columbus, 1874.

gradually to ameliorate. To this end he spared no pains. Much was done to initiate, instruct, and encourage them in the lower and most indispensable parts of civilization. Pasturage was brought into use, agriculture also, to some extent; both together supplanting considerably among them their previous entire reliance for food on hunting, fishing, and wild fruits. To the better and more secure modes of obtaining a livelihood which civilization offers, he sought to win them by example as well as by precept. He brought his slaves from North Carolina, and, under the right conceded to his office, he opened and cultivated a large plantation at the Agency on Flint river, making immense crops of corn and other provisions. He also reared great herds of cattle and swine, and having thus always abundance of meat and bread, he was enabled to practice habitually towards the Indians a profuse, though coarse hospitality and benevolence which gained their hearts and bound them to him by ties as loyal and touching as those of old feudal allegiance and devotion."

Here Colonel Hawkins died in 1816, and was buried on the wooded bluff overlooking the Flint river, a few hundred yards below the point of the present crossing. No stone marks his grave. Among the scattered and almost obliterated mounds in this lonely and forsaken cemetery is one more prominent than the rest. It may designate the precise place of his sepulture.

For several years after the death of this prominent man, who gave impulse and direction to all about him, neglect and decay supervened. New life was infused into the settlement, however, by Francis Bacon, of Massachusetts, who, having married Jeffersonia,—the youngest daughter of Col. Hawkins,—established himself upon the site of the *Old*

Agency, about 1825, and founded the town of Francisville. Traffic with the surrounding country was freely invited. Being a man of means, of intelligence, and of enterprise, matters prospered. Other settlers, attracted by the prospect for gain, purchased lots of about an acre in extent and located themselves on both sides of the public road. Several dry goods and grocery stores, a wagon manufactory, a blacksmith shop, a drug store, a church, a public school, a tavern, and a post-office were in time built. From 1830 to 1850 the town had an average population of about one hundred whites. Much business was here transacted.

Upon the completion of the railway running from Macon to Columbus the resident merchants sought other and more convenient localities. Trade languished, was then wholly diverted, and the town speedily disappeared. Cotton fields now usurp the domain formerly occupied by the village.

The traveler from the south as he crosses the Flint river, ascends a long rocky hill, and passes through a narrow lane on the top, discerns no traces of this dead town. The *Old Agency*,—once so important in the early days of this section,—exists only in tradition. *Francisville*, which was builded upon its ruins, has fallen into nothingness. Tall trees and a tangled undergrowth hide the graves of the dead, and there is little else save silence and forgetfulness. Even the earth-mound which covers the bones of the famous Colonel Benjamin Hawkins is incapable of positive recognition, and rests under the common oblivion which has overtaken all.

V.II.

MISCELLANEOUS TOWNS, PLANTATIONS, &C.

DeBrahm in his History of the Province of Georgia* furnishes us with the following classification of the Towns in the Province:

"Besides the Metropolis of Savannah upon Savannah Stream, 17 miles from the Sea,

Are 4 Sea Port Towns,

Hardwick upon Great Ogetchee Stream
Sunbury upon Midway Stream
Darian } upon Alatamaha Stream
Frederica }

4 Towns upon
navigable fresh water streams

Brandon[a] upon little River, is navigable only to the Cataract above Augusta, 200 miles from the Sea.
Augusta upon Savannah Stream 150 miles from the Sea.
Queensbury in the Fork of Lambert's River and Great Ogetchee Stream, 120 miles from the Sea.[b]
Ebenezer upon Savannah Stream 57 miles from the Sea.

4 Villages of which
two are upon a navigable River,

* Wormsloe, 1849, pp. 25, 26.

(a) Since Gov. Wright's Administration this Place (being deserted in Gov'r Reynolds' time by Edmond Grey) revived again under the name of Wrightsborough inhabited by above 60 Families, and its Township contains about 200 Families all Quakers; they are indulged by the Gov'r; that no Person, but such as they approve, shall be permitted to settle among them.

(b) Queensbury is inhabited by about 70, and its Environs by above 200 Families mostly Irish, from which it is generally called the Irish Settlement.

<table>
<tr><td>Acton</td><td rowspan="2">upon Vernon River</td></tr>
<tr><td>Vernonburg</td></tr>
<tr><td>Hampstead</td><td rowspan="2">upon the Head of Vernon River."</td></tr>
<tr><td>Highgate</td></tr>
</table>

The enumeration contained in "Histoire et Commerce des Colonies Angloises dans l'Amerique Septentionale,"* is essentially similar: "On partage la Georgie en doux divisions. La Septentrionale comprend;

<table>
<tr><td>Savannah</td><td rowspan="3">Villes.</td><td>Old-Ebenezer</td><td rowspan="5">Villages.</td></tr>
<tr><td>New-Ebenezer</td><td>Hampstead.</td></tr>
<tr><td>Augusta</td><td>High-Gate.</td></tr>
<tr><td></td><td></td><td>Abercorn.</td></tr>
<tr><td></td><td></td><td>Skindwe</td></tr>
</table>

La méridionale est moins peuplée, on n'y trouve que deux villes & un village.

<table>
<tr><td>Frederica</td><td rowspan="2">Villes</td><td rowspan="2">Barikmake</td><td rowspan="2">Village."</td></tr>
<tr><td>New-Inverness</td></tr>
</table>

Savannah and Augusta still exist and are justly reckoned among the most opulent, beautiful, and attractive cities of the Empire State of the South. In their locations the judgment of the early Colonists has been sanctioned by the favorable experience of nearly a century and a half. New Inverness has given place to Darien which, amid shifting fortunes, is still supported by the lumber trade and the rice crop of the Alatamaha. Of the memories of Frederica, Sunbury, New and Old Ebenezer, Bethany, Hardwick, and Abercorn, we have already spoken; and it remains for us in a few words to mention some smaller and insignificant towns, projected in the early days of the Colony, which have long since lost their identity

* p. 235. A. La Haye, 1755.

amid the changes of population and the vicissitudes of ownership.

Brandon may be recognized as still maintaining a feeble existence in the later village of Wrightsboro, although its original features and peculiarities have encountered essential modifications. The founder of Brandon was Edmund Grey, a pretending Quaker, who came from Virginia with a number of followers. A man of strong will and marked influence, he was nevertheless a pestilent fellow, and, during Governor Reynolds' administration, was compelled to abandon his little town. He subsequently formed a settlement on the neutral lands lying between the Alatamaha and the St. Johns rivers. Thither flocked criminals, and debtors anxious to escape the just demands of their creditors.*

Brandon on Little river was revived by Joseph Mattock, a Quaker, who having obtained for himself and friends a grant of forty thousand acres of land, called the town WRIGHTSBORO in honor of Governor Sir James Wright, who favored the establishment of the new colony. Mr. Mattock hospitably entertained Mr. William Bartram in 1773, by whom he is described as a public spirited man about seventy years of age, hearty, active, and presiding as the chief magistrate of the settlement.† We recall no special incidents in the history of this town. Its life was uneventful, and at present it can scarcely claim even a nominal existence.

---

*DeBrahm's History of the Province of Georgia, p. 30. Wormsloe, 1849.
Stevens' History of Georgia, vol. I, pp. 406, 407. New York, 1847.

†Travels Through North and South Carolina, Georgia, &c., pp. 35, 36. London, 1792.

Between four and five miles southwest of Savannah, as its limits were at first ascertained, and on rising ground, the village of HIGH-GATE was laid out in 1733. Twelve families,—mostly French,—were here located. A mile to the eastward the village of HAMPSTEAD was formed the same year, and peopled by twelve families,—chiefly German. These settlers were engaged in gardening, and their principal business was to supply the inhabitants of Savannah with vegetables. Francis Moore, who visited these little towns in the spring of 1736, describes them as being "pretty," and says that the "Planters are very forward, having built neat Huts and clear'd and planted a great deal of Land."

It would appear, however, that the prosperity of these villages was of short duration. We are informed that in 1740 but two families remained at High-gate, while Hampstead was entirely abandoned.*

For the protection of the few families to whom a home at THUNDERBOLT had been assigned, a small fort was erected; but as early as 1737 it had fallen into decay.

On the north-east point of SKIDOWAY ISLAND, ten families were placed and a fort built in 1734. This attempt at colonization proved so unsuccessful that four years afterwards the village had disappeared and the fortification was in a deserted and ruinous condition.

---

* For further notices of these villages see "Moore's Voyage to Georgia," p. 32. London, 1744. "An Account Shewing the Progress of the Colony of Georgia," &c., p. 35. London, 1741. "A State of the Province of Georgia, attested upon Oath," &c., p. 10. London, 1742. "Extract of the Rev'd Mr. John Wesley's Journal," &c., p. 61. Bristol, n. d. "A True and Historical Narrative of the Colony of Georgia," &c., p. 109. Charles-Town, 1741. "An Impartial Enquiry into the State and Utility of the Province of Georgia," &c., p. 51. London, 1741.

A similar fatality attended the effort to plant a colony of ten families near the light-house on TYBEE ISLAND the year after Savannah was settled.

So long as FORT ARGYLE was garrisoned, the ten freeholders who established their plantations in its vicinity strove to render their cultivation profitable: but, upon the withdrawal of the Rangers, eight of them removed, and within a short time all signs of industry disappeared.

The labors of the Scottish colonists at JOSEPH'S TOWN were prosecuted but a few years, and that settlement was quickly numbered among the failures which occurred on every hand.

Near fort St. Andrew on the north-east extremity of Cumberland island grew up the village of BARRIMACKÉ, which, about 1740, embraced some twenty-four families. When General Oglethorpe's regiment was withdrawn from the southern frontier, this town speedily died, and for more than a century all traces of its former existence have been entirely wanting.

Similar is the history of the German village of gardeners and fishermen which stood near the southern end of the military road connecting Frederica with St. Simons.

Of the meagre and uneventful lives of Acton and Vernonburgh on Vernon river, of Goshen and Bethany near the Savannah, of Williamsburgh, and Fort Barrington on the Alatamaha, and of Queensbury on the Great Ogeechee, we feel scarce called upon to speak. Were we not dealing exclusively with the *dead* towns of Georgia, we might enumerate others which, in their moribund condition and present dilapidation, perpetuate little more than the names and sites which they at first received.

Of the more prominent plantations established at an early date we may mention those of Colonel Cochran, Captain Gascoin, and Lieutenant Horton on St. Simon's island,—of Messrs. Carr and Carteret on the main,—of Sir Francis Bathurst, Walter Augustine, Robert Williams, Patrick Tailfer, Jacob Matthews, Mr. Cooksey, and Captain Watson on the Savannah river,—of Mr. Houstoun on the Little Ogeechee,—of the Messrs. Sterling on the Great Ogeechee river,—of Messrs. Noble Jones, Henry Parker, and John Fallowfield on the Isle of Hope,—of Oxtead, the settlement of Mr. Thomas Causton on Augustine creek,—of the Hermitage, the abode of Hugh Anderson,—of Mr. Thomas Christie,—of the twenty German families sent over by Count Zinzendorf,—of Mr. William Williamson,—of the Trustees, committed to the care of William Bradley,—of Mr. Thomas Jones,—and of president William Stephens at Bewlie. This last plantation consisted of a grant of five hundred acres at the mouth of Vernon river, and was confirmed by General Oglethorpe on the 19th of April, 1738. Of this place Mr. Stephens, on the 21st of March, 1739, writes as follows: "I was now called upon to give the Place a Name; and thereupon naturally revolving in my Thoughts divers Places in my native Country, to try if I could find any that had a Resemblance to this; I fancied that *Bewlie*, a Manor of his Grace the Duke of *Montague* in the *New Forest*, was not unlike it much as to its Situation; and being on the Skirts of that Forest, had Plenty of large Timber growing everywhere near; moreover a fine Arm of the Sea running close by, which parts the *Isle of Wight* from the main Land, and makes a beautiful Prospect; from all which Tradition tells us it took its Name and was antiently called *Beaulieu*, though now vulgarly *Bewlie;* only by leaving out the *a* in the first Syllable, and the *u* in the end of the last."*

This is the true account of the original cession and *naming* of that attractive bluff rendered memorable in after years by the debarcation of Count D'Estaing on the 12th of September, 1779, and by the erection of formidable batteries for the protection of this approach to the city of Savannah during the Confederate struggle for independence.

These plantations, and others which might be enumerated, have, *with a single exception,* so far as our information extends, lost all traces of primal occupancy and passed into the ownership of strangers. We allude to the beautiful plantation of WORMSLOE on the Isle of Hope. Of this interesting spot we have the following description penned by an intelligent visitor who made his observations in 1743. He was then, in an open boat, journeying towards Savannah from St. Catharine's island, where a short season had been spent in the companionship of the friendly Indians who were dwellers there. "We arrived in somewhat more than two Days at the *Narrows* where there is a kind of *Manchecolas* Fort for their Defence, garrison'd from *Wormsloe,* where we soon arriv'd. It is the settlement of Mr. *Jones* 10 Miles S. E. of *Savannah,* and we could not help observing as we passed, several very pretty Plantations.

"Wormsloe is one of the most agreeable Spots I ever saw, and the Improvements of that ingenious Man are very extraordinary: He commands a Company of Marines who are quarter'd in Huts near his House, which is also a tolerable defensible Place with small Arms. From the House

---

*"A Journal of the Proceedings in Georgia," &c., vol. II, pp. 166, 318, 319. London, 1742.

there is a Vista of near three Miles cut thro' the Woods to Mr. Whitefield's Orphan House, which has a very fine Effect on the Sight."*

After concluding his visit to Savannah, this gentleman "set out in one of Captain *Jones's Scout Boats* mann'd by a Party of his *Marine Company*, and had a very pleasant Passage to Fort *Frederick* on the *Island of Port Royal* in *South Carolina*."†

Noble Jones, the proprietor of Wormsloe, was a Lieutenant commanding thirty men,—volunteers and enlisted from Savannah,—in General Oglethorpe's expedition against St. Augustine. He was subsequently assigned to the command of a scout and guard boat and a company of marines to watch the "Narrows at Skedoway" and the "Inlets of the near adjoining Sea;" more especially "those near him of Wassaw and Ussuybaw, lest any surprise should happen." His guard-boat was armed "with a small swivel Gun" in the bow; and, in February, 1741, upon the appearance of a Spanish Privateer on the coast, "One of our smartest Pieces of Cannon," says Stephens, "carrying a four Pound Ball, and well mounted," was delivered to him to assist in the coast defense.‡

At Wormsloe may still be seen the remains of the Tabby Fortification constructed by Captain Noble Jones. The outline of the work and its general features are well preserved, and constitute, perhaps, the most unique and interesting historical ruin on the Georgia coast.

With all its wealth of magnificent live-oaks, palmettoes, magnolias, and cedars; with its quiet, gentle views, balmy

---

* London Magazine for 1745, p. 552.

† Idem, p. 604.

‡ Stephens' Journal of Proceedings, vol. II, pp. 472, 492, 497.
Idem, vol. III, pp. 13, 16, 17, 124, 206. London, 1742.

airs, soft sunlight, inviting repose, and pleasant traditions, this beautiful residence has at all times remained in the possession and ownership of the descendants of the original proprietor. Mr. G. W. J. DeRenne now guards the spot with all the tender care and devotion of a most loyal son, and to the memories of the past has added literary and cultivated associations in the present, which impart new charms to the name of *Wormsloe.*

In this youthful country, so careless of and indifferent to the memories of other days,—so ignorant of the value of monuments and the impressive lessons of antiquity,—where no law of primogeniture encourages in the son the conservation of the abode and heirlooms of his fathers,—where new fields, cheap lands, and novel enterprises at remote points are luring the loves of succeeding generations from the gardens which delighted, the hoary oaks which sheltered, and the fertile fields which nourished their ancestors,—where paternal estates are constantly alienated at public and private sales,—landed acquisitions are placed at the mercy of speculative strangers, and family treasures, established inheritances, and old homesteads are seldom preserved. Thus it comes to pass that ancestral graves lie neglected, abodes once noted for refinement, intelligence, virtue, and hospitality lose their identity in the ownership of strangers, and traditions worthy of transmission, are forgotten amid the selfish engagements of an alien present.

The utilitarian may smile at this, the Republican rejoice in it as a logical sequence of his cherished theories, and the disciples of Benjamin Franklin pronounce in favor of such a condition of affairs, but there is a deal of sadness about it nevertheless; and if this order of things obtain in the coming years as it has in those which are gone, America will continue to be largely a land without permanent homes,—a country devoid of ancestral monuments.

In planting colonies where proper preliminary surveys have not been made, and where the founders are compelled in large measure to grope their way in selecting points for earliest occupancy, errors of judgement will occur, and changes will be necessitated upon a more intimate acquaintance with the territory and during the progress of development. Locations at first deemed essential become subordinate to others, and sometimes prove of no value. Mistakes are committed with regard to the importance of streams, lines of communication, and the desirability of permanent seats. Defensive positions are rendered useless as the tide of human life advances. Barren fields are exchanged for others possessing greater fertility. Diseases are developed at certain points which compel their abandonment.

Settlements increase to the annihilation or absorption of others in their vicinity. The possessions of the many become concentrated in the ownership of the few. Towns perish for lack of support. Thus nothing is more common than to observe, amid the changes consequent upon the development of new plantations, a mortality among villages and settlements for which, at the outset, growth and lasting prosperity were confidently anticipated.

"It hath been a great endangering to the health of some plantations," says Lord Bacon, "that they have built along the sea and rivers in marish and unwholesome grounds; therefore though you begin there to avoid carriage and other like discommodities, yet build still rather upwards from the stream, than along.

Had this precaution been observed, fewer towns would have died in Georgia.

After all, however, despite the admonitions of the wisest and the foresight of the most experienced, we cannot hope to arrest the potent influence of inherent decay, or to stay that unseen hand which remorselessly worketh change and destruction among human habitations.

> "Out upon Time! it will leave no more
> Of the things to come than the things before!
> Out upon Time! who forever will leave
> But enough of the Past for the Future to grieve
> O'er that which hath been, and o'er that which must be:
> What we have seen, our sons shall see;
> Remnants of things that have pass'd away,
> Fragments of Stone rear'd by Creatures of Clay."

INDEX.